T0301400

Environmental Policy Analysis with Limited Information

NEW HORIZONS IN ENVIRONMENTAL ECONOMICS

General Editors: Wallace E. Oates, *Professor of Economics, University of Maryland, USA* and Henk Folmer, *Professor of Economics, Wageningen Agricultural University, The Netherlands and Professor of Environmental Economics, Tilburg University, The Netherlands*

This important series is designed to make a significant contribution to the development of the principles and practices of environmental economics. It includes both theoretical and empirical work. International in scope, it addresses issues of current and future concern in both East and West and in developed and developing countries.

The main purpose of the series is to create a forum for the publication of high quality work and to show how economic analysis can make a contribution to understanding and resolving the environmental problems confronting the world in the late twentieth century.

Recent titles in the series include:

Environmental Policy Analysis with Limited Information
Principles and Applications of the Transfer Method
William H. Desvousges, F. Reed Johnson and H. Spencer Banzhaf

Environmental Transition in Nordic and Baltic Countries
Edited by Hans Aage

Biodiversity, Conservation and Sustainable Development
Principles and Practices with Asian Examples
Clem Tisdell

Green Taxes
Economic Theory and Empirical Evidence from Scandinavia
Edited by Runar Brännlund and Ing-Marie Gren

The Political Economy of Environmental Policy
A Public Choice Approach to Market Institutions
Bouwe R. Dijkstra

The Economic Valuation of Landscape Change
Theory and Policies for Land Use and Conservation
José Manuel L. Santos

Sustaining Development
Environmental Resources in Developing Countries
Daniel W. Bromley

Valuing Recreation and the Environment
Revealed Preference Methods in Theory and Practice
Edited by Joseph A. Herriges and Catherine L. Kling

Designing Effective Environmental Regimes
The Key Conditions
Jørgen Wettestad

Environmental Networks
A Framework for Economic Decision Making and Policy Analysis
Kanwalroop Kathy Dhanda, Anna Nagurney and Padma Ramanjuram

The International Yearbook of Environmental and Resource Economics
1999/2000
Edited by Henk Folmer and Tom Tietenberg

Environmental Policy Analysis with Limited Information

Principles and Applications of the Transfer Method

William H. Desvousges

Research Professor, Duke University and President, Triangle Economic Research, Durham, NC, USA

F. Reed Johnson

Vice President, Research and Development, Triangle Economic Research, Durham, NC, USA

H. Spencer Banzhaf

Duke University and Consultant-in-Residence, Triangle Economic Research, Durham, NC, USA

NEW HORIZONS IN ENVIRONMENTAL ECONOMICS SERIES

Edward Elgar
Cheltenham, UK • Northampton, MA, USA

Published by
Edward Elgar Publishing Limited
Glensanda House
Montpellier Parade
Cheltenham
Glos GL50 1UA
UK

Edward Elgar Publishing, Inc.
6 Market Street
Northampton
Massachusetts 01060
USA

A catalogue record for this book
is available from the British Library

Library of Congress Cataloguing in Publication Data
Desvousges, William H.
    Environmental policy analysis with limited information:
principles and applications of the transfer method/William H.
Desvousges, F. Reed Johnson, H. Spencer Banzhaf.
    — (New horizons in environmental economics series)
    1. Environmental economics. 2. Natural resources—Cost effectiveness.
3. Transfer functions. I. Johnson, F. Reed, 1946–   . II. Banzhaf, H. Spencer,
1969–   . III. Title. IV. Series: New horizons in environmental economics.
HD75.6.D475   1998
333.7—dc21   98–9844
ISBN 1 85898 655 9   CIP

Printed and bound in Great Britain by Biddles Ltd, Guildford and King's Lynn

Contents

List of figures

List of tables

Preface and acknowledgements

In benefit–cost analyses, natural resource damage assessments and other research, we have frequently employed transfer studies to address a research question with existing information, even when such information may be limited in various ways. We have increasingly come to view this task as a challenge that calls for creativity and resourcefulness, plus all the technical skills needed for original research. In expressing this view, this book offers several suggestions for ways in which the standards for transfers should be raised, illustrating many of these suggestions with a detailed case study.

This book should be of interest to two audiences. The first is economists – especially environmental and health economists – who are engaged in transfer studies. The second audience is those in government or industry who have a stake in the quality of transfer estimates and who wish better to understand the issues involved. We hope that this group will profit from our efforts to explain the intuition of transfer methods as well as the technical details of interest to practitioners.

Research for the case study was funded by Northern States Power Company, and by Madison Gas and Electric Company, Wisconsin Electric Power Company, Wisconsin Power and Light Company and Wisconsin Public Service Company. While we owe them thanks for their support, the views expressed in this book are those of the authors and not necessarily those of the companies.

Many people have helped us at various stages along the way. We especially thank Howard Balentine, Al Bethke, Kevin Dietz, Erin Fries, David Keen, Randolph Russell, Venus Sadeghi, Robert Sandefur, Joel Smith, Jay Snyder and Nicole Wilson for their work. Sheila Martin contributed more directly by co-authoring Chapter 6 with us. In addition, Robert Haveman, Robert Hetes, Erhard Joeres and Kerry Smith provided us with many valuable comments and suggestions.

Tom Mol and Audrey Zibelman at Northern States Power were especially helpful in interpreting the policy issues and in their support for our attempt to achieve technical excellence. Steve Harrison and Chad Koch of Wisconsin Electric, Ed Newman of Wisconsin Public Service, Greg Bollom of Madison Gas and Electric and Kathy Lipp of Wisconsin Power and Light provided useful direction throughout the Wisconsin project. Many agencies also supplied us with valuable data and information. We thank the Minnesota Pollution Control Agency, the Minnesota Department of Natural Resources, the Minnesota Department of Public Health, and the US Department of Agriculture. John Kruse and Darnell Smith of the Food and Agricultural Policy Research Institute provided us with the valuation model for the agricultural damages presented here.

Finally, we have relied on many people for their expert skills in producing this book. We thank Andrew Jessup, and especially Karen Bourey and Elaine Ball. They have shown tremendous grace through all of our (at times seemingly endless) revisions.

William H. Desvousges
F. Reed Johnson
H. Spencer Banzhaf

1.   Introduction

Transfer studies are the bedrock of practical policy analysis. Only rarely can policy analysts afford the luxury of designing and implementing original studies. Instead, they must rely on the limited information that can be gleaned from past studies. In many cases such studies are limited, contradictory, or only tangentially related to the policy question at hand. Nevertheless, information from past studies is the basis for many benefit–cost estimates increasingly required by regulations governing environmental and other policies. Despite the central role they play in public decision making, transfer studies often employ simplistic methods for interpreting, summarizing and integrating available information for the new policy context.

This book offers the contrarian view that competent application of transfer methods demands all the advanced technical skills required in original research and more. In addition to all the basic tools of microeconomic theory and econometrics, transfer analysts must employ great judgement and creativity both in manipulating available information and in presenting results to decision makers. They must also clearly expose the relative roles of data and assumptions, helping decision makers to understand the sources and magnitudes of uncertainties inherent in the estimates.

Furthermore, transfer studies often require analysts to summarize and use results from non-economic studies. Transfer methods should be as applicable for incorporating results from natural science and health science studies as from economics. Indeed, we have found techniques that were developed largely outside traditional economics, such as meta-analysis and Monte Carlo simulations, to be valuable tools for quantifying uncertainty and testing the sensitivity of conclusions to assumptions and analytical judgements in a wide variety of applications.

Contemporary applications of transfer methods to policy analysis in the United States have their origins in the early use of benefit–cost analysis in the US Army Corps of Engineers.[1] The United States began requiring benefit–cost analyses with the Flood Control Act of 1936, which required that 'the federal government should improve or participate in the improvement of navigable waters or their tributaries ... for flood control purposes if the benefits to whomsoever they may accrue are in excess of the

1

estimated costs ...'. From these origins in the US Army Corps of Engineers, benefit–cost analysis attracted the attention of many economists, including Otto Eckstein in his work on water resource management at Harvard (Eckstein 1958). From this beginning in water resources, Resources for the Future, Inc. later led many of the pioneering investigations into important benefit–cost issues, including the work by Kneese (1964), Haveman (1965), Clawson and Knetsch (1966), Krutilla (1972) and Krutilla and Fisher (1975). At the same time, benefit–cost analysis spread to other parts of government policy in response to efforts to introduce efficiency in government.

Likewise, benefit–cost analysis has grown in importance in Europe. The Organization for Economic Cooperation and Development has led numerous investigations using benefit–cost methods. The OECD and the United Nations have also developed guidelines for evaluating projects in developing countries (Little and Mirlees 1969; Dasgupta, Sen and Marglin 1972). Finally, the World Bank has used benefit–cost analysis for evaluating its projects.

The role of benefit–cost analysis took a major leap in the United States with President Reagan's Executive Order 12291, issued in 1981, requiring that all new major regulations be subject to a benefit–cost test. Executive Order 12291 expanded the practices that had begun under Presidents Ford and Carter, most notably the role of the Council on Wage and Price Flexibility, staffed by professional economists, to review proposed regulations. Under Executive Order 12291, agencies such as the US Environmental Protection Agency developed guidelines for staff to conduct regulatory impact analyses.[2] (More recently, President Clinton's Executive Order 12866 has retreated somewhat from the earlier position.)

Within environmental economics, benefit–cost methods also received an expanded role from the 1980 Comprehensive Environmental Response, Compensation, and Liability Act, or 'Superfund', which established liability for damages to natural resources from toxic releases. In promulgating its rules for such natural resource damage assessments, the US Department of Interior interpreted these damages and the required compensation within a welfare-economic paradigm, measuring damages as lost consumer surplus (43 *CFR* Part 11). The regulations also describe protocols that are based on various economic valuation methods.

The number of studies these laws could potentially require threatens to become unmanageable. Accordingly, the practice of benefit–cost analysis itself has been the subject of increased scrutiny. One of the most important questions is at what level the analysis should be applied. Some economists have suggested that benefit–cost studies should themselves be subject to a benefit–cost test (Lerman 1981; Freeman 1984). In principle, a benefit–

cost study should incur expenses up to the point where the marginal cost of increasing the study's quality just equals its expected marginal value.[3] Thus, following the logic of this criterion, some analysts began to consider whether there were alternatives to full-scale assessments involving the collection of original data and the estimation of site-specific models. Smith and Desvousges (1986) called the alternatives to full-scale assessments 'benefits transfer'. They called for agencies to begin to design studies that would make such transfers more informative and reliable.

Transfer studies provide an economical way to conduct research when a full-fledged study is not practical or not necessary. They apply the results of previous studies to a new policy context, perhaps with some adjustment, thereby economizing on the time and expense of primary data collection and new estimation. Commensurate with the increasing demand for benefit–cost studies, the number of transfer studies has increased with time. In establishing guidelines for implementing Executive Order 12291, the US Environmental Protection Agency has authorized transfers, as has the US Department of Interior for small (Type A) natural resource damage assessments and settlements of larger ones. Additional areas giving rise to transfers include methods used by the US Forest Service to manage parks and recreation areas and attempts formally to include environmental costs in the planning decisions of electric utilities. The latter has sparked such externality studies in several American states, as well as in Canada and Europe.[4]

The increasing reliance on transfer studies has provoked calls for improving standards and protocols. In 1992, a special issue of *Water Resources Research* was devoted to the subject, as was a workshop of the Association of Environmental and Resource Economists. This book reviews some of the lessons from those forums and subsequent studies, as well as contributions to the transportation economics literature rarely cited by environmental economists. More importantly, it also extends those lessons by reflecting on a large case study assessing the externalities of electricity generation in the US. This case study illustrates many of the problems and solutions that are encountered in any transfer study. It also includes several refinements in transfer methodology, including meta-analyses designed to summarize information from multiple studies and Monte Carlo methods to assess uncertainty in the transfer.

The remainder of this chapter first overviews the steps and features of a transfer study. The chapter then concludes with two sections placing the transfer method in the context of benefit–cost analysis. Specifically, Section 1.2 briefly introduces the main ideas of benefit–cost analysis and the measures of value that economists use. Section 1.3 reviews the methods used by economists to value non-market goods in particular.

These are the methods that would have to be used in any analysis of an environmental policy, and which are used by many of the studies that will be transferred. The material in both of these sections is geared to the non-economist or, in Section 1.3, to economists unfamiliar with these methods. Freeman (1993) is recommended for readers interested in a more in-depth discussion.

After this chapter, Chapter 2 focuses on several key aspects of the transfer method in more detail. Chapters 3 through 7 then illustrate the method with the case study. Finally, Chapter 8 concludes with an assessment of the usefulness of the transfer method in policy making.

1.1   INTRODUCTION TO THE TRANSFER METHOD

In an introduction to a special issue of *Water Resources Research* on the transfer method, Brookshire and Neill (1992) observe that the contributors to the volume applied a range of meanings to the term. In this book we take a broad view of the term, defining the 'transfer method' as the use of existing information designed for one specific context to address policy questions in another context. We refer to these two contexts as the 'original context' and the 'transfer context' respectively, and further use 'original' and 'transfer' to modify 'estimates', 'study', 'policy', 'site' and other aspects of the two contexts.[5]

Transfer studies are not limited to environmental economics or to benefit–cost studies; they occur whenever economists draw on past studies to predict the effect of trade restrictions, minimum wage and rent control policies, or other policies. Note the potential breadth of this definition. Strictly speaking, all analysis involves transferring some information, whether the information is data such as census counts, the intuition and tools of economics and other disciplines, or the analysts' prior knowledge, assumptions and language. Furthermore, any study must be conducted in a slightly different context from the one in which the policy will take place. For example, it may require simplifying assumptions, involve a sub-sample of the relevant population, or involve a time period different from the policy. To provide a narrower compass, we only use the term 'transfer' when the questions of interest are addressed with information gathered for a different purpose. Thus the term precludes routine transfers of universally available data or relatively objective statistics. It also precludes concern about the simplifying assumptions and the like used in any original study. Still, the term admittedly involves some ambiguity, with an inevitable grey line demarcating original studies and transfer studies.

This definition is also broad in comparison with earlier discussions in the environmental economics literature, which have usually used the term 'benefits transfer', thereby implicitly focusing on the valuation aspects of policy analysis (Smith and Desvousges 1986; Desvousges, Naughton and Parsons 1992). In contrast, our definition includes any of the elements of policy analysis. In the case of environmental policy, these elements usually include the cause-and-effect linkages of a policy, including the initial physical effects, any subsequent downstream physical effects and the behavioural responses of households and firms, together with the final estimates of benefits and costs. For example, Figure 1.1 illustrates the linkages for a change in electricity generation, the case study examined in the following chapters of this book. A policy or plan, such as increasing generation by constructing a new coal plant, changes existing patterns of air emissions. Depending on wind speed and other factors, the new emissions cause different changes in air quality in any given area. This in turn affects the ability of ecosystems to maintain habitat, the productivity of agriculture, the ability of people to maintain their health, and other services, translating into a change in people's value for the air resources after accounting for any behavioural adjustments. In a transfer study, one or more of these links is inferred from pre-existing information from different contexts, although economists have been most interested in the benefits transfer that takes place at the last stage.

While the case study examined in this book involves the full range of linkages just described, other transfer studies may involve a smaller range. At the opposite extreme, some transfers may involve only one link. For example, consider informal predictions of the effect of minimum wage policies based on studies of past experiences (for example, Brown, Gilroy and Kohen 1982; Card and Krueger 1995). These simple transfers involve only one linkage because minimum wage policies have a direct effect on markets without passing through any physical changes. Between these two extremes lie the majority of transfer studies involving two or three linkages.

Identifying the technical linkages and the studies used to transfer information at each of them is but one step in the overall transfer process. This process is sketched in Figure 1.2 as five basic steps. The figure orders the steps to show the conceptual relationship between them; in practice analysts may perform them in a different order or simultaneously, with consistency requiring that decisions at early steps be made with later ones in mind. The first step involves identifying the cause-and-effect linkages and the existing research that can potentially quantify them. Sometimes this research is in the form of computer models, but more often it will be the results from published literature. Although a literature search of

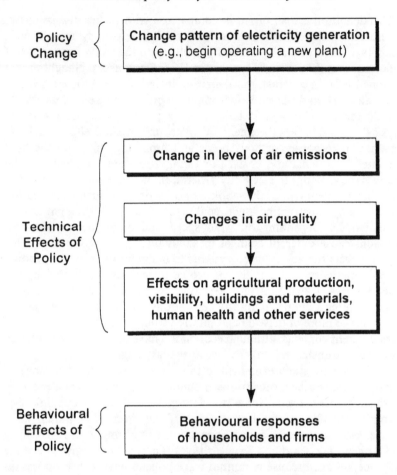

Figure 1.1   Effects and responses of a change in eliminating air pollution

published articles may reveal some candidates for a transfer, some relevant studies may not appear in the normal channels. In particular, some may be hiding in the grey literature (high-quality but not yet publishable studies, studies yet to be published, or special contractual studies).[6] If literature searches unearth several potentially useful studies, analysts must represent the information in some way before transferring it, either choosing to use a single study or summarizing multiple studies in some way.

Often, some of the work in the first step is done by technical consultants or government staff who are familiar with the natural science and engineering aspects of the policy, with the economists' contributions

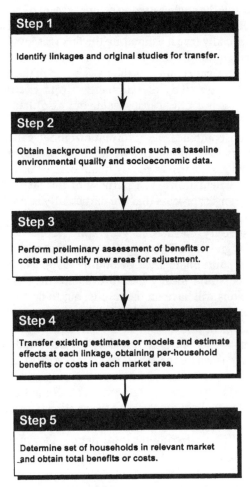

Figure 1.2   Basic steps in a transfer study

occurring at the last, behavioural linkage. But whether or not there is division of labour across these linkages, the estimates at each link all must fit together smoothly. For example, the units measuring environmental quality must be the same when predicting the effects of the policy on the environment and when predicting the effect of environmental quality on service flows. This requirement can sometimes cause difficulty, with the estimates available for transfer at two linkages being sound in themselves, but not readily compatible. For example, the effects of policy on environmental quality may best be measured with objective measures, but generally it is people's perceptions that influence behaviour.

The linkages and the studies used to estimate them often require data on baseline environmental quality, socioeconomic characteristics, and other data. This is especially true if estimating the linkages involves transferring entire estimated equations that include controlling variables. Gathering such data for the transfer context is the second step of the transfer method. For example, the case study of externalities from electricity generation required collecting not only census data, but also data on baseline air quality and incidence of certain illnesses.

The third step combines the information about causal relationships with the necessary data to obtain a preliminary assessment of benefits or costs. Often, this assessment is purely qualitative or involves only 'back-of-the-envelope' calculations. The purpose of this step is to identify the linkages in the transfer process that are particularly important, and where analysts may want to invest more resources in further refinements. It may also serve to identify the needed geographic scope of the analysis or inform other design issues. This step illustrates that the transfer process is often circular, a point highlighted by Smith (1996). The circularity arises because analysts would ideally like to evaluate the influence that their modelling decisions will have on the results, but to do so they would have to have a model already in place. Thus, while we represent this process as a discrete third step, in practice it may be an iterative process involving a cycle of preliminary estimates followed by revisions and new estimates.

The fourth step is where the actual transfer occurs. Armed with insights from these preliminary calculations as well as any relevant prior knowledge, the analysts characterize the existing information and use it to quantify the linkages. In characterizing the existing information, they may choose to use a single study, or to summarize the results of multiple studies. In actually transferring the information, they may transfer only a scalar value or an entire functional relationship, and do so with or without adjustment. These decisions are at the heart of the transfer method, and we will discuss them in particular detail in Chapter 2 and throughout this book.

Usually after all the cause-and-effect linkages are combined, the fourth step yields a per household (or per individual) estimate of benefits or costs in each market area. In the fifth and final step, these per household estimates are multiplied by the relevant number of households within each market to obtain total benefits or costs. This step, while computationally simple, can be difficult conceptually because of the problems that arise in determining the relevant market. Original studies are not performed to determine the relevant market, and techniques for delineating markets for resource services have not been established. Thus the markets are often based on qualitative information and the analysts' judgement.

Unfortunately, assumptions about the relevant market can significantly influence the outcome of the benefit–cost analysis.

While these stylized steps provide a useful summary of the transfer method, they do not necessarily capture all the important problems that arise in designing a transfer. For example, in a study of electricity generation and air quality, the precise definition of the commodity 'air quality' involves a number of dimensions that have implications for the analysis. Considering just the geographical dimension, the commodity could be defined as air quality in an entire state, or it could be sub-divided into smaller geographical units. The latter implies more than just additional markets in which to multiply per household values by the number of households. It also proliferates the number of locations at which to calculate each physical and behaviour linkage and at which to gather the required data. Other important design issues will inevitably arise on a case-by-case basis.

In addition to the obvious time and resource advantages, a careful transfer study following this method has several other advantages. The first advantage of the transfer methodology is that it uses a conceptually correct framework for benefit–cost analysis. Whereas policy makers are frequently tempted to focus on the costs of a policy, which they can monetize more easily, the transfer method systematically incorporates benefits into the analysis. In addition, it calculates costs and/or benefits in a way that is consistent with economic theory, recognizing the behavioural linkages that occur. Thus it differs from the engineer's approach, which neglects behavioural adjustments and estimates all effects as if they were purely technical.

The second advantage is that the transfer methodology organizes the issues and provides a logical framework while remaining flexible. By organizing the calculations in a chain of linkages, it readily allows additional branches to be grafted on as new issues are identified or as new original studies become available. For example, if analysts wanted to include a new health effect in a transfer study of the costs of electricity generation, they could 'tack on' this new effect to the preceding linkages already calculated. Similarly, analysts can replace pieces of the transfer with better original studies as they become available or even with original analysis of the transfer context. The transfer method allows this flexibility because it identifies and uses the appropriate variables for measuring each linkage.

A third advantage of the transfer method is its usefulness as a 'scoping study', preliminary research to identify where more analytical effort will make a difference and where it would be fruitless. In the event that funding becomes available for a primary data study in the future, the transfer study will have identified the most important analytical problems, allowing analysts to concentrate their resources more effectively.

Despite these advantages, the transfer methodology has important limitations. One potential weak point in the methodology is the original studies used. These studies were not designed for the transfer application, and finding suitable studies can be difficult. Sometimes the analysts must resort to studies of dubious quality. As Brookshire and Neill (1992) comment, the transfer can be no more reliable than the original estimates upon which it is based, and can only magnify the uncertainty surrounding the original estimates.

Furthermore, transfer analysts must make a number of assumptions and judgements when employing the method. Smith (1992) notes that analysts must often make assumptions about technical, environmental, economic or political issues to make the types of linkages illustrated in Figure 1.1. For example, they may need to make assumptions about how to measure environmental quality, and how observed changes in environmental quality affect behaviour. Do people react to objective measures of quality? To warnings such as air pollution advisories? To measures more related to perceptions of environmental quality such as visibility? Other assumptions include the delineation of the relevant market and the duration of the policy's effects. Such assumptions introduce subjectivity and greater uncertainty into the analysis.

Of course, as McConnell (1992) stresses, the same could be said of any modelling exercise. The key question is whether the added subjectivity and uncertainty surrounding the transfer are acceptable, and whether the transfer is still informative. If not, the alternatives are to forego a quantitative benefit–cost analysis or to conduct an original study. To help answer such questions, Brookshire (1992) and Deck and Chestnut (1992) distinguish between different purposes of the transfer and the level of accuracy required for each. These different purposes are illustrated along a stylized continuum in Figure 1.3. One purpose is simply fact-finding or obtaining other insights such as identifying critical linkages or markets, a purpose that requires only a relatively low level of accuracy.

At the next highest standard, transfer studies may be a useful screening tool for guiding the design of an original study. Because the transfer results themselves will not be directly used in the policy analysis, the studies need not be highly accurate. Transfer studies that inform policy decisions, such as benefit–cost tests, are at the third step in the continuum. Because real economic commitments hinge on their results, such studies must meet a certain standard of accuracy. However, it is often sufficient if they obtain a bounded result. For example, benefit–cost tests often need only to determine whether or not benefits are greater than costs; they may

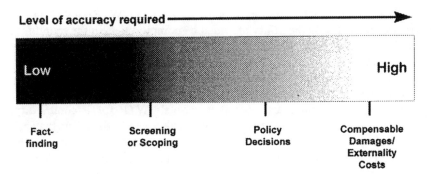

Source: Brookshire (1992).
Figure 1.3   A continuum of decisions settings from least to most required accuracy

not need to establish an exact magnitude. Thus, if costs are already known, some uncertainty is perfectly acceptable in the transfer estimates of benefits so long as they are clearly larger (or smaller) than the known costs. In contrast, at the highest standard of accuracy, an actual magnitude is required. In environmental economics, this category includes determining compensatable damages in natural resource damage assessment cases and identifying externality costs for the purposes of a Pigouvian tax or other mechanism designed to equate marginal social costs and benefits.

1.2   INTRODUCTION TO BENEFIT–COST ANALYSIS

Whether conducted on the basis of existing information or with a new study, benefit–cost analysis seeks to determine whether the benefits of a project or regulation exceed its costs. Closely related are analyses of only the benefits or only the costs of a policy or event, such as the damages caused by a spill of a hazardous substance that injures natural resources.

Economic principles assume that individual judgements are the appropriate basis of value. Thus, when estimating benefits, economics uses individuals' values for the commodity or services the policy would supply, and their values for the resources that would be consumed in producing the commodity or service when estimating costs. Estimates of these values are based on how much each person would be willing to pay for the commodity, or how much each person would be willing to accept as compensation to forego it.[7]

The basis for such measures of willingness to pay (WTP) or willingness to accept (WTA) is the utility provided by commodities. In the economics lexicon, utility is an abstract measure of an individual's well-being or satisfaction. Economics assumes that people make decisions that will maximize their utility. Thus people's behaviour reveals the utility they receive from various commodities and services. Accordingly, by observing behaviour, economists can estimate people's WTP for a commodity, defined as the payment that would leave them indifferent between obtaining the commodity at that price and not obtaining it, that is, the payment that, when accompanied by the commodity, would give the same utility as would be received without the commodity and payment.

Figure 1.4 illustrates an example of a marginal WTP schedule, the line P^oQ^o. It shows how much individuals are willing to pay for one more unit of a commodity when they are already consuming a given quantity. For example, a person already consuming Q units will be willing to pay P* for one additional unit. The downward slope of the line indicates that people are willing to pay less for additional units. This line is also called a compensated, or Hicksian, demand curve. It shows how many units of the commodity individuals would be willing to buy at a given price, contingent on their receiving a compensating payment that would keep them

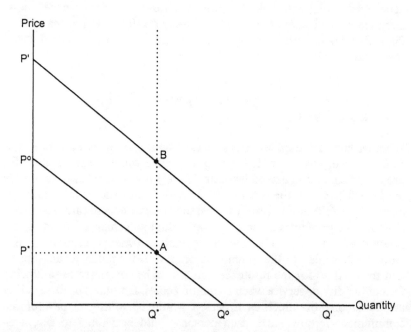

Figure 1.4   Willingness to pay and consumer surplus

at the same level of utility. The vertical line at Q* in the figure indicates that this is the total quantity of the resource available for consumption. If markets are perfectly competitive, the price will be P*. This price ensures that only people who are willing to pay more than P* use the resource, and hence that it is utilized most efficiently.

The total benefit of consuming Q* units is the amount that people are willing to pay over and above that which they actually have to pay, a measure known as Hicksian consumer surplus. In the diagram, this is the area of the triangle P*AP°. Suppose a public policy were to subsidize providing one more unit of the commodity at no cost to the consumer. Then the correct measure of benefits would be the marginal WTP, in this case P*. When markets are not present to allocate resources efficiently, observed prices cannot be used to measure marginal benefits and costs. One example is measuring the damages from closing a beach following an oil spill. If limited beach capacity is rationed by a first-come-first-served rule rather than by price, market forces do not ensure that only people with the highest WTP are injured by the closure. Thus the marginal WTP averaged over all affected individuals is the correct measure.[8] Another example is the health benefits provided by clean air. In this case, the benefits of a reduction in sick days should not be measured at the level of the individual with the lowest value, because all individuals benefit. Instead, it should again be the average of all individuals' marginal WTP. Such average measures are the benefits estimates most often used in this book.

In still another case, however, a policy may be best interpreted as improving the quality of a resource rather than providing an increased quantity. In this case, the entire WTP schedule would shift. The resource now having a higher quality, people are willing to pay more to use it. Figure 1.4 depicts this with the shift in the WTP schedule up to P'Q'. The benefit of such a programme is the change in Hicksian surplus. Assuming the price remains fixed at P*, this is the area (P'BAP*−P*AP°), or the area P'BAP°.

The discussion so far has assumed that WTP schedules are observed and known by the policy analyst. However, measuring WTP is often a challenging task to the economist. One empirical compromise frequently used is to substitute ordinary market demand for Hicksian demand or WTP. Market demands are similar schedules indicating the quantity of a commodity individuals will buy at a given price, but they do not include the hypothetical compensation required to keep utility constant. Thus utility is not held constant along an ordinary market demand curve, but it is such a curve that can actually be 'observed' in the marketplace. However, under certain conditions, it can be shown that for marketed goods, the area under the market demand curve, called ordinary consumer surplus, is bounded by the WTP and WTA measures, and that the approximation is close (Willig 1976).

Even with this compromise, measuring benefits of such non-market goods as environmental quality is difficult. Because there are no markets for these goods, at least in the usual sense, demand cannot be estimated from people's response to prices. However, environmental economists have developed a number of approaches for inferring values from WTP surveys and observed behaviour. The following section reviews some of these methods.

1.3   EMPIRICAL METHODS FOR NON-MARKET VALUATION

WTP surveys, travel-cost, hedonic, averting-behaviour and cost-of-replacement methods are the most common approaches to estimating demands and values for commodities not traded in markets. This section briefly overviews each of these methods for those unfamiliar with them. Freeman (1993) and Braden and Kolstad (1991) provide more detailed discussions.

WTP Surveys

Direct methods use surveys to elicit preferences about non-market commodities in a hypothetical situation. The most common survey method, known as contingent valuation (CV), uses mail, telephone, or in-person surveys to simulate a market for the commodity or to conduct a referendum on a hypothetical policy design to provide a non-market good.[9] More recent iterative methods, sometimes using computers, are called stated-preference or conjoint-analysis surveys. Economists employ CV to infer the values of a variety of public goods, particularly environmental amenities. The survey itself generally consists of five sections:

1. Introduction and statement of purpose
2. Non-valuation questions (for example, attitudes and prior knowledge of the resource)
3. Scenario development, resource definitions and payment-mechanism specification
4. Bidding or valuation questions
5. Special options, closing questions such as demographics, and remarks.

The first two of these sections and the last are self-explanatory and need not be discussed further. The scenario-development and market-definition section is the most critical because it must carefully and credibly present the alternative levels of environmental quality, and a commodity or policy that could deliver an improvement in quality.

The next major section of a CV questionnaire contains the actual valuation questions. The proposed method of payment in a CV survey, the vehicle for the valuation question, is critical. CV studies should use realistic, unobjectionable, and familiar payment vehicles in their valuation scenarios. For example, a CV survey may propose an entrance fee to pay for enhancements at a local park. Such an entrance fee is both realistic and familiar, helping to make the simulated market credible to respondents. Nevertheless, it may still lead to biased responses if it gives respondents implied-value cues (Rowe, d'Arge and Brookshire 1980; Greenley, Walsh and Young 1981; Brookshire, Randall and Stoll 1980; Milon 1989).[10]

Given a payment vehicle, the valuation question may be posed in several ways, raising another critical aspect of the CV survey. One way asks for a response to an open-ended question such as, 'What is the most you would be willing to pay to experience one less headache next year?' Another elicitation method uses payment cards, visual displays showing an array of possible values. A third alternative is a series of yes-or-no questions with successively increasing payment amounts until respondents answer no; this process is called an iterative bidding game. Researchers have identified problems and biases associated with each of these formats (see Mitchell and Carson 1989).

A newer question format, *dichotomous choice*, has become the preferred elicitation format for many researchers. Dichotomous choice, also known as the referendum format, relies on yes-or-no responses to a stated WTP value. Although any one respondent 'votes' on only one or two values, the entire sample of respondents votes on a wide range of randomly assigned values. Dichotomous-choice surveys require larger sample sizes and more sophisticated estimation techniques than other elicitation formats. The dichotomous-choice format is not without problems, particularly the phenomenon known as 'yea saying', in which respondents may agree to values that are not consistent with their actual preferences. Some studies have found an unexpectedly high proportion of yes responses to very high bid levels, leading researchers to conclude that WTP estimates may be sensitive to bid structure (Cooper and Loomis 1992; McFadden and Leonard 1993; Boyle et al. 1996; Kanninen 1995).

One problem encountered in CV surveys is that respondents sometimes have cognitive difficulties in answering valuation questions. Many respondents find questions involving probabilities unfamiliar or confusing, especially the very small probabilities often associated with environmental and health risks. For example, several researchers have found evidence that people tend to over-weight events with small probabilities

(Kahneman and Tversky 1979; Machina 1983). Smith and Desvousges (1987) found that marginal WTP for risk reductions were lower at higher baseline risk levels, a violation of the usual expected-utility hypothesis (but compare Machina 1984). Viscusi, Magat and Huber (1991) found that CV health survey respondents exhibited three other behavioural traits that create difficulties in estimating WTP. First, they found that respondents placed greater emphasis on the most chronologically recent information and tended to emphasize the information mentioned last in the survey (temporal weighting). They also found that the range of risk levels affected respondents' estimates of risks. Wider ranges led respondents to assume worst-case scenarios and to exhibit an upward bias in their estimates of risk. Finally, they found that respondents exhibited biased behaviour when presented with skewed probability distributions. When the distribution was skewed toward low levels of risk, respondents' mean response was much higher than the actual mean, but when high levels of risk were emphasized in the distribution, respondents' mean response matched the true mean. Thus, worst-case scenarios seem to dominate survey participants' perceptions.

Difficulty with risk perception is not the only cognitive problem that arises in CV research. Preference-formation processes and bounded rationality also pose challenges for most CV surveys. Research by Fischhoff (1991), Slovic, Griffin and Tversky (1990) and Tversky, Sattah and Slovic (1988) suggests that respondents who value unfamiliar goods must form new preferences, rather than state existing ones, and that the process of developing these preferences may be sensitive to the context in which the survey presents the problem. The valuation process required in a CV survey may exceed people's cognitive limitations by asking them to decide between conflicting values (Shepard 1964), by presenting so many attributes for consideration that respondents experience information overload (Keller and Staelin 1987; Shields 1983; Sundstrom 1987), or by presenting them with a valuation task so unfamiliar that they resort to simplifying heuristics and rules of thumb (Schkade and Payne 1994). Partly for this reason, the case of using CV to value non-use services has been particularly controversial and has raised doubts about CV reliability.[11]

Market-research methods known as stated preference (SP) or conjoint analysis employ preference-elicitation methods based on commodity attributes.[12] The value of a car, for example, depends on its acceleration, gas mileage, storage space, electronic features and price. People have preferences for each of these attributes, and are willing to accept trade-offs among them. Likewise, recreation-area attributes may include beauty, accessibility, picnic facilities and water quality. Ill health may be described in terms of symptoms, duration of symptoms, mobility restrictions and so forth. SP surveys ask people to choose among commodities, repeating over commodities with different attribute combinations. The resulting observed trade-offs among attributes, including price, are the basis for estimating marginal WTP for each attribute. This is an advantage over traditional contingent valuation, which can only measure total WTP for a given commodity.[13]

The Hedonic Method

Accustomed to observing behaviour in markets, economists have often been sceptical of WTP estimates based on survey data, preferring indirect methods that infer values for a non-market commodity based on observed behaviour in connected markets. One such approach is the hedonic method to value both air quality and health, a method first formalized for non-market valuation by Sherwin Rosen (1974).[14] Not unlike SP methods, this method interprets the non-market attribute of interest as one of several perceived attributes of a market good. For example, houses are differentiated from each other by square feet, number of bathrooms and so forth, plus the air quality of the neighbourhood. The hedonic method can be used to see how, holding other attributes constant, the price of houses varies with air quality. This relationship is the hedonic price function, and can be estimated by regressing prices for the differentiated commodity on its attributes.

Formally, Rosen's model is as follows. A differentiated commodity, say houses, has a vector of **n** attributes $(x_1, \ldots, x_n)$ and a price that is a function of those attributes, $p(x)$. Let x_1 be air quality. Households care about air quality and the other attributes of their homes as well as a composite of other goods and services z, whose price we normalize to be one. Thus, the households' utility function is $u(z, x_1, \ldots, x_n)$, which they maximize subject to available income y. The first-order conditions for this problem are that the marginal rates of substitution between an attribute and the composite good be equal to the ratio of their marginal prices. With the price of the composite good normalized to be one, this means:

$$u_{x1}/u_z = dp/dx_1 \qquad (1.1)$$

If z is money, marginal willingness to pay is equal to the derivative of the hedonic price function with respect to the attribute.

Valuing non-marginal changes is more difficult. Because WTP is only equal to the derivative of the hedonic price function at the margin, valuing non-marginal changes requires additional information about household WTP functions. Reasoning from the fact that the price function results from the interaction of households and firms, Rosen originally suggested that household WTP could be identified with second-stage regressions in a way not unlike ordinary demand estimation. Since then, several authors have noted that the identification problem is not so straightforward. One reason is that unlike the usual case for identifying market demands, where consumers choose a quantity at a given price, here consumers choose a point on the hedonic price function, thereby simultaneously choosing quantities and prices.[15] However, Bartik (1988b) and Kanemoto (1988) have shown that the marginal WTP from the hedonic regression still gives an upper-bound estimate of benefits.

The hedonic method has frequently been used to value natural resources, with air quality being the most common application (see Smith and Huang 1995 for a bibliography). It also has been used to value health, an application stressed in the case study. For example, Kip Viscusi and others have used hedonic wage models to estimate how much people are willing to pay, in the form of lower wages, for a job with lower health risks. As discussed in Chapter 5, the approach has been especially popular for valuing mortality risks (Viscusi 1992, 1993).

Averting-behaviour Method

The averting-behaviour method uses the household-production frame-work to estimate the value of environmental quality.[16] First suggested by Gary Becker, the household-production model postulates that households behave like firms, combining environmental quality together with one or more market goods to 'produce' a service such as good health or cleanliness.[17] By looking at the way households trade off between market goods at different levels of environmental quality, it allows economists to infer the value of the natural resource.

Suppose utility is a function of health, h, and a composite good z, $U(h, z)$. Households use air quality, q, and a market commodity a, such as air filters, with price p_a, to produce good health according to the production technology $h = \phi(q, a)$. Intuitively, since in this simplified model air quality affects utility only through health, it follows that the WTP for a marginal improvement in air quality is equal to the marginal effect of air quality on health times the value of health. Using the implicit function theorem, this in turn is equal to the negative of the marginal adjustment of averting expenditures in response to a marginal change in air quality:

$$WTP(dq) = p_a \frac{\phi_q}{\phi_a} = -p_a \cdot a_q \qquad (1.2)$$

The benefits of a marginal improvement in q are the savings in averting expenditures that maintain the original level of health.

The averting-behaviour method can also be used to infer the value of health effects *per se*, a simpler calculation.[18] In this model, the value of health effects is just the price of averting behaviour divided by its efficacy in producing health:

$$WTP(dh) = \frac{p_a}{\phi_a} \tag{1.3}$$

See for example Dickie et al. (1987). This method has also been used to estimate the value of reduced mortality risks based on the use of seat belts (Blomquist 1979), and smoke detectors (Dardis 1980).

While the averting-behaviour approach has these theoretical strengths, it can suffer from various empirical difficulties. First, some averting behaviours, such as the purchase of air filters, are binary choices (that is, the choice to buy one or none). In these circumstances, many people receive benefits from the air filter above the cost they pay for it, making the expense an inexact measure of WTP. Åkerman, Johnson and Bergman (1991) address this concern by employing conditional logit models. Second, averting behaviours may involve joint products. An air conditioner, for example, clearly involves a contribution to utility through cooling in addition to improved health. Other things equal, such joint production suggests that averting-behaviour approaches yield upper bounds on WTP. A third problem with implementing the averting-behaviour method involves measurement. Calculating marginal WTP requires measuring the marginal cost of averting behaviour and the marginal product of that behaviour (that is, the reduction in sick time or symptom severity). Both of these quantities may be difficult to observe. For example, some averting behaviours, such as spending time indoors, do not involve market goods, making it difficult to infer their cost. A final problem is that households' perception of physical relationships between averting behaviours and health may differ from the technical relationships used by the analyst. In one attempt to circumvent this problem, Chestnut et al. (1988) based their calculations of WTP to avoid an angina attack on a survey of people's perceptions.

Travel-cost Methods

The travel-cost method is similar to the averting-behaviour method in that it also uses the household-production framework, but it is generally used to value recreation services instead of health or cleaning services. The travel-cost method presumes that households use environmental quality, together with market goods, to produce recreation services. The intuition underlying the travel-cost method is simple, and was first proposed by

Harold Hotelling in 1949. The intuition is that recreators pay an implicit price through the costs of travel and time to acquire access to a site. All else being equal, people will continue to visit a site until the marginal value of the last trip is exactly equal to the travel expenses and the opportunity of the time spent travelling. Because recreators visit a site from many different points of origin, they face different prices, and so their demand for the site's services can be estimated from their travel behaviour. With demand thus estimated, consumer surplus for the site can be calculated.

In the past, the traditional travel-cost model used one equation to model the number of recreation trips people take to a single recreation site. The number of trips is assumed to be a function of travel costs, characteristics of the recreator, and sometimes variables to account generally for available substitute recreation opportunities. Such single-site models are easy to construct but oversimplify the choice problem. The major flaws of this model are its inability adequately to account for substitution among recreation sites and its inability to determine the importance of individual site characteristics. If there are substitutes for the site, an increase in travel costs would induce people to visit another site rather than forego recreation altogether. This substitution means that not all the value of the trip is lost. It is only reduced by the difference in satisfaction given by the second-choice site relative to the first-choice site. Because the travel-cost model does not incorporate this substitution in any meaningful way, the method overstates the benefits of the recreation site.

Attempts to compensate for these drawbacks have included estimating multiple-site models, which use a series of demand equations to estimate the number of trips taken to several sites with different attributes and quality. While these models are an improvement over the single-site models, they can still only value a trip as a whole. They cannot value an improvement of one specific attribute of a site, such as environmental quality.

While still using the same basic intuition, a more recent approach that takes a more realistic view of the choice process has largely taken the place of the traditional travel-cost model. These conditional logit models, originally developed to study transportation choices, posit that the benefit an individual receives from a given activity is observable with some degree of uncertainty. For this reason, they also are called random utility models (RUMs). A second difference from the traditional travel-cost model is that, instead of estimating the number of trips that an individual will take to a site, they estimate the probability that an individual will choose any given site as a function of its attributes and travel cost.

Specifically, let the utility of person i for recreation choice j be a function of attributes of the site, $\mathbf{a}$, including environmental quality q, and travel cost t. Utility is also a function of a composite good z, which is just income y minus travel costs. The utility of a visit to site j is then:

$$u_{ij} = u(y_i - t_{ij}, \mathbf{a}_j, q_j, \mathbf{c}_i) + \varepsilon_{ij} \qquad (1.4)$$

where $\mathbf{c}$ are personal characteristics used to estimate the utility parameters and ε is the random component of utility which is unobserved by the analysts.

The probability of an individual choosing site j is simply the probability that the utility from j is greater than the utility from all other sites. McFadden (1973) has shown that if the ε are distributed Weibull, then the probability of an individual choosing site j is

$$\text{Prob}(\text{choice}_i = j) = \frac{e^{u(y_i - t_{ij}, \mathbf{a}_j, q_j, \mathbf{c}_i)}}{\sum_j e^{u(y_i - t_{ij}, \mathbf{a}_j, q_j, \mathbf{c}_i)}} \qquad (1.5)$$

With this framework, the parameters of the utility function can be estimated from observed site choices using methods of maximum likelihood.

From the structure imposed by the functional form of the utility function in Equation (1.4) and the estimated parameters, welfare measures of a change in a site's attributes are obtainable. First, the marginal utility of money is calculated from the parameter on travel cost. Then, for any utility change induced by a change in site attributes, it is possible to calculate the money payment that would leave utility unchanged. This money payment is the person's WTP for the change in attributes. Unlike the traditional travel-cost model, this is not the WTP to take a trip to a site with the improved attributes. Rather, it is the WTP for the opportunity to have a site with those attributes among one's menu of options. Because utility is partly a function of unobserved error terms, the analyst must determine the payment that will leave utility unchanged in an expected value sense (see Bockstael, McConnell and Strand 1991).

Restoration- and replacement-cost Methods

A final alternative for measuring natural resource costs and benefits is to use the replacement- or restoration-cost method. The restoration-cost method values environmental quality in a natural resource as costs of improving quality, often as appraised by an engineer. For example, it might value clean water as the cost of filtering it or cleaning up contaminants. The replacement-cost method similarly determines the value for natural resources as the cost of obtaining alternative sources of the resource's services.

The greatest advantage of the restoration-cost method is that it is relatively simple to use. But as noted earlier, the method ignores the behavioural responses of individuals to changes in the natural resource. It also obscures the distinction between benefits and costs: there is no guarantee that people are actually willing to pay the estimated cost. These objections are decisive: restoration costs are just arbitrary values that may bear little relationship to true social values. Users' willingness to pay for the restoration of the natural resource may be more or less than the cost of replacement.

However, one related method often used in health economics, the cost-of-illness method, has some merit over other restoration-cost approaches. Cost-of-illness studies measure foregone income and the costs of medical treatment – including doctor visits, hospital visits, medication and other expenses – and add them together to calculate the out-of-pocket expenses of an illness. This differs from other restoration-cost approaches because it observes actual expenditures people are making rather than an expert's appraisal of the costs. If individuals are bearing the full cost of the treatment, this guarantees that they are willing to pay at least this treatment cost to restore full health.[19] Of course, they would also be willing to pay, in money, up to the same quantity of income lost from the illness. Thus cost-of-illness approaches can at least yield a lower bound on WTP, whereas other restoration-cost approaches have no necessary relationship with WTP. The issue of a lower bound is discussed in more detail in Chapter 5, which specifically addresses health valuation for the case study.

NOTES

1. Much of this history is based on Krutilla (1981) and Grubb, Whittington and Humphries (1984), who stress aspects related to environmental economics. Porter (1995) discusses some of the history before the Flood Control Act and subsequent administrative developments.

   The theoretical development of benefit–cost analysis and welfare economics generally has not been as smooth as this simple history suggests, with the economics profession wavering between competing desires for methodological purity and for operationalism and applicability. As a microcosm of this debate consider, for example, the series of correspondence that appeared in *The Economic Journal* in 1938 and 1939 including Harrod (1938), Robbins (1938), Hicks (1939) and Kaldor (1939).

2. Morgenstern (1997) summarizes the more significant analyses that EPA has conducted.

3. In terms borrowed from the economics of information, studies of different quality are different message services each with a cost and an expected value (for example Hirshliefer and Riley 1992).

4. Studies include Ontario Hydro (1990), Harrison et al. (1993), Thayer et al. (1994), Rowe et al. (1994), European Commission (1995), Lee, Krupnick and Burtraw (1995) and Desvousges et al. (1995a, 1995b).

5. This terminology differs from the more standard 'study site' and 'policy site' introduced by Desvousges, Naughton and Parsons (1992). We find the new terminology more

straightforward and less likely to cause confusion, since both the original and the transfer work involve studies and both may involve policies.

6. In environmental economics, economists have compiled several useful bibliographies that include many studies from the grey literature that would otherwise be difficult to find. These include Carson et al. (1994a) and MacNair (1993). In addition, the US Environmental Protection Agency has compiled a bibliography that is available electronically.

7. See Hanemann (1991) for a technical discussion of the difference between these two measures.

8. Note that this average across individuals of marginal WTP is different from the overall average WTP. The latter would include all the trips of each individual. In Figure 1.4, this would be total Hicksian surplus divided by the number of trips, or $(P^o - P^*)/2$. This measure is inappropriate, as individuals would still enjoy the benefit from trips at other times; only marginal trips during the closure period are lost.

9. See Mitchell and Carson (1989), Arrow et al. (1993) and Bjornstad and Kahn (1996) for an introduction to current CV methods and evaluations of CV research.

10. Implied-value cues are information in the survey suggesting values that the respondent may interpret as conventional, socially acceptable, or required to cover costs of provision.

11. Non-use services include such values as one obtains for the mere existence of a resource, even if never planning to visit it or use it in another way. For example, one may have values for the Grand Canyon as a natural wonder or national treasure, even without ever visiting it.

12. Technically, CV also is a 'stated-preference' method. However, CV was developed by environmental economists quite independently of market-research SP techniques. We use SP to designate only procedures that employ systematic variations in commodity attributes.

13. Recently two of the authors have applied SP techniques to value morbidity associated with heart and lung disease episodes. See Johnson et al. (1996). This study was specifically designed to facilitate transferring health-benefit estimates.

14. Helpful reviews of the large literature on the hedonic method include Palmquist (1991) and Freeman (1993).

15. For discussion of this and other problems, see Brown and Rosen (1982), Epple (1987), Bartik (1987), and McConnell and Phipps (1987).

16. For more on the averting-behaviour method, see Courant and Porter (1981), Gerking and Stanley (1986) and Harrington and Portney (1987). See Cropper and Freeman (1991) for a review.

17. For a discussion of household-production models and environmental-benefits estimation under different assumptions about the technical relations between environmental services and market goods, see Smith (1991).

18. The term 'averting-behaviour study' or method can create some confusion because different authors have used it to mean up to three things. It can mean an attempt to estimate WTP for quality, WTP for specific impacts such as health effects, or simply adding up observed averting-behaviour expenses. As explained in Chapter 5, the latter provides a lower bound on WTP. See Harrington, Krupnick and Spofford (1989), Abdallah, Roach and Epp (1992), and Desvousges (1995b) for examples.

19. Typically patients pay only a portion of the full cost of treatment, with the remainder covered by public or private health insurance. Third-party payments thus complicate the interpretation of cost of illness as a lower bound on WTP.

2. Critical aspects of the transfer

Both the art and the science of transfer studies consist in how analysts implement the steps summarized in the previous chapter. Many of these steps can be taken in different ways, using available information differently, requiring various levels of effort, and thus involving different ways of interpreting the transfer. For example, one critical aspect of transfers that has received much attention is how to determine which information should be transferred. What studies should be chosen, based on what criteria? How can multiple studies be transferred? This chapter addresses these and other critical aspects of the transfer.

2.1 DEGREE OF AGGREGATION

At the first step of the transfer process, analysts identify linkages and search for existing research to quantify them. In practice, even in cases where there are multiple cause-and-effect linkages, analysts may sometimes aggregate the linkages and transfer them simultaneously. At the most aggregate level, analysts may simply identify the final benefits and costs of previous policies and transfer the final estimate to a new policy, combining all the steps into one transfer. For example, for the case study of externalities of electricity generation in the midwestern US, we could simply have transferred the results of previous estimates (which, in this case, themselves use the transfer method) of the externalities of electricity generation in California or Nevada. More commonly, after separately estimating physical effects, analysts might combine the effects on services and the value of those services. For example, after estimating a change in air quality we could simply transfer willingness-to-pay (WTP) estimates for air quality itself without considering the many services affected. Such estimates might be available from hedonic models of housing markets (see Smith and Huang 1995 for a bibliography) or contingent-valuation studies (Loehman, Boldt and Chaikin 1984). This approach assumes that the effects of all the linkages are incorporated into observed, revealed or stated preferences. Alternatively, at the most disaggregate level analysts can quantify each linkage separately, which is the approach taken in the case study. In the remainder of this book we refer to the latter two approaches as 'aggregate' and 'disaggregate' transfer studies respectively.[1] The case study is an example of a large disaggregate transfer.

One concern that arises in the disaggregate transfer is whether different types of effects can realistically be monetized separately and then added together. This is another facet of an issue raised by Hoehn and Randall (1989), who question the appropriateness of evaluating multiple policies with separate benefit–cost analyses, and by Randall (1991), who applies the reasoning to estimating separately the different conceptual components of welfare (use value, non-use value, and so on). Hoehn and Randall show that, even in theory, independent estimation and summation (IES) does not lead to the same result as would a more holistic estimation procedure.

Following Randall (1991), consider a household with the utility function

$$u = u(s_1, s_2, s_3, q, \mathbf{z}) \tag{2.1}$$

where s_1, s_2 and s_3 are three service flows from an environmental resource, q is the quality of the resource, and $\mathbf{z}$ is a vector of all other commodities. With this utility function, the solution to the household's cost-minimization problem yields the expenditure function $e(p_1, p_2, p_3, q; u)$. The correct total value (TV) of the resource is the change in expenditures required to keep utility constant at some reference level u^o when the service flows are eliminated:

$$
\begin{aligned}
TV &= e(p_1^*, p_2^*, p_3^*, q^o, u^o) - e(p_1^o, p_2^o, p_3^o, q^o, u^o) \\
&= e(p_1^*, p_2^*, p_3^*, q^o, u^o) - e(p_1^o, p_2^*, p_3^*, q^o, u^o) \\
&\quad + e(p_1^o, p_2^*, p_3^*, q^o, u^o) - e(p_1^o, p_2^o, p_3^*, q^o, u^o) \\
&\quad + e(p_1^o, p_2^o, p_3^*, q^o, u^o) - e(p_1^o, p_2^o, p_3^o, q^o, u^o)
\end{aligned} \tag{2.2}
$$

where o superscripts denote baseline levels and $*$ superscripts denote the choke price – the implicit price at which demand for the service falls to zero. Extending this result to the value of quality changes is straightforward.[2]

The equation shows that the total value can be decomposed into three sequential valuations. The IES approach, however, does not consider each effect sequentially, but rather, as the name suggests, independently. That is, valuing one service flow at a time from the same baseline, the approach gives:

$$
\begin{aligned}
IES &= e(p_1^*, p_2^*, p_3^*, q^o, u^o) - e(p_1^o, p_2^*, p_3^*, q^o, u^o) \\
&\quad + e(p_1^*, p_2^*, p_3^*, q^o, u^o) - e(p_1^*, p_2^o, p_3^*, q^o, u^o) \\
&\quad + e(p_1^*, p_2^*, p_3^*, q^o, u^o) - e(p_1^*, p_2^*, p_3^o, q^o, u^o)
\end{aligned} \tag{2.3}
$$

In general, these two estimates will be different. Hoehn and Randall (1989) further show that, in the limit, as the number of steps becomes large, the independent estimation and summation approach overstates the true benefits.

Hoehn and Randall's argument implies that when it evaluates each effect independently, the disaggregate transfer implicitly ignores the changes in substitution opportunities and budgets brought about by all the other effects. However, while this is an important caveat, it does not necessarily imply that aggregate transfers are preferable to disaggregate ones. In practice, seemingly aggregate estimates may not actually capture all the benefit categories involved. For example, transferring estimates of the WTP for air quality from household hedonic regressions would not include agricultural effects or health effects resulting from exposure at work or elsewhere away from the home. Furthermore, aggregate revealed- or stated-preference approaches require heroic assumptions about market efficiency, cognitive capabilities and statistical realities. A possible strategy is to transfer both aggregate and disaggregate estimates, providing a sensitivity analysis of assumptions or a range of estimates.

2.2   SELECTING CANDIDATE STUDIES FOR THE TRANSFER

In transferring its estimates, analysts must transfer an original study's methodology and assumptions as well. Thus, they should examine the existing studies they have identified for quality and relevance to the new context. Several resource economists have suggested criteria for evaluating existing studies, including Boyle and Bergstrom (1992); Brookshire (1992); Desvousges, Naughton and Parsons (1992); Kask (1992); Luken, Johnson and Kibler (1992); McConnell (1992). Table 2.1 summarizes these criteria.

The first type of criterion for transfer candidates is that, in Freeman's (1984) words, they must 'pass scientific muster'. If the original study uses flawed methodology and assumptions, the transfer estimates will also be flawed. While the specific criteria will vary greatly depending on the type of study, some general principles apply to most cases. The study should use sound empirical practices for avoiding bias and its underlying data should be a representative sample of adequate size. Likewise, its analysis should follow a framework guided by the appropriate theory, and its statistical methods should be appropriate and rigorous. In econometric estimates, for example, errors can arise if the wrong functional form is used, if variables are omitted, or if variables are measured with error. For

Table 2.1 Criteria for evaluating the transferability of existing studies

Category	Specific criteria
Scientific soundness	Data collection procedures Empirical methodology Consistentency with scientific or economic theory Statistical techniques
Germaneness	Change in environmental quality Baseline environmental quality Affected services or commodities Site characteristics of affected commodity Duration and timing of effects Exposure path and nature of health risks Socioeconomic characteristics of the affected population Property rights
Richness of detail	Definition of variables and means Treatment of substitutes Participation rates Cost of time Standard errors

Sources: Boyle and Bergstrom (1992); Brookshire (1992); Desvousges, Naughton and Parsons (1992); Kask (1992); Luken, Johnson and Kibler (1992); McConnell (1992).

example, in tests of the effect of model specifications on transferability, Train (1979) and Koppelman and Wilmot (1986) find that more complex specifications provide better predictions in the out-of-sample transfer context. In general, the best practices for research vary by discipline and application, but guidelines are often established in the literature. For example, Mitchell and Carson (1989) and Arrow et al. (1993) provide guidelines for contingent-valuation studies.

The second type of criterion, germaneness or relevance, involves the similarity and applicability of the original study to the transfer context. The first criterion in this category is that the magnitude of the effects should be similar for the original and transfer policies, to avoid extrapolating outside the range of data. A similar criterion is that the baseline levels of environmental quality should be comparable in the original context and the transfer context. Health effects resulting from a one-unit increase in air pollution in London may be higher than the same increase in rural Minnesota because of an already greater health burden. Similarly, the WTP for a given improvement in health is sensitive to baseline health levels (Alberini et al. 1994; Johnson, Fries and Banzhaf 1997). In addition to background environmental quality, the affected commodities should be similar in other ways. In the case of health risks, for example, differences in exposure pathways, risk levels, the voluntariness of the risks, and other aspects may all influence an individual's response (Slovic, Fischhoff and Lichtenstein 1979). In the case of WTP studies of outdoor recreation, the sites should be similarly accessible, have similar amenities, and involve similar substitute alternatives. Likewise, the socio-economic characteristics of the affected populations should be similar, as these may influence behaviour, preferences and, in the case of health effects, physical responses. A final criterion is the assignment of property rights. Although the assignment is often arbitrary, if property rights in environmental improvements are given to people so that willingness to accept is the appropriate welfare measure instead of WTP, transferred studies should use willingness to accept.[3] In sum, the original study's context and that of the transfer policy should match as closely as possible.

The third category of criterion involves the richness of the information available from the existing study. To facilitate transferring entire equations, studies would ideally provide precise definitions and units of the variables in the analysis, as well as their means. As discussed later, knowledge of the covariance matrix or parameters is also essential for bootstrapping and Monte Carlo simulations of confidence intervals. At the benefits or cost stage of the transfer, they would ideally include information on the available substitutes for the commodity and how they were modelled. They would also reveal participation rates, the extent of the relevant geographic market and, in the case of travel-cost studies of recreation demand, report assumptions about the opportunity cost of time. All studies should provide standard errors or other measures of dispersion. Although rarely reported, the entire variance–covariance matrix of parameters facilitates hypothesis tests and Monte Carlo simulations of confidence intervals when transferring a model.

2.3   SUMMARIZING EXISTING INFORMATION

Some of the discussion in the previous section and in other treatments has tacitly assumed that analysts are looking for a single best estimate to transfer at each linkage. And indeed, often only a single study is available. But when multiple studies are available, conducting a literature review and choosing the 'best study' is only one approach to transfers. Using only the information from the chosen study, this approach neglects other valuable information available to be transferred. To capitalize on all the information, other approaches use information from multiple studies.

One such approach is to use several studies to provide a range of possible estimates. An original study with a low estimate provides the lower bound of the transfer estimate; another with a high estimate provides the upper bound. An alternative approach summarizes the studies with simple descriptive statistics such as the mean and standard error. With this approach, uncertainty is usually quantified by averaging 95 per cent values to provide an overall 95 per cent confidence interval. Still other approaches use qualitative judgements about the central tendency of the studies in the manner of a traditional literature review.

As Krupnick (1992) notes, no protocol currently exists for using multiple studies. In part, this probably follows from the failure of most of these approaches to represent adequately the existing information available to be transferred. Of the three approaches suggested above, the first generally does not use all the available original studies, the second treats them all equally, and the third implicitly weights the original studies for quality or applicability in a subjective and often unreported way. None provides a rigorous assessment of uncertainty and none takes advantage of the richness of the information that can be provided by multiple studies performed under different settings.

For those services and their linkages that back-of-the-envelope calculations suggest will have particular influence on the final estimates, an ideal approach would be to obtain the data from the original studies and estimate a pooled model. For example, Morton and Krupnick (1988) pooled data from four experiments on the relationship between ozone levels and health effects, estimating a single model. This pooled model could then be transferred to the new context, capturing all the available information. However, pooled models are rare, as the data are often unavailable or not measured in compatible units.

If a pooled model is infeasible, the next best approach is to use meta-analysis techniques.[4] Meta-analysis, although common in the natural and applied sciences and in other social sciences, has been used less often in economics.[5] Those analyses that have been done have usually explored the influence of various modelling decisions on final estimates; only rarely do they attempt to synthesize estimates and economic relationships in a way that is useful for policy making or transfers. Despite being rarely used, meta-analysis has significant potential. First, it can derive underlying statistical distributions from which study-specific findings may have come, providing a more rigorous estimate of overall central tendency and dispersion than simple averaging. In addition, through regression techniques it can explore systematic relationships between the estimates at each linkage in the transfer and other parameters, such as the background environmental quality, the commodity's attributes and socioeconomic characteristics of the affected population. This information can be useful in adjusting for differences in these parameters between the original and transfer contexts.

There are several general approaches to formalizing the analyst's beliefs about the nature of the problem and the relationship between the evidence and factual outcomes. Because the 'true' values of interest may differ among studies undertaken in different statistical contexts, each of these approaches incorporates specific assumptions about the underlying process that gives rise to the estimates. Alternative approaches include the equal-effects model, fixed-effects model, the random-effects model and Bayesian approaches.

The equal-effects model presumes that the same parameter value underlies all the available studies. Thus either the statistical circumstances among studies are the same, or any differences have no effect on estimates. To the extent that estimates vary according to observed, known factors, it is only necessary to make appropriate adjustments for systematic differences between the original contexts and the transfer context. In most cases, however, the true value will vary systematically according to observed and unobserved factors specific to each study.

The Fixed-effects Approach

In the general case where differences in study results arise from unobserved factors, analysts may choose between fixed-effects and random-effects approaches. The fixed-effects approach summarizes a group of estimates using a set of weights. This approach aims to replicate the statistical variation that would be observed if the same studies were performed under the same circumstances. For example, suppose the analyst uses equal weights to summarize epidemiological evidence across multiple locations. The result indicates the expected health outcome in a population drawn randomly from the set of possible locations. If the weights are proportional to location populations, then the result indicates the expected health outcome for an individual drawn randomly from the set of possible locations.

Suppose the individual studies estimate a parameter of interest b, variation in which can be explained by a regression model of the form

$$b_{ij} = \alpha_i + \gamma' \mathbf{x}_{ij} + \varepsilon_{ij} \qquad (2.4)$$

where i indexes different studies, j indexes observations within studies, the constant α_i varies across studies, and ε_{ij} is a common random error term with an expected value of zero and constant variance. The explanatory variables in **X** may include both dummy variables that control for observed differences in study methodology and behavioural or technical determinants of b, such as differences in background, environmental quality or population characteristics across studies. Thus, after controlling for observable determinants of differences among studies, remaining differences can be explained by a set of study-specific constants, α_i, that capture unobserved, systematic study-specific differences. This case is the fixed-effects model.[6]

Chapter 5 describes a meta-analysis of willingness-to-pay values for acute morbidity. The data come from five studies that report a total of 53 estimates. In Chapter 5, we report only the equal-effects model used in the case study. However, another model that could be tested is a simple fixed-effects specification:

$$\text{WTP} = 957 \cdot S_1 + 945 \cdot S_2 + 886 \cdot S_3 + 1386 \cdot S_4 + 1095 \cdot S_5$$
$$\quad (3.5) \qquad (3.2) \qquad (3.2) \qquad (4.5) \qquad (4.0)$$

$$\qquad - 1228 \cdot \text{QWB} + 3.32 \cdot \text{DAYS}$$
$$\qquad (-3.2) \qquad\qquad (3.8) \qquad\qquad\qquad\qquad (2.5)$$

where WTP is the estimated willingness to pay to avoid a particular illness, S_1 to S_5 are dummy variables for the five study-specific fixed effects, QWB is the quality-of-well-being health-status index for the illness, and DAYS is the duration of the episode of ill health. The t-ratios are shown in parentheses and indicate that all coefficients are significant at the 1 per cent level. Full details of the analysis can be found in Johnson, Fries and Banzhaf (1997), where a random-effects model is also reported.

Transferring a predicted value from a fixed-effects model raises the question of which fixed effect to include in the prediction. This question appears to require analysts again to decide which is the single 'best' study, a judgement we hoped to avoid by using meta-analysis. While it is not possible or appropriate to completely avoid judgements about study quality, one possible strategy is to construct a single, composite constant term that is the average of the fixed effects, possibly weighted by the number of observations each study contributes to the regression.

The Random-effects Approach

Alternatively, a random-effects approach assumes there is a 'mother distribution' of true outcomes common to all the studies. Thus the observed studies represent random draws from the underlying distribution and an estimate of the distribution summarizes the relevant information in the studies. Uncertainty about the truth in this case arises not only from differences in sampling error among studies, but also from the inherent randomness of the underlying parameter values that give rise to particular study estimates. A random-effects approach to summarizing results thus attempts to predict what might happen in a new setting subject to the same underlying randomness as the existing studies.

In particular, suppose now that the underlying relationship takes the form

$$b_{ij} = \alpha + \gamma' \mathbf{x}_{ij} + u_i + \varepsilon_{ij} \tag{2.6}$$

where the respective studies now share a common constant term, α, and u_i is a random error term specific to each study with mean zero and variance σ_u^2. After controlling for systematic, observed factors that vary among studies, remaining differences arise from draws on the distribution of each u_i.[7] The expected value of b and its standard error, β^* and σ^*, are the mean and standard error of the underlying mother distribution from which the individual study estimates are drawn.

Chapter 4 describes a random-effects meta-analysis of studies of mortality rates associated with exposure to particulate matter. The studies share a similar estimation protocol and each estimates a parameter b_i that is the percentage increase in mortality for a 1 $\mu g/m^3$ increase in daily particulate matter – PM_{10}. Suppose then that there is no variation in $\mathbf{X}$ among studies (or that the γ coefficients are all zero). This random-effects model assumes that the estimated coefficients and variances for each study, b_i and s_i^2, are determined by the means and variances β_i and σ_i^2 of the city-specific distributions from which they are drawn. It further assumes that the city-distribution parameters are drawn from a common mother distribution with parameters β^* and σ^* that is the source of all the estimates and that is independent of the range of exposure.

Using the technique described in Chapter 4 to recover the underlying parameters from the eight particulate studies, we estimate the underlying meta-coefficient, or the mean of the mother distribution, to be 0.1014, with a standard error of 0.0424. That is, we estimate that the underlying physical relationship is a 0.1014 per cent increase in mortality for a 1 $\mu g/m^3$ increase in daily PM_{10}. Figure 2.1 illustrates the random effects model estimated here. It shows the mother distribution derived from the eight individual-study coefficient distributions (labelled by city).

The random-effects model has the advantage over fixed-effects models of not using up degrees of freedom with the study-specific dummy

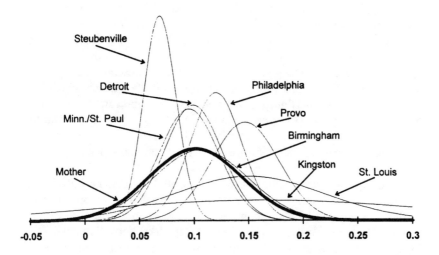

Figure 2.1 Illustration of random-effects model of mortality studies

variables. In the data set used here, for example, only one observation is available from each study, making fixed-effects regressions impossible. In other cases, multiple estimates from each study will provide a true panel (or longitudinal) data set. One disadvantage of the random-effects model is the assumption that the shocks for each study u_i are independent of any other regressors. Hausman (1978) provides a test of this assumption.

Bayesian Approaches

The equal-effects, fixed-effects and random-effects models minimize the judgements and assumptions necessary to summarize results from multiple sources. These approaches use the relative frequency of outcomes in the original studies to determine the probability that a summary result is correct. In fact, analysts may hold well-informed opinions about study biases, relevance, validity or overall quality. Incorporating such judgements implies a different view of the transfer problem. Bayesian approaches use analysts' prior beliefs about how likely or unlikely each original study's outcome is to form a probability distribution over possible values of the underlying parameter. Bayesian analysis helps structure such beliefs by requiring analysts to specify subjective probability distributions for parameters of interest.

In conventional or classical statistics, the parameter of interest is considered to be fixed with a single value. The Bayesian view is that the parameter is a random variable whose probability distribution expresses the analyst's current degree of uncertainty about its true value. Thus this approach presumes some prior understanding about a given parameter, ranging from complete uncertainty (a so-called 'flat' or non-informative prior) to certain knowledge of its true value. Additional evidence is then evaluated in light of this prior, producing a modified assessment of the likely probability distribution, or 'posterior' distribution, for the parameter. This updated assessment can then serve as a prior for evaluating another source of evidence. The process proceeds until all available evidence has been assimilated into an overall summary posterior judgement about the probability distribution.

Let the parameter of interest be represented by β. The initial prior distribution for β is $f(\beta)$. Observed estimates of β from one or more studies are denoted by b and contain information about the true value of β. The likelihood function $L(b|\beta)$ indicates the likelihood that b would be observed, given a particular judgement about the distribution of β. Bayes's theorem links the posterior distribution $f(\beta|b)$ with the prior distribution and likelihood function.

$$f(\beta|b) = k \cdot L(b|\beta) \cdot f(\beta) \tag{2.7}$$

where k is a normalizing constant that adjusts the area under the probability density function to equal one. If the relevant distributions are normally distributed, the posterior distribution of β is normally distributed with mean and variance[8]

$$E[\bar{\beta}|b] = \frac{\dfrac{\beta}{\sigma_\beta^2} + \dfrac{b}{\sigma_b^2}}{\dfrac{1}{\sigma_\beta^2} + \dfrac{1}{\sigma_b^2}} \tag{2.8}$$

$$\mathrm{Var}[\bar{\beta}|b] = \frac{1}{\dfrac{1}{\sigma_\beta^2} + \dfrac{1}{\sigma_b^2}} \tag{2.9}$$

Thus the posterior mean and variance are weighted averages of the prior and study means and variances, where the weights are the inverses of the prior and study estimate variances. The prior variance indicates the analyst's relative confidence in the prior compared to the study estimate.

The problem of transferring a particulate mortality coefficient from the previous section can serve as an example of the Bayesian approach. In addition to the eight studies used in the random-effects model, there is an additional study of particulate-induced mortality in Santa Clara,

California (Fairley 1990). This study employs a somewhat different methodology and different measure of particulate exposure. Both the coefficient and its standard error are roughly half that of the eight-study mother distribution.[9] The estimated coefficient is 0.054, with standard error of 0.024. If this were the only available study and the analyst's prior were completely uninformative, $1/(\sigma_\beta^2) \to 0$ in Equations (2.8) and (2.9). The posterior estimates $\bar{\beta}$ and $\bar{\sigma}^2$ would be the same as the study estimates. Thus the transfer would consist simply of applying the Santa Clara estimates in the transfer context.

Suppose instead that we have strong confidence in the mean mother-distribution estimate for β, and are somewhat sceptical of the relevance of the Santa Clara study. Nevertheless, we are unwilling to discount the Santa Clara results entirely. If our relative confidence in our prior ($\sigma_b = 0.024$) relative to the additional study is, say, ten to one, then set $\sigma_\beta = \sqrt{\sigma_b^2/10} = 0.0076$.[10] The posterior mean coefficient decreases slightly from 0.101 to 0.097, with the posterior standard error also falling slightly to 0.0072.

Critiques of Meta-analysis

The most important advantage of meta-analysis is that it requires analysts to document judgements and assumptions used in summarizing research results and facilitates sensitivity analysis of such judgements. Nevertheless, meta-analysis has been criticized. Some of the concerns of meta-analysis critics include: selection bias, heterogeneity and violations of statistical assumptions, inadequate responses to inconsistent reporting conventions, and tendency to emphasize quantity over quality (see Wachter 1988; Gaver et al. 1992; Rosenthal 1991; Thacker 1988).

Selection bias, availability bias, or the so-called 'file-drawer problem' refers to the tendency of journal editors to publish positive and statistically significant results. Thus the consignment of negative and insignificant results to researchers' file drawers results in a biased sample of results to include in a meta-analysis. Rosenthal and Rubin (1988) suggest procedures for quantifying and adjusting for such potential bias. Rosenthal (1991) also reviews several studies that have attempted to assess actual differences between published and unpublished studies. The results generally suggest that potential biases are much smaller than critics often assert.

Heterogeneity, or the 'apples-and-oranges' problem, is related to the argument that meta-analysis misuses statistical techniques designed for experimental data collected under controlled conditions by applying them to study estimates based on heterogeneous samples and estimation methodologies. While inappropriate use of statistical techniques in any context is to be deplored, there are, as we have discussed, appropriate techniques for controlling for fixed and random effects across studies. While meta-analysis poses several statistical challenges, careful use and interpretation of statistical analysis of study results can be a valid application of quantitative techniques.

While it is possible to control statistically for systematic differences among studies, such procedures assume that such differences are measurable, based on information provided in research articles and reports. In fact, the lack of established reporting conventions or differences in conventions among disciplines and journals often makes it difficult to measure relevant study attributes. Analysts are consequently forced to choose among eliminating some relevant studies (increasing the risk of selection bias), imputing missing information (increasing the risk of measurement error) or omitting explanatory variables (increasing the risk of specification error). This criticism is a serious one and has motivated numerous appeals to editors to adopt more uniform standards for reporting research results. Even if successful, such appeals would do nothing to remedy reporting inconsistencies in past research.

Finally, critics have argued that the emphasis on statistical methods to summarize research inevitably favours quantity over quality. Thus research summaries are dominated by a large number of mediocre studies and are insufficiently sensitive to the smaller number of high-quality studies. This argument seems to assume a mechanistic application of statistical methods. Gaver et al. (1992) caution that all forms of meta-analysis require combining data with judgement. If either the data or the judgement are of poor quality, then meta-analysis may produce worse answers than if no meta-analysis were undertaken.

It is important to put such criticisms of meta-analysis in the appropriate context. Our particular interest is in applying meta-analysis to inform and improve using estimates obtained in one context for predicting outcomes and values in a different context. While there are many problems in using meta-analysis, the alternatives may be subject to even greater concerns. Selecting a single 'best' estimate from among many potential candidates, simply averaging all the available estimates, or applying undocumented 'professional judgement' provide fewer opportunities for assessing the validity of the transfer or quantifying the possible uncertainty than using meta-analysis.

2.4   TRANSFERRING EXISTING INFORMATION

After synthesizing the available information in some way, whether adopting a single 'best study' or performing a meta-analysis, the second part of the actual transfer is to apply this information to the new context. At this point, there are four possible levels of complexity forming a hierarchy of transfer types. In the basic, least complex transfer, analysts simply apply a scalar-valued estimate to the new context. For example, at the valuation linkage, a best-study estimate or the mean of several studies may estimate the value of a day of fishing to be $30, and so the total benefit of the transfer policy is the estimated increase in the number of fishing days times $30. More generally, let $E(\hat{Y}_{oc})$ be the expected value of an estimate $\hat{Y}$ in the original study's context, and let Y_{tc} be the true value in the transfer context. The original estimate is 'perfectly transferable' if

$$E(\hat{Y}_{oc}) = Y_{tc}, \qquad (2.10)$$

that is, if the original estimate provides an unbiased estimate for the transfer. If $\hat{Y}$ is a predicted value from a regression analysis, it is typically evaluated at the means of the independent variables. At a minimum, Equation (2.10) of course requires that the original estimate be unbiased within its own context. Thus, it should meet the standards for soundness highlighted in Table 2.1.

To test if it is also unbiased across contexts, Brookshire (1992) suggests examining the regression equations explaining $\hat{Y}_{oc}$. If elasticities are high with respect to the independent variables, especially those at different magnitudes than at the transfer context, then the transfer is likely to be biased. Alteratively, if studies using similar methodologies repeated over different contexts find different values for $\hat{Y}_{oc}$, again the estimate from a very different original context is likely to be biased in the transfer context.

As Boyle and Bergstrom (1992) note, if transfer analysts conclude that Equation (2.10) does not hold, they may either elect to forego the transfer, accept the bias, or make some adjustments to the estimate $\hat{Y}_{oc}$. Note that foregoing the transfer is not the necessary response to the failure for Equation (2.10) to hold. If standard errors are small, the equation may fail to hold statistically even if the difference between the estimates is small. But it is the difference in estimates that will determine the quality of the policy analysis.[11] As noted in the introduction, the ultimate test of the appropriateness of the transfer method is that the expected benefits of a policy based on original research relative to a policy based on (possibly biased) transfer estimates be smaller than the relative cost of conducting an original study. If the transfer passes this test, analysts may choose to accept the bias.

Alternatively, to improve the quality of the transfer, the analysts may make some adjustments to the estimate. This is the second level of complexity. The adjustment is usually *ad hoc* and largely depends on the analysts' judgement. At best, judgement can be guided by the considerations suggested by Brookshire (1992), with the analysts inspecting the differences between results across contexts and imputing a value for the transfer context.

Making these adjustments more systematic, the next level of complexity transfers an entire functional relationship, usually expressed as a regression equation. With this approach, analysts apply the values of the independent variables in the transfer context to the estimated coefficients from the original study. In this way, they can control for differences between the original and transfer contexts with respect to environmental quality, site attributes, socioeconomic characteristics, and other aspects listed in Table 2.1 as related to the relevance of the original studies. Analogous to Equation (2.10), the original model is perfectly transferable so long as the specification is identical and

$$E(\hat{\beta}_{oc}) = \beta_{tc}, \tag{2.11}$$

that is, the regression coefficients from the original context are unbiased estimates of the true coefficients in the transfer context.

In the particular case of the transfers at the behavioural linkage, this approach may involve transferring WTP equations from contingent-valuation studies, or, more likely, demand equations.[12] Loomis (1992) notes that not only does transferring an entire demand equation control for the characteristics of the commodity and affected population, but it also has the advantage of simultaneously capturing both the quantity and price dimensions of consumer surplus. That is, the demand equation itself provides all the information needed for welfare estimates. This is in contrast to transfers of average WTP per unit of the commodity (a scalar entity rather than a function), which analysts would multiply by the estimated quantity demanded to arrive at the overall welfare estimate. The latter approach typically estimates the quantity demanded with data and behavioural assumptions differing from those used to estimate average WTP. Transferring the demand function maintains the internal consistency of the welfare measure.

Note that this type of transfer can often be linked to the meta-analysis techniques described in the previous section. Even if the original studies do not themselves control for important commodity characteristics or socioeconomic variables, if they report their mean values, then the meta-analysis can explain differences in the results across studies as a function of differences in these and other variables. Thus another purpose of meta-analysis is to summarize information in a format that facilitates a complex transfer. For example, in Chapter 4 we present two alternative meta-analyses of studies relating particulate air pollution to mortality risks. One meta-analysis controls for age-specific effects, differentiating effects for the elderly from the rest of the population; the other controls for differences in background particulate levels across study areas.

Even with equations from individual studies or meta-analyses, analysts may still believe that the parameters from the original equation are not fully applicable to the transfer context (that is, Equation (2.11) does not hold). As with a transfer of scalar values, they may then forego the transfer, accept the biased equation as an approximation, or make adjustments to the parameters. The strategy of making adjustments to the equation parameters is the fourth and highest level of complexity in the hierarchy of transfers. These adjustments again may be *ad hoc*, but Atherton and Ben-Akiva (1976) and Cameron (1992) suggest a number of protocols for making such adjustments systematically so long as some data are available in the transfer context.

One suggestion is for the special case of transferring choice-based models such as the multinomial or conditional logit where the set of choices remains constant across contexts. In this case, Atherton and Ben-Akiva suggest transferring the model coefficients but adjusting the choice-specific constants. If only zonal or other aggregate data are available for the transfer context, the constants could be adjusted so that the original equation predicts the aggregate data in the transfer context. If a small sample of individual choice data is available, the constants could be re-estimated by re-estimating the whole model but constraining the co-efficients to their values from the original equation.

These adjustments may work for intertemporal transfers or in such policy contexts as transportation where the choice set may be small and constant across many areas. In environmental economics, however, where the choices might represent recreation opportunities such as lakes, analysts may often want to transfer the model to a context where choices are added to or eliminated from a large number of alternatives, or even to a context with a completely different set of choices. In such cases, the model should not include the constant terms, as it would then not be appropriately calibrated to the transfer context. For these cases, Cameron (1992) proposes a protocol based on the intuition that adjustments should account for differences in the data across contexts. She suggests using a weighted exogenous sample maximum likelihood estimator (WESML) frequently used in conditional logit models (Manski and Lerman 1977; see also Ben-Akiva and Lerman 1985 and Amemiya 1985). A compromise estimator, WESML, is unbiased and consistent but not asymptotically efficient. Still, it is highly practical.

For this application, the WESML estimator works as follows. Let

$f_{ox}(\mathbf{x})$ represent the joint density of the exogenous variables in the original context, with $\mathbf{x}$ a vector of individual-specific parameters such as environmental quality, site characteristics or especially socioeconomic characteristics. Similarly, let $f_{tc}(\mathbf{x})$ represent the joint density in the transfer context. The latter density may be available from such common sources as the US Census, or may be estimated from a small sample taken at the transfer site. With these densities, the WESML estimator weights the observations in the original study by $f_{tc}(x)/f_{oc}(\mathbf{x})$ for each individual's values of $\mathbf{x}$. These weights recalibrate the data from the original study to better represent the transfer context. If, as is most likely, a continuous joint density cannot be estimated, a tractable alternative is to partition the data into cells and estimate the density non-parametrically.

A final suggestion for adjusting the transfer equation is to pool data from the original context with a small sample from the transfer context, updating the original (prior) estimates. Aigner and Leamer (1984) and Leamer (1995) have employed this approach with a random-coefficients model using a Bayesian approach. Aigner and Leamer use the approach to estimate the response of households to electricity-pricing policies. The coefficients of the demand equation are random, distributed as

$$\beta_i \sim N(\bar{\beta}, \Gamma) \tag{2.12}$$

where i indexes the different study contexts. The most likely value for the parameters in either context is $\bar{\beta}$, and the variance–covariance matrix of the parameters, Γ, determines the degree of transfer from one context to the other. As Γ goes to an infinity matrix, the contexts become more different and must be modelled separately; no transfer can take place. As it goes to a zero matrix, the contexts become identical (and equal to $\bar{\beta}$), and can be estimated as a pooled GLS model.[13] Aigner and Leamer refer to this approach as 'data transfer', but it differs from our use of the word because here the direction of the transfer is mutual among all contexts, with the model being estimated jointly.[14] In contrast, by 'transfer' we usually mean a one-way transfer of information from existing studies to a new context. From this perspective, we can consider the Aigner–Leamer approach a kind of generalized transfer. As Aigner and Leamer note, 'transfer', as we use it, is just a special case of their approach, the case when no data are available in the new context. In this case, $\bar{\beta}$ is estimated from the other contexts and directly transferred.

A similar approach has also been used by Leamer (1995) to test the convergence hypothesis: the hypothesis that poor countries should grow faster than wealthy ones, *ceteris paribus*, with wealth eventually equalizing. Designed to account for the uneven quality of data collection across countries, this approach has the refinement of allowing the analysts to specify their prior subjective beliefs about the quality of information from each context, as well as the degree of similarity between contexts.

Specifically, consider the model

$$Y_i = X_i(\beta_i + \theta_i) + \varepsilon_i \tag{2.13}$$

where θ is the bias vector resulting from the quality of the data, a way to introduce errors-in-variables into the model. The θ vector introduces severe multicollinearity (with each exogenous variable entering the equation twice), but the model can be estimated with information about the priors. Without presenting the actual estimator, consider the intuition of this model. Again assuming random coefficients, the coefficients are distributed (in the two-context case):

$$\begin{bmatrix} \beta_1 \\ \beta_2 \\ \theta_1 \\ \theta_2 \end{bmatrix} \sim N \left(\begin{bmatrix} \bar{\beta} \\ \bar{\beta} \\ 0 \\ 0 \end{bmatrix}, \begin{bmatrix} U & \rho U & 0 & 0 \\ \rho U & U & 0 & 0 \\ 0 & 0 & V_1 & 0 \\ 0 & 0 & 0 & V_2 \end{bmatrix} \right) \tag{2.14}$$

Here, the parameter ρ represents the correlation of the structural parameters across the two contexts and the covariance matrix U measures the departures from the most likely parameter values $\bar{\beta}$. The variance–covariance matrices V_i represent the reliability of the data in each context, with a small prior reflecting an analyst's beliefs that the data are reliable.

This model allows a great deal of flexibility in modelling the transfer. For example, with large U and ρ near 1, the model allows a relatively large confidence interval for β while constraining the values for β in the two contexts to be close.[15] In addition, large values of V discount the information from a given context. In this way, several studies can be combined and transferred, but not all need be given equal weight. Cameron (1992) notes that from this perspective transfer analysts who reject a given study are essentially assigning it an infinite variance, thereby discounting the information. This approach has the advantage of forcing the analysts to make such subjective judgements more explicitly and systematically.

The range of choices available to analysts in transferring estimates in some ways mirrors the choices they have in making policy recommendations with original studies. In addition to choices about modelling strategies, with original studies they may still face a choice about whether to base recommendations on a sample mean, an econometric estimate with the sample data, or an econometric estimate predicted on the population rather than the sample characteristics. In the same way, transfer analysts face a hierarchy of choices for the transfer. Several studies have compared the predictive ability of transfers across levels of this hierarchy (Atherton and Ben-Akiva 1976; Loomis 1992; Kirchhoff, Colby and LaFrance 1997). Not surprisingly, they have consistently found that more complex transfers give better predictions. We review these studies in Chapter 8 in an assessment of the transfer methodology.

2.5   EXTENT OF THE MARKET

Markets are the geographic domain over which all of the linkages are calculated. Three interdependent components of the relevant market are the geographic extent, the affected households or firms within the geographic boundaries, and the availability of substitutes. Identifying geographic or political boundaries such as watersheds or counties may be one way to establish the relevant geographic market. If the decision-making authority is only interested in the impacts within such boundaries, this may be the most appropriate way. However, if all affected parties are considered to be relevant, this may be a less accurate approach because the point where benefits fall to zero may not necessarily correspond to these boundaries.[16] Air pollution, for example, may cross state or national boundaries.

In some cases, the geographic extent of the market is simply determined by the estimates of the physical linkages in the transfer. For example, wherever a policy affects air quality, that is where it affects people because they have no choice (or extremely limited choices) about the air they breathe. In other cases, such as if and where they participate in outdoor recreation, people have more choice. In such cases as this, the set of people likely to consider a site in their choice set constitutes the relevant market. Usually, determining this set is another area that calls for judgement on the part of the analyst, as well as one that can influence the results of the study.

As a first approximation, analysts may make a judgement about whether the affected market is local, regional or national in scope. From there, they can begin to determine more exact boundaries. To inform such judgements, analysts can often draw on some information from the transfer context. They may be able to find previous surveys of users of the resource, indicating the geographic extent. Or, if they have enough time and money, they may be able to conduct their own survey just for the purpose of obtaining this information. More qualitatively, they may conduct interviews with 'key informants', experts who are knowledgeable about the users of a resource and about who is likely to be affected by a particular policy. For example, in a study of outdoor recreation, Dunford, Mathews and Banzhaf (1995) interviewed owners of retail shops that sell or rent recreation equipment, lifeguards, operators of charter fishing boats, and presidents of local recreation clubs.

Another approach is to transfer the extent of the market along with other aspects of transferred studies. The extent of the market is estimated as a function of site characteristics, demographic variables, availability of substitutes and geographic variables and then transferred. Unfortunately, the extent of the market is often as arbitrary in the original studies as in a transfer. If the information is available, analysts may use raw data from existing studies to model the extent of the market. One strategy for doing this follows a technique introduced in the industrial organization literature by Elzinga and Hogarty (1973). Elzinga and Hogarty examine geographic zones of consumers purchasing a commodity from a particular firm and sort them by the highest percentage of consumers. They then compile the cumulative frequencies and tentatively delineate the market as the group of zones providing the top 75 per cent of consumers. To verify the market definition, they check that at least 75 per cent of the total shipments for all firms in the area fall within its boundaries and that no more than 25 per cent of the consumers go outside the area for the commodity. This strategy has been used to determine the market area for hospitals (Cruz 1986) and in other applications, and could easily be applied to non-market commodities such as recreation trips. Recreation sites would be analogous to the firms and recreators to the consumers. Recreation surveys usually collect Zip codes, which could be used as the zones. Thus existing data sets are probably available to test the applicability of the Elzinga–Hogarty strategy.

Closely related to the geographic extent of the market is the number of affected households or firms. If all households within an established geographic market participate in the affected services, as would be true with air quality, this component is trivial. If not, it requires an adjustment for market participation. As noted by McConnell (1992), this adjustment may be implicit if the analysts transfer a per household estimate of benefits that already involves an assumption about participation, or it may be explicit if they transfer an estimate of benefits per user.

Finally, substitutes affect the extent of the market and the per household level of benefits. *Ceteris paribus*, resources have higher values if alternatives are fewer. In the case of water quality, the value of one lake's water quality will be higher if few other lakes or rivers are available for recreation. In the case of air quality, substitution opportunities are much more limited, but still include purchasing air filters and other technologies or even moving to an area with better air quality. As these examples illustrate, substitutes are a matter of degree. Incorporating such substitution effects into the transfer process can be a major challenge.

As with the geographic extent of the market, analysts may use existing information about the transfer commodity to assess the set of available substitutes. Again, this may involve surveys, key informant interviews or transfers from original studies. Smith (1992) suggests that, when wrestling with how to define the commodity extent of the market, transfer analysts may benefit from using a residual-demand approach introduced by Baker and Bresnahan (1988) to define marketable commodities. A residual-demand analysis uses the demand curve for a hypothesized relevant product that would be faced by the firms in the industry if they were a single firm. The residual demand measures the extent to which cost shocks can be passed on to consumers through price increases, thereby testing the substitution possibilities. If the cost increase can largely be passed on without affecting quantity sold (requiring that the residual-demand curve be inelastic), the hypothesis about the relevant product is valid. In contrast, if the cost increase cannot be passed on without affecting quantity (for example, the residual-demand curve is elastic), the product market is too narrowly defined. Applying this framework to resource service markets may aid in determining the extent of services affected. For example, suppose that a cost increase affected the demand for superior game fishing but not rough game fishing. Defining the affected service as all fishing is incorrect because that delineation is too broad.

Estimating the extent of the market is often an important problem in transfers because few original studies incorporate this consideration. In the main, they assume political jurisdiction within which to draw a statistical sample. Even in those few cases where original studies have assessed the extent of the market, sufficient information may not be available to transfer the findings. Thus the extent of the market is often one area where some original information is required, or where sensitivity analyses will be particularly important.

2.6 THE ROLE OF UNCERTAINTY IN TRANSFER STUDIES

Although it is an inescapable aspect of statistical analysis, uncertainty does not mean randomness or indeterminacy. Uncertainty means that a range of likely results can be inferred from observed data, where some outcomes are more likely than others. Thus the term 'uncertainty' refers to the statistical reliability of estimates. If estimates are reliable, then repeating a study with new data should produce statistically comparable results. As we noted in our discussion of meta-analysis, however, variations in estimates can arise from various sources. Transfer estimates are most useful to decision makers when the causes of uncertainty are clearly identified and quantified. In this section, we discuss possible sources of uncertainty and methods for constructing statistical confidence intervals for various kinds of transfer problems.

Sources of Uncertainty

Finkel (1990) identifies four sources of uncertainty that arise in estimation:

1. Measurement
2. Modelling
3. Parameters
4. Judgement.

Measurement uncertainty may arise from measurement errors or from errors in the sampling procedure. Measurement errors are often difficult to quantify unless the analyst has detailed information about the measurement process and an unbiased source of information to use as a standard for comparison. Sampling error, in contrast, follows well-known statistical principles.

Random sampling methods seek to construct a sample that represents the entire population of interest. For example, a study of the incidence of respiratory discomfort from exposure to NO_2 in the general population should use well-known random sampling techniques to ensure that the sample is representative of the general population. A sample of only adult women or people of a particular ethnicity would be unrepresentative of the general population for most purposes. In many cases, however, the only available data come from a statistical sample that is not representative of the target population. For example, a study of student nurses often used to assess the health effects of SO_2 and NO_2 may be subject to bias because it is based on a single occupation with predominantly young, female subjects. It is possible that there are certain health, socioeconomic, lifestyle, and ethnic characteristics that are more prevalent among these nurses than in the population at large, and that these differences may influence the estimated results.

To the extent that such factors mediate the incidence of observed outcomes, unrepresentative sampling is a source of uncertainty in transferring results to the general population. Moreover, even random sampling does not ensure representativeness if the sample is small. A sample of 20 nurses out of a nurse population of 10 000 is an unreliable basis for estimating even nurse-specific effects. A second sample of 20 nurses is likely to yield quite different estimates.

Model uncertainty arises from choices related to estimation techniques. When estimating a model, analysts can choose among many techniques and functional forms. The guidelines for choosing relevant variables and an appropriate functional form are not always clear-cut. There may or may not be theoretic arguments that favour one choice over another. Furthermore, a functional form that theory suggests may perform less well statistically than another functional form. It is ultimately the analyst's responsibility to weigh theoretical consistency versus statistical performance.

An example of model uncertainty in the case study is the choice of the ISCST2 model (US EPA 1992a) that estimates the dispersion of air emissions in the atmosphere. As noted in Chapter 3, there are several different models available for performing dispersion analysis, and they differ in their complexity and in the way they handle sources and distances. It is unclear whether the ISCST2 model provides the most accurate results; however, it is widely used by both industry and government, including the EPA, and is generally considered the most appropriate choice for modelling dispersion from point sources such as those in the case study.

Parameter uncertainty occurs when estimates are subject to variability in ways that are possibly unknown to the observer. For example, older epidemiological studies may not be as relevant to populations today as they were at the time of their publication. Changes in dietary habits and outdoor exercise regimens may mean that subjects today would respond differently to changes in ambient air quality. Similarly, a contingent-valuation survey of willingness to pay for environmental amenities may have a limited 'shelf life' because of changing environmental attitudes, changing relative prices, and changing availability of substitutes.

Finally, judgement uncertainty encompasses an array of non-modelling decisions. Some are practical choices, such as the exposure measure to use in a concentration-response function (one could use daily, weekly, monthly or yearly averages). Various strategies for coping with inadequate information are additional sources of uncertainty. For example, choosing to exclude effects for which there are no data is a practical necessity. Nevertheless, the absence of evidence does not guarantee that an effect does not exist. In many cases, the available evidence is of dubious quality. Decisions about including or excluding questionable evidence or judgements aimed at resolving conflicting evidence introduce additional uncertainty about the relationship between estimates and reality.

Thus sources of uncertainty can be classified and often assessed; they cannot be eliminated entirely. This does not mean, however, that uncertain findings of a transfer study are invalid or unreliable. By carefully tracking and quantifying the uncertainty in their analysis, analysts can identify the most likely range of effects and thus help decision makers to interpret and use the analysis appropriately.

Accounting for Measurement Uncertainty

Statistical inference uses the attributes of a sample to obtain information about the attributes of the group as a whole. If the mean is taken as the estimate that best describes a most likely value, then such statistics as standard error and confidence intervals are measures of how precise or 'noisy' the estimate is.[17] Calculating the degree of precision is the essence of uncertainty analysis, and probability and statistics provide the basis for such calculations. Suppose, for example, a team of epidemiologists conducts a study on the effects of airborne particulates on bronchitis in children and arrives at the following estimate:[18]

$$\text{Cases of bronchitis in children} = \exp(0.036 \times \Delta PM_{10}) \times \text{base cases}$$

$$(2.15)$$

The estimate in this example is the coefficient 0.036. It is the most likely value of the true relationship based on available data.

In addition to this coefficient, the study also produces several measures of the degree of error in the model. Among these is the standard error of the coefficient. The standard error is used to construct a confidence interval that reflects the variability of the observed response relative to the variability of the explanatory variables. A confidence interval is the range of values within which some percentage – say 90 per cent – of repeated studies would fall. Viewed in another way, a 90 per cent confidence interval provides a range in which the true value would fall with 90 per cent certainty. In this example the coefficient estimate is normally distributed with mean 0.036 and standard error 0.041. The 90 per cent confidence interval for the coefficient is calculated as $0.036 \pm 1.645 \times 0.041$, for a range of 0.00 to 0.103.[19]

Analysing uncertainty becomes more complicated when several uncertain estimates are combined, as we have done in the case-study analysis of externality costs. In such a complex transfer study, estimates are assembled from a large number of estimated parameters and values. These estimates include concentration-response functions, valuation functions, exposure simulations, and other estimates. Estimates, each of which has its own confidence interval, are multiplied and summed. The question that arises from this approach is how combining these estimates affects the overall level of uncertainty of the final results.

Unfortunately, there is no simple formula for the variance of the product of two random variables. One common approach to calculating upper and lower bounds for combinations of estimates is to combine all the individual lower bounds for an overall lower bound and all the individual upper bounds for an overall upper bound. However, these calculations do not produce a 90 per cent confidence interval of the combined estimates. Rather, they correspond to a wider confidence interval because the probability of all the lower (upper) bounds occurring simultaneously is very small. Instead, some estimates are more likely to be high at the same time that others are low.

Monte Carlo simulations provide a more rigorous approach to uncertainty. A Monte Carlo simulation draws a large number of random samples from each of the underlying distributions of values, then calculates the corresponding combined values for each draw.[20] Figure 2.2 illustrates this procedure, with each curve representing a probability distribution over possible values. The figure shows draws being taken from the range of possible estimates for pollution data, concentration-response functions, demographic data and WTP values.[21] The mean of

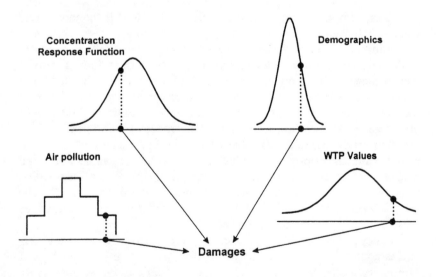

Figure 2.2   Monte Carlo simulations

the combined values from all the draws together is then calculated, along with the 90 per cent confidence interval. The case study employed a Monte Carlo simulation that constructs confidence intervals from 500 draws on possible combinations of underlying values.

The random draws used in the Monte Carlo simulations provide a way to quantify the uncertainty and variability around each type of input.[22] In the previous section, we provided an example of a calculation for chronic respiratory disease. In that calculation, we used only the most likely values, but any values could be drawn from the distributions illustrated in Figure 2.2. Consider now another example. Suppose the annual average of PM increases by $0.1\,\mu g/m^3$ at a certain Zip code. According to our concentration-response function, the number of adult cases of bronchitis a year after change in concentrations is equal to $\exp(0.036 \times \Delta PM_{10}) \times BC$, where ΔPM_{10} is the change in concentrations and BC is the number of base cases of bronchitis (the number before the change in concentration). Suppose we estimate that there are 500 base cases of bronchitis among adults each year at this Zip code. Then we would estimate the number of cases a year after the change to be $\exp(0.036 \times 0.1) \times 500 = 501.8$. Subtracting 500, this is an increase of about 1.8 cases. With a willingness to pay of $148.07 per case, the annual damages from bronchitis effects at the receptor would be about $267.

These calculations all use the most likely estimates. In a Monte Carlo simulation, we allow each of these estimates to vary according to the amount of uncertainty surrounding them. In a given draw, we might randomly pick a concentration-response parameter of 0.045 instead of 0.036, an estimate of 440 base cases, and a willingness to pay of $175. For this draw the estimated increase in the number of cases of bronchitis in the receptor would be $\exp(0.045 \times 0.1) \times 440 - 440$, or about 3.0 cases. At a willingness to pay of $175, this is a damage estimate of $350. The Monte Carlo simulation repeats this process many times, with changes being higher than the mean for some draws, as with this one, and lower than the mean for others. The interval in which 90 per cent of the estimates falls defines the 90 per cent confidence interval. For other effects many other variables may enter the calculation, including other demographic variables, other parameters from the concentration-response function, and ambient concentrations.

Although discussion thus far has related to products of uncertain estimates, calculations may also involve sums of uncertain estimates. The damage-cost model requires computing both products and sums; however, temporal, spatial and pollutant aggregations require many more sums than products. Figure 2.3 shows the probability distributions for a hypothetical example involving the sum of two estimates, A and B.[23]

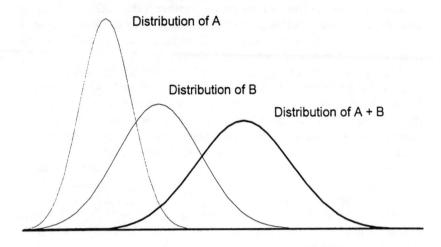

Figure 2.3   Sum of two uncertain estimates

Table 2.2 compares the two approaches for calculating confidence intervals. Suppose effects A and B are estimated to have damages of $100 and $250, respectively, with the confidence intervals shown. Simply summing the individual 90 per cent confidence-interval estimates gives a lower bound of $168.50 and an upper bound of $531.50. However, the Monte Carlo draws range between $205.41 and $492.75. Thus the simple-sum approach overstates each bound by about $38. Note that the Monte Carlo mean is about $349 rather than $350. The precision of the point estimate can be improved by using a larger number of draws, but in most cases several hundred draws usually produce an acceptable approximation to the true distribution.[24]

Table 2.2   Confidence interval example

| | 90 per cent confidence | | |
	Lower bound	Mean	Upper bound
Effect A damages	50.50	100.00	149.50
Effect B damages	118.00	250.00	382.01
Total damages			
A + B	168.50	350.00	531.51
Monte Carlo	205.41	349.08	492.75

Unfortunately, not all studies report standard errors for parameter estimates. In some cases it is possible to construct standard errors from reported confidence intervals. In others, it is necessary to rely on judgemental methods. In such cases, analysts can choose standard errors that reflect their subjective degree of confidence in the estimate, or that are consistent with arbitrarily chosen confidence intervals such as plus or minus 50 per cent. Continuous density functions provided by standard errors are not necessary. Instead analysts can assign probabilities to a discrete number of alternative estimates, representing a range of possible values. This is similar to a high–medium–low approach in more naïve treatments of uncertainty, except that not all low or all high estimates will occur together in the random draws of the Monte Carlo simulations.

Accounting for Other Forms of Uncertainty

As we have seen, uncertainty analysis starts with an assessment of the probable confidence interval for each estimate. Most of the previous discussion related to measurement uncertainty, with confidence intervals derived statistically. Even in instances where standard errors are reported in the original study, we have seen that there may be additional sources of uncertainty. Thus analysts may wish to employ wider confidence intervals than indicated by sampling theory alone. This range may be obtained from meta-analysis or professional judgement. Other forms of uncertainty are analysed similarly, once the appropriate confidence interval has been determined.

Section 2.3 discussed using Bayesian analysis to combine prior beliefs about a parameter distribution with new information in meta-analysis. This approach is also suitable for quantifying non-sampling uncertainty of various kinds. The posterior distribution can thus be interpreted as a way of combining multiple sources of uncertainty. Rewriting Equation (2.9):

$$\text{Var}[\bar{\beta}|b] = \frac{1}{\sum_i \frac{1}{\sigma_{bi}^2}} \tag{2.18}$$

where now σ_{bi} is the analyst's assessment of the standard error around estimate b due to uncertainty of type i.[25] Thus the overall confidence in the estimate is a function of the sum of the inverses of the subjective variances.

Sensitivity Analysis

It is not always apparent which assumptions and analytical decisions are merely convenient, and have little effect on overall results, and which are crucial to the final conclusions of the study. Sensitivity analysis is a way to examine results under a range of alternative assumptions. Monte Carlo analysis is actually a type of sensitivity analysis that relies on random draws from probability distributions to induce variation in results. In common usage, however, sensitivity analysis refers to variation in results induced by systematic choice of a range of more or less plausible assumptions. For example, analysts often try to choose 'conservative' assumptions to avoid overstating benefits of a programme. Excessively conservative assumptions, however, risk biasing estimates downward to the extent that they are of limited usefulness for decision making or benefit–cost analysis. Sensitivity analysis helps distinguish among computationally important and unimportant assumptions and thus aids choosing a set of assumptions that are both plausible and conservative in a meaningful sense.

Including such calculations has several additional benefits:

1. Sensitivity analysis helps identify areas where additional effort in either obtaining further information or conducting additional analysis is likely to be relatively cost-effective.
2. Sensitivity analysis helps distinguish between results that rely primarily on data and results that rely primarily on professional judgement.
3. Sensitivity analysis allows decision makers to play a role in identifying plausible sets of assumptions.

Transfer studies, like most policy analysis, are often subject to strong time and budget constraints. Achieving the most accurate and useful results possible under such constraints is challenging. It is useful, therefore, to know which areas of uncertainty have the greatest effect on the precision and reliability of the analysis. Sensitivity analysis may indicate where limited analytical resources can best be allocated to produce the greatest improvement in the quality of the estimates.

Similarly, policy analysis is a craft that employs data and judgement in varying amounts. While bad data are not necessarily superior to good judgement, the analyst should make clear to what degree results depend on assumptions rather than empirical information. Finally, where there is no clear analytical reason for preferring one set of assumptions over another, there may be an important role for decision makers in evaluating alternative assumptions.[26] Sensitivity analysis provides a basis for examining such alternatives.

Although uncertainty is intrinsic in all forms of empirical analysis, it is a particular concern in transfer studies. This type of analysis often requires creative use of limited information. Thus professional judgement and simplifying assumptions necessarily play a central role. Consequently, a transfer study must be regarded as incomplete if it lacks a careful evaluation, quantification and discussion of uncertainty. We have seen that quantification of uncertainty can help clarify the effects of various forms of uncertainty and assist decision makers in interpreting and using transfer estimates appropriately.

NOTES

1. Brucato, Murdoch and Thayer (1990), reviewed in Chapter 8, compare these two transfer methods for the air quality case.
2. The value for a change in quality to q' is

$$TV = e(p_1^o, p_2^o, p_3^o, q^o, u^o) - e(p_1^o, p_2^o, p_3^o, q', u^o)$$
$$= e(p_1^*, p_2^*, p_3^*, q', u^o) - e(p_1^o, p_2^o, p_3^o, q', u^o) - [e(p_1^*, p_2^*, p_3^*, q^o, u^o) - e(p_1^o, p_2^o, p_3^o, q^o, u^o)]$$

3. For practical reasons, willingness-to-accept studies are rare. Applied economists seem generally to have settled for WTP measures, regardless of property-rights considerations.
4. Glass (1976) first coined the term 'meta-analysis' to describe statistical procedures to combine results from multiple studies.
5. See Eddy, Hasselblad and Shachter (1992) and Rosenthal (1991) for introductions to meta-analysis. Examples of meta-analysis in environmental economics include Smith and Kaoru (1990); Walsh, Johnson and McKean (1992); Boyle, Poe and Bergstrom (1994); Smith and Huang (1995); Smith and Osborne (1996); Loomis and White (1996); Johnson, Fries and Banzhaf (1997).
6. Because residuals are typically heteroscedastic in such models, it is appropriate to estimate the models by generalized least squares using the inverse of the variances as weights. The usual standards for testing functional forms and criteria for including or excluding explanatory variables of course also apply.
7. Estimation of the random-effects model requires generalized least squares. (See any standard econometrics text; for example, Greene 1993.)
8. The analysis is greatly complicated if priors and sample distributions have different functional forms or if σ_β^2 is unknown. This exposition treats only the simplest case. See Zellner (1971); Judge et al. (1988); Greene (1993); Morgan and Henrion (1990).
9. See Chapter 4 for details on these studies.
10. The empirical standard error from the mother distribution is actually 0.042. The Bayesian approach allows analysts to define the prior variance according to the relative degree of certainty in the estimate, rather than the result of a statistical calculation from a sample. Of course, analysts are free to use the statistical estimates from one or more studies as the basis of the prior if that is the best representation of belief. An alternative approach for constructing σ_β is to determine the likely 90 per cent confidence interval, then calculate the variance consistent with those error bounds from $\sigma_\beta = (\text{upper bound} - \beta)/1.645$.
11. Ben-Akiva (1981) refers to these as 'statistical' and 'importance' tests respectively.
12. Loomis (1992) traces the development of this approach to Burt and Brewer (1971) and Cicchetti, Fisher and Smith (1976). These authors estimate multi-site travel-cost models

and transfer the demand coefficients for that recreation site judged to be the nearest substitute to the proposed new site. From this transfer, they then estimate the set of price reductions for those predicted to visit the new site and estimate benefits as reduced travel costs.

13. To see this, inspect the estimator for β_i and $\bar{\beta}$ under the assumptions about Γ. They are given as

$$\hat{\beta}_i = (\sigma_1^{-2} X_i' X_i + \Gamma^{-1})^{-1} (\sigma_1^{-2} X_i' y_i + \Gamma^{-1} \bar{\beta})$$

$$\hat{\bar{\beta}} = \left[\sum_i (\sigma_i^{-2} X_i' X_i + \Gamma^{-1})^{-1} (X_i' X_i \sigma_i^{-2}) \right] \left[\sum_i (\sigma_i^{-2} X_i' X_i + \Gamma^{-1})^{-1} (X_i' y_i \sigma_i^{-2}) \right]$$

14. See also their index of transferability on p. 211.
15. With ρ near 1, the variance matrix of $(\beta_1 - \beta_2) = 2U(1 - \rho)$ is small.
16. See Whittington and MacRae (1986, 1990) and Trumbull (1990) on the question of who has standing in benefit–cost analysis.
17. In some cases the median or mode might be preferable representations of the most likely value, rather than the mean. As we shall see, however, the mean has distinct advantages in Monte Carlo simulations.
18. This is the estimate obtained by Dockery et al. (1989) that is used in the case study. See Chapter 4 for additional details.
19. Although $0.036 - 1.645 \cdot 0.041 = -0.031$, zero is the lowest plausible value. Negative values would indicate that PM reduces the number of bronchitis cases. Because the confidence interval includes zero, the estimate implies that it is possible that PM has no effect on the number of cases of bronchitis.
20. See Fishman (1996) and Halton (1970). Most commercial statistical software packages include procedures that can be adapted for Monte Carlo analysis. In addition, spreadsheet programs such as Excel can perform random draws on normal distributions for simple Monte Carlo simulations.
21. This procedure assumes that each distribution is independent of the others.
22. The bootstrap is an alternative resampling approach that can be useful in quantifying uncertainty. Whereas Monte Carlo analysis involves resampling from an assumed parametric distribution, the bootstrap resamples from the data themselves, with replacement. Thus this procedure simulates multiple draws from the same underlying population, assuming the original data are representative of that population (Efron and Tibshirani, 1993).
23. The variance of a linear combination of n random variables x_i does have an analytical solution:

$$\text{var}\left(\sum_{i=1}^{n} a_i x_i \right) = \sum_{i=1}^{n} a_i^2 \, \text{var}(x_i) + 2 \sum_{i>j}^{n} \sum_{j=1}^{n} \text{cov}(x_i, x_j)$$

For independent random variables $\text{cov}(x_i, x_j) = 0$ and the second expression thus drops out.

24. Means are always normally distributed with expected value of the mean equal to itself. The standard error is the standard deviation of the distribution. Other distributions, such as environmental quality variables, may not be normally distributed. Ramberg et al. (1979) report an algorithm for constructing empirical distributions of general form.
25. We are assuming that the uncertainty affects only the variance around b, not its expected value. If, in addition, the analyst suspects that uncertainty of a given type also involves potential bias, then both Equations (2.10) and (2.11) are relevant.
26. The risk of such involvement on the part of decision makers is that they will choose the assumptions that correspond to the results that they like, rather than the assumptions that are most consistent with the facts. Nevertheless, sensitivity analysis makes clear what the connection is between decisions and the analytical assumptions consistent with such decisions.

3. Designing the transfer study

In the practice of transfers, high principle confronts empirical realities. Analysts frequently face unexpected road blocks at each step. They may also find that the order of steps and linkages may not be as clean as implied by the first two chapters. For example, data limitations at a final step may require adjustments at an earlier step to ensure consistency.

To illustrate many of the problems that can arise, the next five chapters of this book focus on a large case study using the transfer method to estimate the externalities of electricity generation. This chapter begins the case study with the first basic step in the transfer, identifying the relevant linkages. In particular, it first defines the policies for electricity generation to be evaluated and then discusses criteria for identifying which path of linkages probably has the greatest impact on natural resources and service flows. Before turning to the task of identifying the available information to transfer at each linkage, however, this chapter next looks at one aspect of the study design that, at least in this case, transcends several of the usual steps and linkages, namely the geographic extent of the market and the degree of resolution of analysis. This includes not only the total area covered in the analysis, but also the geographic and temporal units for which calculations are made. This aspect of the study design defies procedural classification because it serves as the framework upon which the other procedures are all built. Finally, the chapter concludes with the first two linkages in the transfer, the effect of the policies on emissions of pollutants and the effect of those emissions on air quality throughout the study area. Later chapters take up the subsequent linkages on service flows and values for those services.

3.1 DEFINING THE POLICY

An electric utility expecting growth in the demand for electricity to exceed its current capacity will be forced to turn to new resources. The utility may choose to build new power plants, purchase power from other utilities or from independent power producers, extend the life of existing resources beyond currently scheduled retirement dates, or avoid or defer new capacity requirements by devoting resources to decreasing demand

('demand-side management'). US utilities consider all these interrelated options when developing an integrated resource plan. This plan identifies the type, size and timing of demand- and supply-side resources that are required to meet utilities' basic objective of providing reliable electric service at least cost to customers, subject to institutional constraints. Because generating electricity can affect environmental resources (most notably air quality), different plans will probably be associated with differing externality levels.

The current planning process already incorporates environmental concerns to the extent that existing environmental regulations constrain the technological choices available to utilities and limit the emissions that can be released into the environment. Nevertheless, many regulatory agencies are concerned that existing safeguards do not adequately account for the full social costs of electricity generation. In the state of Minnesota, the Public Service Commission required the integration of external costs into resource-planning decisions. As part of meeting this requirement, our study estimates the likely externalities under three potential resource-planning scenarios for one major utility, Northern States Power Company (NSP).

The first step in designing the transfer study is to identify the resource-planning decisions whose external costs are of interest. The choice of planning scenarios has important implications for the design of the study. The scenarios specify where plants would be located, the types of plants that are planned, and the operating conditions for the system. All these factors influence the relevant geographic scope of the study, the resources and services that may be affected, and the magnitude and location of potential damages.

The scenarios should be designed to best address the most important policy questions. Four criteria were used to select scenarios in this study:

1. The scenarios should involve building new power plants.
2. The scenarios should reflect technologies that are primarily associated with air emissions.
3. The scenarios should bracket the likely range of potential externality costs.
4. The scenarios should reflect a broad range of planning locations.

Although the benefits of demand-side management policies are often of policy interest, this study focuses on the externalities of new plants. This emphasis imposes consistency in the analysis among scenarios, thus facilitating comparisons. The second criterion, to focus on air quality, simply recognizes the realistic choices available to many electric utilities. While hydroelectric power, wind generation or nuclear power are all potential possibilities in the strictest sense, fossil-fuel plants represent the most feasible way to produce a significant amount of power under current political and regulatory environments in the US. The third criterion, to bracket the likely range of potential externalities, is important in identifying the potential range of costs associated with alternative plans. The final criterion, that the scenarios should represent a range of geographic locations, is related to the previous one, inasmuch as locating plants in more urbanized areas tends to increase externality costs. Moreover, it enables the study to be generalized to the whole service area.

Defining a planning scenario first and foremost requires specifying power plants at specific locations and with specific attributes, including stack height and diameter, gas exit velocity, gas exit temperature, operating profile and emission rates for each pollutant. But it also requires establishing a modelling perspective from which to evaluate the planning option. Specifically, resource decisions may be modelled in isolation from other decisions (a 'partial equilibrium' analysis), or as part of an integrated set of plans (a 'general equilibrium' analysis). Modelling each plant in isolation from the rest of the system is the simpler approach. If the goal of the research is to identify the damages for each ton of pollution from specific plants in a utility's system, this may be the best approach as well.

However, if the goal is to identify the overall impact of a planning decision such as building a new plant, a system-wide approach might be preferable. This kind of approach recognizes the fact that building a new plant would also change the way other plants in the utility's system – or even elsewhere on the grid – operate. The system-wide approach differs from the individual-plant approach, not necessarily in the number of plants that initially change their emissions, but in identifying indirect changes in emissions throughout the system.

While more realistic, the system-wide approach has the disadvantage of requiring resource planners to model and estimate the indirect effects of each scenario on the operation of other power plants, a potentially lengthy endeavour. Moreover, with emissions changing at many plants at one time, it can yield results that are difficult to interpret. For example, under some conditions, adding a new plant might actually reduce externality costs if the planning model predicts that, somewhere else in the system, generation from a relatively clean technology displaces the generation from a relatively dirty one. Although we began with the system-wide approach in our research, these problems, together with a sceptical view of some of the predictions of the indirect effects, led us eventually to report potential damages only from the individual-plant perspective. This implies that our estimates are geared more to identifying the external costs of emissions under different scenarios than to estimating the cost of particular policies.

We evaluate three scenarios relative to a baseline scenario. These are:

1. Rural scenario, which involves the addition of a 400 MW pulverized coal plant, plus four gas-fired combined cycle units, in the western, rural part of Minnesota.
2. Metropolitan fringe scenario, which involves the same plants located just to the west of Minneapolis/St Paul.
3. Urban scenario, which involves an increase in the emissions of two older coal plants in the Twin Cities area.

The precise location of the key sources in each of these scenarios is shown in Figures 3.1 through 3.3.

Figure 3.1   New source locations for the rural impact scenario

Figure 3.2 New source locations for the metropolitan fringe impact scenario

By expanding what are, relatively speaking, dirty technologies in the centre of an urban area in one scenario, and building relatively cleaner plants in a more rural location in another scenario, these scenarios bracket the likely range of effects on people. In the same way, the scenarios provide a means of testing the sensitivity of damages to various factors, such as a plant's distance from an urban area. The scenarios could be designed to test other facts as well. For example, in a separate study performed in Wisconsin (Desvousges et al. 1995b), the scenarios were somewhat more complicated. They provided tests for the sensitivity of damages to rural versus urban locations and to natural gas versus coal technologies, as well as a scenario that involved a short move (approxi-

Figure 3.3   New source locations for the urban impact scenario

mately 50 km) for eight stacks from natural gas facilities without any
change in emissions.

3.2   IDENTIFYING THE RELEVANT LINKAGES

After defining these policy scenarios, identifying the relevant linkages is
the next step in the transfer (see Figure 1.1). The first linkage is the effect
the scenarios have on air emissions; the second is the effect of these
emissions on the quality of various natural resources. Fossil-fuel-burning
scenarios will of course affect air quality, but they also have the potential
to affect soil and water resources, for example, through acid deposition.

Moreover, because they involve the release of different pollutants, they can affect air quality in various ways. The third linkage is the effect on the service flows provided by each resource. These three linkages are the technical effects of the scenarios.

Identifying the affected resources and services is in some ways a circular process. Ideally, analysts would like to employ their final model to determine which effects will be the most significant, but this is of course impossible because the model itself is based on these determinations. A pragmatic solution is to establish qualitatively whether the available scientific evidence shows that a pollutant affects a given resource service and assess whether the potential damages from the effect are likely to be significant enough to justify the cost of studying them. To be conservative, it is prudent to include the effect when the magnitude of potential damages is uncertain. Finally, because the costs and/or benefits of effects must eventually be quantified, to include an effect in the formal analysis there must be information that can link together all the key steps of a transfer study, including the technical linkages and the behavioural linkage determining the value of the affected services to people. In cases where this information is unavailable it may be useful to perform sensitivity analyses with hypothetical values or assess their importance qualitatively.

In our transfer, the first step of this process screened a number of potential effects categories. For example, we investigated whether air pollution might not affect livestock, especially milk production, an important part of the Minnesota economy, but found no literature linking the two. In other cases, rather than a mere absence of evidence, a preponderance of contrary evidence eliminated consideration of an effect. For example, a convincing body of literature links both ozone (O_3) and sulphur dioxide (SO_2) to lower crop yields (for example, Sommerville et al. 1989), but most studies of nitrogen dioxide (NO_2) and crop yields show no effect, at least at concentrations commonly found in Minnesota (for example: Irving, Miller and Xerikos 1982; Gupta and Sabaratnam 1988; Elkiey, Ormrod and Marie 1988). See Chapter 6.

The second requirement, that an effect be likely to be significant, is more difficult to determine. Significance is a relative concept that has to be weighed against analysis costs. For example, research indicates that exposure to PM may increase the number of cases of croup (a respiratory disease marked by a hoarse cough, inspiratory stridor and dyspnoea) in children, but only by small quantities (Schwartz et al. 1991). Yet once it is decided to model PM emissions and dispersion to account for its other effects, modelling the damages from croup requires little extra effort.

Accordingly, we include croup effects in our analysis. Likewise, research indicates that exposure to chromium, arsenic and other trace elements released from coal can cause cancer. However, the risk is quite small: according to one case study (Constantinou and Seigneur 1991), the cancer risk from the chromium emissions of one coal plant is only 3.1×10^{-8}, or about one in 32 million, well below the risk levels at which the US EPA typically considers protection. But in this case, because capturing these small cancer risks would require modelling additional pollutants, we do not include them in our transfer.

Finally, the absence of information necessary to link together the key steps of the transfer study also eliminates several effects that we could include if the data were available. For example, we do not quantify damages for the effect of fossil-fuel combustion on water quality (and the services it provides) because of the complicated exposure pathway between the initial emission and final effects. Mercury emissions provide the most salient example. To affect people, the mercury emitted from fossil-fuel combustion (mostly divalent mercury) must first disperse through the atmosphere, fall or wash out to the ground, be transported to a water body, undergo a chemical transformation into methyl mercury (methylation), enter into the food chain and finally, by contaminating fish so that they become unfit for eating, affect people's recreational enjoyment or health. Moreover, the process is further complicated by the characteristics of the individual water body, which significantly affect the extent of methylation and bioaccumulation that occurs, by the process of establishing advisories and by the public's information and perception of mercury risks.

Deciding whether the available information is sufficient to include an effect will always be a matter of judgement. To avoid producing purely speculative estimates, it is important to include effects that can be estimated with functions supported by the scientific community at each step. However, it is also important to summarize and adapt the available information as fully as possible. In this case study, we estimated health, materials, visibility and agricultural damages from PM, SO_2, nitrogen oxides (NO_x), ozone, carbon monoxide (CO) and lead. Table 3.1 lists the effects and pollutants included.

3.3 DETERMINING THE RELEVANT MARKET AND RESOLUTION OF THE ANALYSIS

We review the specifics of the first two technical linkages, the effect of the scenarios on emissions and the effect of emissions on air quality, at the end of this chapter. In the following chapters we review the affected services

Table 3.1   Effects and pollutants included in externality study

Effects category	Pollutant	Quantified effects
Health	PM	Mortality, chronic respiratory disease (includes emphysema, chronic bronchitis and asthma), chronic cough, bronchitis, croup, upper respiratory symptoms, cough days
	SO_2	Chest discomfort
	NO_x	Eye irritation
	Ozone	Asthma, lower respiratory symptoms, upper respiratory symptoms
	CO	Headache
	Lead	IQ decrements, hypertension, pre-term deliveries
Agriculture	SO_2	Corn, soybeans, wheat
	Ozone	Corn, soybeans, wheat, hay, potatoes
Other	PM	Soiling, visibility
	SO_2	Materials
	NO_x	Visibility

and their valuation. But before proceeding to the actual transfers at these linkages, we consider one aspect of the overall study design that relates to every step of the study: the geographic extent of the market and the resolution of the analysis. The geographic scope of the case study is Minnesota, western Wisconsin, and South Dakota, an area large enough to capture the effects within 100 km of any of NSP's power plants. This scope was partly a consequence of the study's policy context. The utility was primarily interested in the way its decisions would affect its customers, and the regulatory agency was primarily interested in the way decisions would affect the citizens of Minnesota. A different policy perspective could have justified a wider geographic scope and produced larger damage estimates. Damages are particularly sensitive to PM concentrations, which, because of long-range transport, can be important at longer distances, suggesting that damages could have been significant in Milwaukee, Chicago and Detroit, which lie just outside the geographic scope of the study.[1]

A related point is how the market is sub-divided into different regions where the linkages are made. This is important because the degree to which a natural resource is affected by a policy typically varies from place to place. In the case of air quality, the locations where the pollution concentrations are linked to people and resources are called 'receptors', a term which comes from air modelling. To link the information appropriately, the receptors must be defined in a way that is consistent with the data on population characteristics, agriculture and other resources. The geographic unit also needs to be small enough to be sensitive to varying background air quality and capture the gradient of air quality changes induced by the scenarios. Postal Zip codes provide a small unit that yields a tight resolution that is consistent with US Census information. We identified 618 Zip codes as receptors in the NSP study area. Using Census information, we identified the number of people in each receptor as well as the demographic characteristics such as age group, race, education and income levels necessary to transfer concentration-response functions quantifying the relationship between air quality and health effects. However, agricultural statistics are not available by Zip code, so we estimate agricultural damages at the county level.

Zip codes are a conveniently small unit for many purposes. However, if the geographic scope is sufficiently large, the number of Zip codes can become unmanageable. To define a tractable number of receptors, a logical rule is to specify a denser array of receptors in areas close to power plants (where pollution concentrations are likely to change more abruptly) and in areas with higher populations (where damages are likely to be higher). This selection rule locates receptors as efficiently as possible, without wasting them in areas where additional receptors would not provide additional information or where damages are likely to be small anyway. To begin the receptor analysis, 50 and 100 km radii were drawn around each current and proposed power plant. Receptors were then defined in each county based on the population in the county and the number of radii overlapping the county. Specifically:

1. In counties falling farther than 100 km from any of the modelled power plants, one receptor was assigned to the Zip code with the largest population.
2. In counties falling within one or more 100 km radii but not a 50 km radius, receptors were assigned to all Zip codes with 2500 or more people (as of the 1990 US Census).
3. In counties falling within one to two 50 km radii, receptors were assigned to all Zip codes with 1300 or more people.
4. In counties falling within three to four 50 km radii, receptors were assigned to all Zip codes with 1000 or more people.

5. In counties falling within five or more 50 km radii, receptors were assigned to all Zip codes with 800 or more people.

In cases where different parts of the county fall under different criteria, a conservative solution is to use the criterion yielding the largest number of receptors. The selected receptor sites represent 89 per cent of the area's population, with the remaining people being allocated to receptors in their county of residence. The receptor locations are shown in Figure 3.4.

Determining the temporal resolution of the study is just as important as determining the geographic resolution. For example, temporal resolution can be important if, because of non-linear concentration-response functions, damages are especially sensitive to peak periods of pollution, which can be washed out by long averaging times. Previously, most studies of

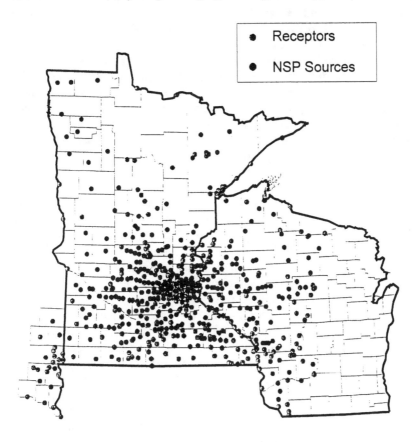

Figure 3.4   Source locations and modelling receptors

the external costs of electricity generation have used annual average pollution concentrations (Rowe et al. 1994; Harrison et al. 1993; Thayer et al. 1994). However, annual averages are not always the relevant exposure period for the effects of interest. Shorter averaging times are required by some concentration-response functions of acute effects, with daily averages being the most common. In these cases, annualizing the data effectively linearizes the concentration-response functions, because day-to-day peaks in pollution concentrations are levelled by averaging. Other concentration-response functions require even more complicated exposure times. For example, one epidemiological study of upper and lower respiratory symptoms uses the daily maximum concentration of ozone as the exposure variable (Ostro et al. 1993). To estimate agricultural injuries from air pollution, the commonly used National Crop Loss Assessment Network (NCLAN) uses an average of pollution concentrations over the daytime hours of a crop's growing season (Heck et al. 1982; Sommerville et al. 1989).

To maintain the consistency of the data between each step of the transfer process, it is appropriate to allow the original studies being transferred to determine the temporal resolution of the study. In this case, if a particular epidemiological study estimates injuries with daily maxima, we use daily maxima for that effect; if another uses annual averages, we use annual averages. To maintain this kind of flexibility, we require data at a very low level of temporal resolution, which can then be aggregated in various ways to estimate concentrations over the various averaging times. We use hourly data on emissions provided by NSP to model the change in air concentrations (hereafter, 'deltas') at each receptor for each hour of the year and then aggregate these data into each of the relevant averaging times.

The combination of a fine geographic and temporal resolution can make a study data-intensive. With 618 receptors and 8760 hours in a year, this case study had over 5.4 million deltas per pollutant per scenario (a total of 97.4 million deltas). While such resolution increases the accuracy and precision of the estimates, the quantity of data can also lead to a number of difficulties in estimating damages at each receptor. For example, the data were too extensive to use as tables that would be compatible with software familiar to potential end-users. One approach to this problem is to sample from the full data set. If samples small enough to be tractable are not sufficiently accurate, another approach is to construct distribution functions to summarize the data. Appropriate functional forms can be chosen on the basis of central moments (Kendall and Stuart 1963) and flexible distributions are available (for example, Ramberg et al. 1979). We use non-parametric step functions to summarize the deltas in the case study.

Another difficulty posed by using Zip codes is obtaining all the data that the concentration-response functions require at the Zip code level. While general demographic information is available from the US Census at this level, many health concentration-response functions identify only a percentage increase in the incidence of a health condition, and thus require information about background incidence rates (or number of 'base cases'). The base-case variable implicitly controls for baseline air quality because, other things equal, the incidence of an effect will be higher in areas with worse air quality. Good base-case information is not available for some health effects such as eye irritation and bronchitis. In such cases it is necessary to use a national average or the average reported in the epidemiological study, although it is preferable to transfer an equation relating base cases to the demographic characteristics of the population (for example, Gold et al. 1993).

If they are defined in absolute rather than relative terms, non-linear functions require information about ambient air quality instead of base cases. We collected 1991 annual average ambient concentrations of PM, SO_2, ozone, NO_x and CO for all monitors in Minnesota, Wisconsin and South Dakota. Table 3.2 shows the background concentrations for

Table 3.2   Ambient PM concentrations in Minnesota

Aerometric Information Retrieval Systems identification code	Name	Average PM concentration ($\mu g/m^3$)
27-017-0013	Cloquet	15
27-037-0020	Dakota Co.	27
27-037-0423	Rosemount	21
27-037-0424	Inver Grove Heights	22
27-037-0426	Dakota Co.	21
27-053-1007	Minneapolis	23
27-053-2006	St Louis Park	21
27-053-3004	Richfield	31
27-109-0015	Rochester	23
27-123-0021	St. Paul	27
27-137-0027	Duluth	22
27-137-0032	Duluth	25
27-141-0011	Sherburne Co.	13
27-141-0013	Sherburne Co.	13

PM. Although these states have a relatively large number of air-quality monitors, such information is of course not available by Zip code. To interpolate ambient conditions for each receptor, a 'kriging' model generated concentration estimates at each site as a weighted average of the known data points, with distance determining the value of the weights.[2] The kriging model is only as good as the known data points, so if the US EPA monitors areas that it suspects have high pollution concentrations, the model will overstate concentrations in the interpolated areas.

Moreover, because it is not feasible to run the kriging model for every hour of the year, most estimated ambient concentrations are annual averages. However, PM and CO require background concentrations for shorter time periods. To obtain the necessary temporal resolution, we estimated Weibull concentration distributions at known data points and regressed the Weibull parameters on the annual average. This function is used to construct predicted Weibull parameters at each receptor, and thus generate the desired temporal variation. This is another example of a strategy to use when facing data constraints. Here, instead of summarizing a large quantity of data with distributions as we did with the deltas, we use distributions to expand a small quantity of data.

3.4   FIRST TWO LINKAGES: ESTIMATING CHANGES IN AIR QUALITY

The first linkage in the case study connects the generation scenarios to the resulting change in air emissions. In this case the first linkage is relatively simple because the emission rates from each source are specified as part of the scenario itself. These emission rates incorporate assumptions about the emissions factors per unit of heat input, expressed as pounds of pollutants per million BTUs per hour, and the operating profile of the plants – the hourly heat input rate over the model year. The second linkage is from the change in emissions to the resulting changes in air quality at each of the receptors. Estimating this linkage requires an air-quality dispersion model that can predict the concentrations of various pollutants at each receptor from the emissions rates and other data. Such a model is an example of the complex type of transfer because an entire functional relationship is transferred and applied to data from the transfer context.[3]

Several models are available to estimate this linkage for non-reactive pollutants, pollutants assumed merely to disperse without undergoing chemical transformations. Particulate matter, nitrogen oxides, sulphur oxides, carbon monoxide and lead are all assumed to be non-reactive. This simplifying assumption abstracts from the process in which nitrogen oxides and sulphur oxides undergo reactions midstream to form particulate matter, thereby overstating nitrogen oxide and sulphur oxide concentrations and understating particulate matter concentrations. It also requires modelling all nitrogen oxide emissions, though nitrogen dioxide is often the primary pollutant of concern. In contrast to these assumed non-reactive pollutants, ozone is strictly a secondary pollutant formed from nitrogen oxides and volatile organic compounds (VOCs), and is modelled separately.

In evaluating the models for non-reactive pollutants, we considered three criteria. First, the model should be able to estimate concentrations at each of the receptors scattered over the study area. Second, it should be able to estimate concentrations at the temporal resolution required for the concentration-response functions at later linkages. To be flexible enough to aggregate up to different averaging times, this requires that it be capable of estimating hourly concentrations. Third, it should provide relatively accurate and precise estimates near each source where pollution impacts are likely to be highest while still being capable of estimating concentrations throughout the area.

Three short-term models are available for estimating this linkage, the SCREEN2 model (US EPA 1992b), the MESOPUFF-II model (US EPA 1984), and the ISCST2 model (US EPA 1992a). Of these, the SCREEN2 model is a simplistic screening model designed to estimate worst-case impacts in a single downwind direction. Accordingly, it is not able to estimate concentrations over a grid of receptors, nor to estimate multiple hourly concentrations. Both the MESOPUFF-II and ISCST2 models do meet these requirements. Of these, the MESOPUFF-II model is primarily designed to estimate pollution impacts far downwind from a source (further than 50 km). In particular, it has the advantage of more accurately estimating the long-range transport of particulate matter, as well as its formation in the atmosphere from nitrogen oxides and sulphur oxides. In contrast, the ISCST2 model is primarily designed to estimate maximum concentrations within 50 km. Accordingly, it has the advantage of more accurately estimating concentrations near the sources, where impacts are likely to be highest. ISCST2 is the US EPA-recommended model for estimating impacts from multiple sources in non-complex terrain and also has the advantage of being extensively tested.

The choice between these two models may have an important influence on the estimates of concentrations, and comes down to the analysts' judgement. We used the ISCST2 model in our transfer because accuracy at short distances was the most important goal. Because policy concerns were limited to Minnesota and certain surrounding areas, we assumed that long-range transport of particulate matter would not be a significant concern. In hindsight, however, the inability of the ISCST2 model to account for secondary formation of particulate matter from nitrogen oxides probably resulted in a significant underestimate of nitrogen oxide damages. We discuss this issue further in Chapter 7 in presenting the results of the case study.

Implementing the ISCST2 model requires hourly estimates of wind speed and direction, temperature, mixing height and stability class at each pollution source. Wind speed and direction and temperature, routinely collected at US airports by the National Weather Service, are available from the National Climatic Data Center. Five sites in the study region supply the surface meteorological data for this transfer, with the data for each generating source coming from the closest meteorological site. Two other sites provide twice-daily estimates of atmospheric mixing heights, while stability class is estimated in the US EPA's RAMMET meteorological pre-processor program (US EPA 1977) from time of day, wind speed, cloud base height, cloud coverage, and estimated incoming solar and outgoing long-wave radiation. We use 1991 meteorological data for all variables, a reasonably representative year.

With these data, the ISCST2 model estimates hourly concentrations for particulate matter, nitrogen oxides, sulphur oxides, carbon monoxide and lead under the assumption that they are non-reactive. In contrast, ozone is clearly a reactive pollutant, formed in the atmosphere from nitrogen oxides and VOCs in a series of complex photochemical reactions. The basics of these reactions can be summarized with a three-reaction cycle: known as the photolytic cycle:

$$hn + NO_2 \rightarrow NO + O^x \tag{3.1}$$

$$M + O^x + O_2 \rightarrow O_3 + M \tag{3.2}$$

$$NO + O_3 \rightarrow NO_2 + O_2 \tag{3.3}$$

where hn is a unit of solar energy, M is an inert air molecule, O^x is an uncharged oxygen atom (free radical), O_2 is ordinary molecular oxygen, and O_3 is ozone. As shown in the first two reactions, during the day NO_2 molecules break apart in the presence of sunlight to produce oxygen free radicals, which in turn react with molecular oxygen to form ozone. Ozone is destroyed again in the third reaction, as NO recycles back to NO_2. VOCs complicate this cycle by splitting apart in the presence of sunlight to form free radicals, providing an additional pathway for ozone to form independently of the photolytic cycle.

Four general classes of models are available to simulate ozone formation: grid models, box models, trajectory models and empirical models. Grid models such as the Urban Airshed Model (Morris et al. 1990) contain complex algorithms simulating meteorological, physical, and photochemical processes. While grid models are the most accurate, they are also extremely expensive to set up and operate, and require extensive field data. Thus grid models are generally not feasible for use in a transfer study. Box models such as EKMA (Whitten and Hogo 1978) use simpler representations of the processes of ozone formation. However, they assume only a single air parcel and so do not provide any spatial resolution to their estimates. To overcome this limitation, trajectory models use similar simple representations of air chemistry but allow for multiple boxes. However, they rely heavily on data about the background concentrations of ozone and its precursors within each area. Such data are often not available in a transfer.

An alternative is to fit ozone levels to observed concentrations of precursors using regression analysis or another statistical technique. Three empirical models are available for transfer (Sillman, Logan and Wofsy, 1990; Trainer et al. 1991, 1993). To determine which model provided the best fit, we compared predictions based on these models to observed ozone concentrations in the relevant market area. Of the three, the model from Sillman, Logan, and Wofsy (1990), which predicts ozone levels from nitrogen oxides and VOCs, provides the best fit. Accordingly, we transfer an adaptation of this model, eliminating some unavailable independent variables from the regression, to predict ozone concentrations from 2 to 7 p.m., May through September, when the model is most accurate and ozone levels highest. Specifically, we transfer the following equations:

$$
O_3 = \begin{cases}
35.2 - 2.30(NO_x\sqrt{VOC}) - 0.05\sqrt{\dfrac{VOC}{NO_x}} & \text{if } 0 < NO_x \le 0.3 \\[3mm]
-3.5 + 1.47(NO_x\sqrt{VOC}) + 5.70\sqrt{\dfrac{VOC}{NO_x}} & \text{if } 0.3 < NO_x < 4.5 \\[3mm]
81.8 + 8.29\left[\dfrac{VOC^2}{VOC + NO_x}\right] - 7.90{*}VOC & \text{if } 4.5 \le NO_x < 11.0 \\[3mm]
-24.7 + 0.74\left[\dfrac{VOC^2}{VOC + NO_x}\right] + 0.78{*}VOC & \text{if } 11.0 \le NO_x < 30.0
\end{cases}
$$

$$(3.4)$$

Table 3.3   Change in annual concentrations of four pollutants at a sample urban receptor ($\mu g/m^3$)

Scenario	Sulphur dioxide	Particulate matter (PM_{10})	Lead	Ozone
Rural	0.0014	0.0006	3E-7	−0.0013
Metropolitan	0.0078	0.0032	2E-6	−0.0017
Urban	0.3445	0.0228	7E-6	0.0413

Table 3.4   Step function of PM_{10} deltas at two sample receptors for the urban scenario ($\mu g/m^3$)

Receptor	0	1.6E-7	5.4E-5	7.4E-4	0.0028	0.0058
431 (rural)	256	12	15	12	10	13
73 (Minneapolis)	249	9	10	11	6	5

Receptor	0.0097	0.0145	0.0208	0.0294	0.0425	0.0657	0.1518
431 (rural)	6	10	10	10	4	7	0
73 (Minneapolis)	4	8	5	8	4	13	33

See Desvousges et al. (1995a) for more details on this model and its development.

The ISCST2 model and the ozone-formation model generate estimates of hourly deltas at each receptor. These hourly data are then aggregated up to additional averaging times as required by the various concentration-response functions (including the daily maximum concentration, daily averages, six-week averages, averages over the afternoon hours of a crop's growing season, and annual averages). For example, Table 3.3 shows the estimated changes in annual average concentrations for four pollutants at a sample urban receptor in Minneapolis for all three scenarios. The table illustrates two patterns in the data. First, note that concentrations for the non-reactive pollutants are higher in the more urban scenarios. This follows from the geographic placement of the new generating sources in each scenario, with the new sources being closest to Minneapolis in the urban scenario and furthest in the rural scenario. Second, note that ozone deltas are actually negative for some scenarios. This follows from the ability of increased NO_x emissions sometimes to break apart, or scavenge, existing ozone into NO_2 and molecular ozone (Expression 3.3). In general, ozone deltas did not follow clear or expected patterns across scenarios or across receptors. We discuss this result further in Chapter 7.

As noted above, shorter averaging times such as daily averages are summarized with a step function or histogram because of the large number of individual data points that would otherwise be required. Table 3.4 gives an example of such a function, summarizing daily PM_{10} deltas at two receptors for the urban scenario. The first row in the table shows the change in PM_{10} concentrations represented by each step, or bin, of the step function. One bin represents a day with no change in concentrations; the remaining twelve represent increasingly greater changes.[4] Below the first row, the next two rows show the number of days at each receptor falling in each bin. Again, notice the expected geographic trend in the data: the urban receptor, closer to the new source, experiences larger deltas than does the more distant rural receptor.

With these deltas, we can now predict the next linkage in the transfer, the change in the level of health and other services.

NOTES

1. On the other hand, the models for long-range transport are not as well tested as the short-range models, and so would have increased the uncertainty of the damage estimates.
2. RADIAN Corporation performed the kriging model in SURFER® (Golden Software 1991).
3. Air-modelling specialists at RADIAN Corporation, an environmental engineering firm, performed this task.
4. These twelve bins were estimated by dividing all the observed receptor days into twelve equal groups and representing each group by its mean. We used this non-parametric approach because we were unable to identify a parametric distribution that would be flexible enough for all scenarios.

4. Estimating changes in health services

The environment provides a number of services that people value, and change in environmental quality affects the level of such services. These services include better health, higher agricultural yields, cleaner buildings and materials, greater visual range, and better opportunities for outdoor recreation such as fishing. Changes in the services provided by the environment and the associated effects are the reasons that people are willing to pay for policies to clean up the environment (or to avoid policies that dirty it). Accordingly, the next link in the disaggregate transfer discussed in Chapter 2 is from the change in environmental quality to the change in services. For example, in the previous link, suppose a given policy is estimated to increase concentrations of particulate matter at a given receptor by $1 \mu g/m^3$. To estimate the associated change in health services, it is necessary to assess the change in the incidence of diseases and symptoms associated with particulate matter, such as cough, emphysema and mortality rates.

Conceptually, the salient aspect of this step is that such effects are the things people value. Analytically, it is for such effects that analysts often have willingness-to-pay information. For example, in studying health, analysts may estimate that people are willing to pay, on average, $20 to avoid a day of cough and $360 to avoid a 0.01 per cent increase in mortality risks. Thus, by measuring the change in health services by cough days and increments of mortality risks, analysts can match the information on physical effects with the available valuation information. This is one illustration of an important principle for the transfer process, which, although noted elsewhere, cannot be overemphasized. Namely, at each step the information estimated must link up with the information from both the preceding and following steps. Thus analysts must be able to estimate effects based on the information they have about the change in environmental quality. Likewise, they must define effects in such a way that they will be able to value them. It is essential to keep this principle in mind when choosing between various ways to quantify this and other links in the transfer process.

In this chapter, we turn to estimating the effects on services in the case study, specifically estimating the health effects that result from changes in air quality discussed in the previous chapter. The chapter focuses on health effects for the present in order to fix ideas, postponing discussion of other types of effects until Chapter 6. The chapter begins with a general discussion of concentration-response functions, which quantify the level of the effects as a function of pollution concentrations. It then reviews the health effects associated with air pollution, beginning with particulate matter and proceeding through each major pollutant in turn. Along the way, it highlights various transfer issues as they arise.

This chapter provides a good opportunity for these discussions because it raises many of the most important concerns in transferring information from original studies to a new context. The first of these concerns is the basic requirements for including an effect in a transfer study and quantifying it. Recall from Chapter 3 that these minimum requirements are that scientific evidence should document that an effect exists at ambient levels, that the effect is significant enough to justify quantifying it, and that sufficient information is available to quantify each linkage, including concentration-response functions and willingness-to-pay information.

Each of these criteria is relevant for some of the effects reviewed in this chapter. Other important transfer issues include the criteria for choosing among studies, the possibility of summarizing and transferring an entire body of literature instead of individual studies, and the adjustments that analysts may make when moving between policy contexts. We also discuss the implications of choosing among various functional forms. The discussion focuses primarily on particulate matter, which affords an opportunity to explore a variety of transfer problems for a pollutant that is at the same time associated with both the widest range of health effects and the bulk of environmental costs associated with the scenarios. Other pollutants receive a briefer treatment.

Note that this chapter does not attempt a comprehensive review of the health-effects literature, or even a complete discussion of the decisions and judgements we have made. Instead, it supplies only minimal documentation of each decision for those readers following the case study in detail, reserving more detailed discussion for those situations that highlight general transfer issues.[1] For more comprehensive reviews of these pollutants and their health effects, see the US EPA's Air Criteria Documents, cited in each section below, and Desvousges et al. (1995a,b).

4.1 CONCENTRATION-RESPONSE FUNCTIONS

Generally speaking, two types of studies can help identify the health effects resulting from exposure to air pollution: toxicological studies and epidemiological studies. Toxicological studies are laboratory experiments that expose people or animals to precisely measured quantities of a pollutant under a specific protocol. They also study groups of individuals with common backgrounds in order to avoid the effects of confounding differences in age, sex and so forth. Typically, they measure health effects as objective physiological changes, such as alterations in one-second forced expiratory volume (FEV_1), the maximum amount of air a subject can exhale in one second, though sometimes they may also ask human subjects to describe subjective symptoms that they experience. Epidemiological studies evaluate the effects of pollution and other factors on large populations of people, substituting statistical analysis for experimental controls. These studies typically rely on community-wide measures of air quality, suggesting that individual exposures are measured with some degree of error.

Well-controlled toxicological studies provide reliable evidence of a causal link between exposure to pollution and health effects, and so can help analysts determine if a given health effect exists and should be transferred. However, epidemiological studies are probably more suitable for providing the specific concentration-response functions that analysts will transfer. This is true for at least three reasons. First, they study effects in large, diverse populations rather than small, unrepresentative groups. Second, by studying people in their normal settings, they study the effects of exposure under more realistic conditions. For example, they study populations with people exercising as they normally do, rather than imposing a protocol such as 15 minutes of cycling followed by 10 minutes of rest. Similarly, and particularly important for benefit–cost analysis, they allow for people's behavioural adjustments. For example, rather than forcing a control group and an exposure group to follow the same exercise regimen, as would a toxicology study, they would capture the effect of some people foregoing exercise, or exercising indoors, as a response to a smog alert.

This distinction raises an interesting point about the place of health effects in a disaggregate transfer: namely, this step in the transfer combines both a physical and a behavioural linkage. Like the preceding impacts on environmental quality, it is physical; the body reacts in a certain way to exposure. But also like the preceding valuation step, it is behavioural; people have some control over their level of exposure and can adjust to different circumstances. This dual nature of health effects can cause complications in selecting appropriate concentration-response functions, as we shall see below. Note, too, that this insight may apply in differing degrees to other effects as well, depending on how adaptable the affected resource is. Buildings, for example, are more or less permanent fixtures that, once built, are exposed to the ambient air quality. Nevertheless, such adaptations and adjustments as painting and cleaning are still possible.

Regardless of the type of study on which they are based, the mathematics of the concentration-response functions can be characterized by several different functional forms, each of which defines the shape of the plotted relationship. The most common functional forms are linear, semi-log, and double-log. Figures 4.1 and 4.2 illustrate various non-linear forms. A feature of non-linear functional forms is that the derivative of the effect with respect to the pollution variable depends on the level of the pollution variable and on other variables that are in the concentration-response function. Thus, to use these concentration-response functions, it is necessary to gather current data on the ambient pollution levels that will change under each scenario. This was the purpose behind the kriging model discussed in the previous chapter. An alternative approach is to linearize the concentration-response function. While linearizing simplifies the function and the subsequent calculations so that ambient concentrations are not needed, it will still be necessary to gather enough background data to determine the point at which the function should be linearized. This may be acceptable if the transfer involves a narrow range of data and the function is linearized at the appropriate point, but may be less acceptable if the transfer must occur across a wide range of data.

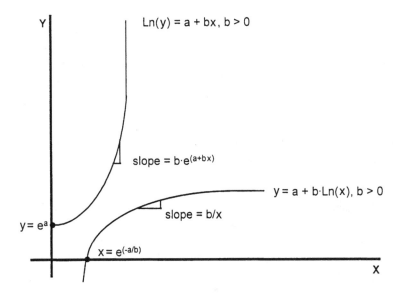

Figure 4.1   Semi-log functional forms

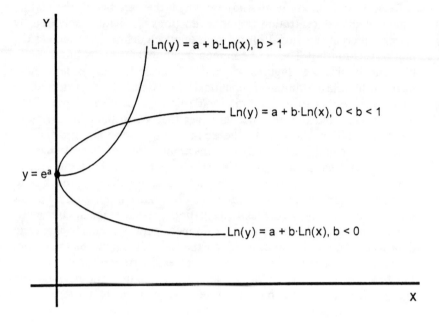

Figure 4.2   Log-linear functional forms

At least three concerns are relevant when selecting a functional form to represent a relationship. The first concern involves the scientific theory behind the problem being studied: for example, does theory suggest that the body can become acclimatized to the presence of a pollutant? The second concern is empirical: when fitting a function, analysts must also explore which functional forms give the best statistical fit to the sample they have at hand. Third, the relevant range of the variables is also important, because various functional forms may be good at describing the data in one part of the range, but not in another. For example, scientific theory suggests that, over a wide range of the level of lead in the air, the relationship between the amount of lead found in the blood (a measure of exposure) and air concentrations is best described by the semi-log function, $y = a + b \cdot Ln(x)$. However, note in Figure 4.1 that this curve is extremely steep at very low values of x. Thus if it is only this low range of x that is of concern, a different functional form should be used. Researchers generally agree that at relatively low air lead levels, a simple linear functional form best approximates the relationship between air lead and blood lead.

Up to this point, we have treated the health effect as a continuous variable that can increase or decrease with a change in the explanatory variables. However, in many cases only a dichotomous measure of a health endpoint is available. For example, study respondents either do or do not report experiencing respiratory symptoms following exposure to ozone. In such cases, a function is needed that can describe the probability of the effect occurring at different concentrations of the pollutant, with the probability obviously having to be constrained to lie between zero and one.

A commonly used specification for discrete effects is a binomial logistic functional form. In its simplest form, such an equation predicts that the probability of observing a symptom, $P(S)$, is

$$P(S) = \frac{1}{1 + \exp(-a - bx)} \tag{4.1}$$

This equation can be rewritten so that the right side is linear, but the left side is the log of the odds of the symptom occurring, that is,

$$\mathrm{Ln}\left[\frac{P(S)}{1 - P(S)}\right] = a + bx \tag{4.2}$$

The derivative of the odds is then

$$\frac{d\left[\dfrac{P(S)}{1 - P(S)}\right]}{dx} = b \cdot \exp(a + bx) \tag{4.3}$$

The likelihood of observing the effect after a change in x is usually compared to the likelihood under a reference level of x. The 'odds ratio',

$$\frac{P(S)_1/[1 - P(S)_1]}{P(S)_0/[1 - P(S)_0]}$$

where the subscript 1 indicates the probability after some change in the explanatory values and the subscript 0 indicates the probability before the change, is commonly used to test for the existence of an effect in epidemiological studies. If this ratio is statistically significantly greater than 1, then the change is considered to be associated with a higher prevalence of the observed effect in the population.

Now, if $P(S)$ is small, or if $P(S)_1 \approx P(S)_0$, then:

$$\frac{P(S)_1}{P(S)_0} \approx \exp(b \cdot \Delta x) \tag{4.4}$$

$$P(S)_1 \approx \exp(b \cdot \Delta x) \cdot P(S)_0$$

This equation is commonly used to predict the *relative risk* of an effect.[2] It measures the risk associated with an increase in concentrations relative to the risk before the increase. In contrast, other risk measures give only the probability of an adverse event occurring at a given level of exposure. Relative risk is reported as a multiple of the prevalence of the effect at a lower, reference level of exposure, $P(S)_0$. Thus, concentration-response functions given as relative risk require background information on $P(S)_0$ in the policy region, frequently measured by finding the number of base cases of the effect in the population and dividing by the total population. Note that these functions do not require gathering background information about ambient air quality – Equation (4.4) utilizes only the change in exposure and the base rate of incidence of the health effect. However, they implicitly control for background air quality through this base-incidence variable, because areas with higher pollution concentrations have higher values for the base incidence, other things equal.

The remainder of this chapter turns to some of the specific concentration-response functions estimated by health researchers to quantify the relationship between air pollution and health. These functions are the potential candidates for transferring at this link in the transfer study. In reviewing the functions, we discuss the importance of functional form and other factors in choosing how best to transfer the concentration-response information to the current policy context.

4.2   PARTICULATE MATTER

Background

Particulate matter (PM) is a common atmospheric pollutant of variable composition. It is categorized by the size of the particles, measured in micrometres (μm) of diameter. Total suspended particulates (TSP) include particulates of any size. PM_{10} signifies all particles less than 10 μm in diameter, $PM_{2.5}$ particles less than 2.5 μm in diameter, and so on. PM has both natural and anthropogenic sources. Its natural sources include wind erosion and wildfires. Its anthropogenic sources include fugitive dust from roads and agriculture, which account for up to 90 per cent of PM emissions in the US; vehicle exhausts; and fuel combustion from industry and utilities, with electric utilities accounting for about 1 per cent of all primary US emissions (US EPA 1995). However, sulphur oxide and nitrogen oxide emissions from utilities can form secondary particulate matter.

The primary US National Ambient Air Quality Standards (NAAQS) are designed to protect humans from adverse health effects caused by exposure to outdoor air pollution. Originally based on TSP levels, the NAAQS began to target PM_{10} concentrations in 1987 and $PM_{2.5}$ concentrations in 1997 after research indicated that these smaller particles, which are more likely to penetrate the airways, present the greatest risk to human health. The current US NAAQS for PM_{10} are a maximum annual arithmetic mean of 50 $\mu g/m^3$ and no more than one single day with a 24-hour concentration above 150 $\mu g/m^3$. The NAAQS for $PM_{2.5}$ are an annual mean of 15 $\mu g/m^3$ and a 24-hour concentration of 65 $\mu g/m^3$. Still based on TSP, the World Health Organization standards range from 60 to 90 $\mu g/m^3$.

The air-quality monitors in the case-study area generally indicate low PM_{10} levels relative to these standards. According to the Aerometric Information Retrieval Systems (AIRS),[3] the air-quality monitor with the highest 24-hour PM_{10} value recorded in 1991, the year modelled in the study, was in St Paul, with a reading of 137 $\mu g/m^3$. A monitor in Rapid City, in western South Dakota, however, twice exceeded the 24-hour standard, with a high of 174 $\mu g/m^3$, suggesting that some of the drier areas in the west of the study region may have had higher ambient PM levels. No monitor in the area reported annual averages within 20 $\mu g/m^3$ of the annual standard in 1991, with the highest being 31 $\mu g/m^3$. Using data from the kriging model reported in Chapter 3, the mean annual average concentration across receptors in the study area was 22 $\mu g/m^3$. These data are consistent with US averages nationally, though some regions, such as southern California and major urban centres, have annual averages of about 50 $\mu g/m^3$. Concentrations are higher in Europe, often in the 50–100 $\mu g/m^3$ range, and higher still in many developing countries, reaching 200 $\mu g/m^3$ in some cities in China.

Exposure Issues

Exposure to particulate matter is a straightforward matter of particles entering the respiratory tract along with air. In general, smaller particles are more likely to penetrate deeper into the airways and lung than large particles, which tend to be deposited in the nasal region or upper airways where they are trapped or filtered by small hairs and abrupt directional changes. However, any particles are more likely to penetrate deeper during oral breathing and heavy exercise. In the tracheobronchial and pulmonary regions, PM may interfere with breathing and cause pulmonary-function changes, acute respiratory symptoms and infections, and chronic effects (such as lung-function changes, chronic obstructive pulmonary disease and chronic respiratory symptoms). Among the elderly and those suffering from pulmonary or cardiovascular disease, PM exposure may contribute to mortality.

In researching these effects, epidemiological and toxicological studies have used various measures of exposure to particulates, including TSP, PM_{10}, $PM_{2.5}$, SO_4, coefficient of haze (COH) and British or black smoke (BS). TSP, the method of choice for monitoring purposes for many years, was generally replaced by PM_{10} in the 1980s. COH and BS are both measures of opacity, and can be used only as indicators of small-particle (less than about 4.5 μm) concentrations. To review and eventually summarize studies using these measures, it is necessary to convert measures to a common metric of particulates. It is commonly assumed that BS levels are equivalent to PM_{10}, and COH levels to TSP. TSP is usually converted to PM_{10} by using ratios varying from 0.45 to 0.66, but the most common are 0.45 and 0.55 (US EPA 1982). The case study uses 0.55 for conversion purposes.[4]

Review of the Literature Linking Mortality Risks to Exposure to PM[5]

A large body of evidence supports the existence of a number of health effects for particulate matter, with an effect on mortality rates heading the list. In 1930, a dense fog containing large amounts of PM covered the Meuse Valley of Belgium. In two days, approximately 6000 people became ill and died, an increase of over 1000 per cent above the normal death rate. Similar incidents subsequently occurred in Donora, Pennsylvania, and in London. In the London incident in 1952, some 4000 deaths above normal were due almost exclusively to respiratory and cardiovascular disease, primarily among the elderly. These events leave little doubt that high concentrations of particulate-based smog are associated with increased mortality rates, at least among vulnerable individuals.

Since this anecdotal evidence, many studies have shown a positive relationship between particulates and mortality, with ten estimating concentration-response functions to quantify that relationship, often controlling for weather and other types of pollution. Seven of these studies, loosely referred to as the 'Schwartz studies' for the role played in them by Joel Schwartz, used a similar methodology (Dockery, Schwartz and Spengler 1992; Pope, Schwartz and Ransom 1992; Schwartz 1991a, 1991b, 1993a; Schwartz and Dockery 1992a, 1992b). These studies matched the daily count of all non-accidental deaths to the 24-hour average of either TSP or PM_{10} from all population-based monitors in each location. Because mortality is a relatively rare event, they used Poisson regressions for fitting models. Three other studies used different methodologies. Schwartz and Marcus (1990) examined the relationship between BS and mortality in London for the winters of 1958 through 1972, where pollution levels were much higher than in the other studies, though average concentrations dropped markedly over time. The authors accounted for serial correlation in their data, seasonal trends and weather. In another study, Fairley (1990) used COH as the exposure variable. Finally, Shumway, Azari and Pawitan (1988) employed state–space, non-parametric and parametric models to investigate associations among mortality and COH. They processed the data using a low-pass filter, with the resulting series subsampled weekly to produce smoothed observations of daily mortality, pollution and weather variables. They then fitted autoregressive models, regressing mortality on logged COH and controlling variables.

In all these studies, the model takes the form:

$$y = \exp(\mathbf{x'b}) \tag{4.5}$$

where y is mortality and $\mathbf{x}$ is a vector of explanatory variables, most importantly PM, but sometimes also including weather, time trends and other pollutants. Denoting PM levels as x_k, it follows that

$$\frac{\partial y}{\partial x_K} = b_K \exp(\mathbf{x'b}) = b_K y$$
$$b_K = \frac{\partial y / \partial x_K}{y} \tag{4.6}$$

so that b_K is the percentage change in mortality for a given change in particulates. Thus the concentration-response function is similar to the relative risk given in Equation (4.4) above, requiring information about base mortality rates in the population to which the information is being transferred.

Table 4.1 presents a summary of these ten studies. The table lists the cities in which the studies were conducted and the study's sample size. It also gives the mean level of daily mortality in the city, the original units used to measure particulates, the mean exposure in those units, and the equivalent PM_{10} measure of both mean exposure and the range of exposures. Finally, the table shows the estimated coefficient and standard error for the percentage change in mortality. The average PM_{10} or PM_{10} equivalent exposures in the ten US cities varied between 28 and 61 $\mu g/m^3$ PM_{10}, several of them below the NAAQS threshold of 50 $\mu g/m^3$. The average London exposure between 1958 and 1972 was about 174 $\mu g/m^3$, nearly three times the highest average US exposure. The change in daily mortality for a 1 $\mu g/m^3$ increase in PM_{10} exposure ranges between about

Table 4.1 Results of ten studies on the relation of particulates and mortality

Study	City, years	Sample size	Mean daily mortality	Original PM units	Mean PM exposure	Coefficient (standard error)	PM$_{10}$ equivalent		
							Mean PM$_{10}$ exposure	Range PM$_{10}$ exposure	Coefficient in percentage terms (standard error)
Schwartz (1991a)	Detroit, MI 1973–82	3650	53.0	TSP	87	0.000546 (0.000145)	48	30–67 (10–90%)	0.0993 (0.0264)
Schwartz and Dockery (1992b)	Steubenville, OH 1974–84	4016	3.0	TSP	111	0.000381 (0.000082)	61	20–115 (10–90%)	0.0691 (0.0149)
Schwartz and Dockery (1992a)	Philadelphia, PA 1973–80	2726	48.0	TSP	77	0.000661 (0.000131)	42	24–64 (10–90%)	0.1203 (0.0238)
Schwartz (1991b)	Minneapolis/ St Paul, MN 1973–82	2800	27.0	TSP	78	0.000525 (0.000150)	43	25–70 (1st–5th quintile)	0.0955 (0.0273)
Pope, Schwartz and Ransom (1992)	Provo, UT 1985–89	1436	2.7	PM$_{10}$	47	0.00147 (0.00031)	47	1–365	0.1471 (0.0310)
Dockery, Schwartz and Spengler (1992)	St Louis, MO 1985–86	311	56.0	PM$_{10}$	28	0.0015 (0.0069)	28	1–97	0.1501 (0.0691)
	Kingston/ Harriman, TN 1985–86	330	16.0	PM$_{10}$	30	0.00160 (0.00149)	30	4–67	0.1601 (0.1491)
Schwartz (1993a)	Birmingham, AL 1985–88	1087	17.0	PM$_{10}$	48	0.00104 (0.00043)	48	21–80 (10–90%)	0.1044 (0.0431)
Fairley (1990)	Santa Clara, CA 1985–86	549	20.0	COH	67	0.0059[a] (0.0026)	37	3–210	0.0540 (0.0241)
Shumway, Azari and Pawitan (1988)	Los Angeles, CA 1970–79	508	175.0	COH	34	9.01[b] (1.88)	35	52–180	0.1463 (0.0305)
Schwartz and Marcus (1990)	London 1958–72	1680	292.0	BS	174	2.3100[c] (0.1598)	174	20–1500	0.0299 (0.0021)

Notes: [a] $b \cdot COH$
[b] $b \cdot Ln(COH)$

84

0.07 per cent and about 0.16 per cent for the US cities, while the London estimate of 0.03 per cent is less than half of the lowest US estimate.

Analysts considering a transfer study will often find their plans frustrated by a lack of available studies from which to transfer information. But in this case, an embarrassment of riches is the greater problem: all ten of these studies provide high-quality information that could be used in a transfer. One response to this situation is to pick the 'best study', whether on a scientific and methodological basis (for example, the study that used the most appropriate sampling procedures or statistical analysis) or on the basis of a comparison with the new policy context (for example, the study that analysed pollution concentrations closest to those in the study area). Often the decision is not an easy one, and requires a subtle understanding of the literature being evaluated. Accordingly, we review briefly some of the criticisms of and unresolved questions about these epidemiological studies, which could provide criteria for choosing a 'best study'.

The first unresolved question is: What components of PM are responsible for the mortality effects? With the exception of SO_4, none of the commonly used PM measures discriminates among various types of particulates. The measures generally contain a variable mix of particulates that range from inert to highly reactive, different chemical properties that presumably have quite different, but currently undetermined, health implications. Studies have differed on the impact of different types of particles. These results demonstrate the complexities that may arise when transferring information between contexts. In the case study, we estimate a policy's effect on air quality partly as measured in terms of PM concentrations. But PM is not a homogeneous entity, and different mixtures may be associated with different effects. Ideally, in transferring information at this stage analysts would look for studies involving a mix of particles similar to those in the ambient air of their transfer region, or emitted in the transfer policy. Alternatively, they could try somehow to adjust for important differences. If the data informing such judgements are unavailable, they may be better off assuming that the PM in the policy to be evaluated has the same health effects as the particulate mix in the study regions. The case study relies on that assumption.

A second question surrounding these epidemiological studies involves their inability to pinpoint a threshold at which mortality risks begin. Although some studies find statistically insignificant effects at low PM concentrations (for example, Özkaynak and Thurston 1987; Lipfert et al. 1988), five of the Schwartz studies (Pope, Schwartz and Ransom 1992; Schwartz 1991a, 1991b; Schwartz and Dockery 1992a, 1992b) find no difference between the effects at low levels and at high levels when the data are grouped and compared by quintiles. In general, the linear and exponential functional forms employed by most researchers do not suggest a strong attenuation of effects at low levels. Nevertheless, the state of the science cannot rule out the possibility of some attenuation. If for one reason or another analysts are convinced by the arguments in favour of a threshold, they may choose to impose a threshold on the functional forms before transferring them, or choose a study with a functional form predicting no effects at low levels. Other analysts may choose a study with concentrations near those in their study region. For our purposes, for example, Table 4.1 shows that the studies in St Louis and Kingston may be the most appropriate, with mean ambient PM levels of 28 and 30 $\mu g/m^3$.[6]

A third unresolved issue is how best to control for the effects of weather, important because high temperatures are generally considered to be a factor in mortality. The majority of studies do find a relationship between particulates and mortality even when controlling for temperature. However, when controlling for temperature and humidity in a study of seven years of July data, Katsouyanni et al. (1993) found that a dummy variable for high-particulate days was not a statistically significant explanatory variable for mortality in Greece, but that a term representing interaction between smoke and temperature was suggestive. Weather can also affect health in more complex ways. For example, Kalkstein (1991) found elevated mortality rates as a function of the number of sequential hot and humid days. These two studies seem to suggest that some of the effects attributed to PM may be due to previously uninvestigated effects of weather. However, particulate concentrations tend to increase during the winter, and several studies only use data for winter months.

A fourth area where there have been inconsistent findings between the studies is in the time lag between PM concentrations and mortality effects. Fairley (1990) found the best fit to be a two-day lag, Schwartz and Dockery (1992b) a one-day lag, and Schwartz and Marcus (1990) contemporaneous exposure. In fact, all these measures are imperfect proxies for actual exposures, which are dominated by indoor air quality. Differences in statistical significance among measures may be a consequence of variations in the mix of particulate components, or of uncontrolled behavioural or architectural differences among cities and over time that affect indoor PM concentrations and personal exposures. However, for benefit–cost analysis, whether effects are observed on the same day or with one or two days' lag matters little, as people's willingness to pay will be the same.

A fifth and final area of uncertainty and potential criticism concerns which age groups are most susceptible to PM's mortality effects. Schwartz and Dockery (1992a) divided their sample population into two groups, people aged 65 and older and people younger than 65, and estimated a regression for each group. Fairley (1990) also divided his population into two age-based groups, those 70 and older and those younger than 70. Both studies found that the older group was much more significantly affected. This pattern matches that seen in London in 1952, where the sharp increase in sudden deaths occurred mostly among older or sickly individuals. It is also consistent with evidence linking PM's effects to the pulmonary system and heart. Schwartz and Dockery (1992a) found that the most significant cause of death was chronic obstructive pulmonary disease (COPD) followed by pneumonia and cardiovascular disease, results confirmed by Schwartz (1993b).

Some researchers have gone so far as to suggest that these five concerns cast doubt on the causal connection between PM and mortality risks. While they do raise worries, no one has offered a credible alternative explanation for the high degree of consensus among results that have been replicated in diverse communities. If the association were due to an omitted covariant or misspecified weather model, the impacts of the missing variable would have to be the same across all the locations, or the correlation between weather and PM_{10} would have to be the same. Neither is likely. Associations between particulates and daily mortality have been found in locations with low and high annual temperatures and with PM levels that peak at different times of year. Likewise, associations have been reported in dry climates (Utah Valley and Santa Clara) and humid climates (eastern US). In a similar way, they have been found for different mixes of particles. The similarity of regression coefficients across locations with considerable variability in particulate levels, particulate types and weather suggests that the results of these studies are sufficiently reliable for benefit–cost analysis.

But while they may not be enough to discredit some causal relationship, these concerns are all factors to consider when choosing a 'best study' to transfer. Any best study would have to take them into account as much as possible. But by now it should be obvious that it is not always clear how to do so, for the choice of how to account for these factors depends critically on the unresolved questions. Furthermore, almost certainly some studies will be best (or most appropriate) in some respects, while others will be best in other respects. Consequently, picking a single study to transfer and ignoring the others unavoidably means casting away valuable information. But analysts engaged in a transfer study should never let too much information become an obstacle. Instead, they should seek to make the most out of whatever information is available. Rather than as an embarrassment, therefore, analysts should view an abundance of information as an opportunity.

Accordingly, the literature linking PM and mortality offers an opportunity to use meta-analysis techniques. In this way, we can avoid throwing away useful information, allowing all the concentration-response functions to contribute to the final form of the function. Of course, we could also achieve this with simpler approaches, such as taking a simple mean of all the coefficients listed in Table 4.1. But while this would incorporate all the studies, it would also treat them equally, ignoring real differences that exist among them. With a meta-analysis, we can weight them by the standard error of each study's estimates, control for differences in ambient exposures, and potentially account for other differences as well, including methodological differences.

Meta-analysis of Mortality Estimates

One approach to meta-analysis assumes that the various studies are all measuring essentially the same physical relationship, but with random disturbances. That is, the relationship is not determinant, but may differ – or at least appear to differ as far as we can measure it – from city to city. But there is still an underlying distribution to the relationship, an underlying mean and variance. Thus each city is associated with its own physical relationship between particulates and mortality, which research can infer from a study in a given city, but they all fit into a pattern according to the underlying distribution. In more technical terms, this random-effects model assumes that the estimated coefficients and variances for each study, b_i and s_i^2, are determined by the means and variances β_i and σ_i^2 of the city-specific distributions from which they are drawn. It further assumes, in turn, that the city-distribution parameters are drawn from a common 'mother distribution' with parameters β^* and σ^{*2} that is the source of all the estimates and that is independent of the range of exposure. The goal of this kind of meta-analysis is to estimate these underlying parameters, using maximum-likelihood techniques, from the observations of each city.

When observations are independently and identically sampled from a normal population, sufficient statistics for describing each study are the number of observations (n_i), the sample mean (b_i) and the sample variance (s_i^2). The contribution to the likelihood function of a sample mean and variance, in terms of the population mean and variance $(\beta^*$ and $\sigma^{*2})$ is derived in Kendall and Stuart (1963):

$$L_l(b_i, s_i^2 | \beta^*, \sigma^{*2}) = \left[\frac{1}{\sigma^*} \exp\left(-\frac{n_i(b_i - \beta^*)}{2\sigma^{*2}} \right) \right] \frac{1}{\sigma^{*n_1 - 1}} s_i^{n_i - 3} \exp\left(-\frac{n_i s_i^2}{2\sigma^{*2}} \right)$$

$$(4.7)$$

Maximizing the likelihood yields parameter estimates of the mother distribution:

$$L^* = \prod_{i=1}^{m} L_i(b_i, s_i^2 | \beta^*, \sigma^{*2}) \tag{4.8}$$

where m is the number of results synthesized in the meta-analysis, in this case eight (the seven Schwartz studies, with separate results for two cities from Dockery, Schwartz and Spengler 1992, as noted in Table 4.1). This technique is further discussed in Eddy, Hasselblad and Shachter (1992).

Using this technique to estimate the underlying parameters, we estimate the underlying meta-coefficient, or the mean of the mother distribution, to be 0.1014, with a standard error of 0.0424. That is, we estimate that the underlying physical relationship from which the cities deviate is a 0.1014 per cent increase in mortality from a 1 $\mu g/m^3$ increase in daily PM_{10}. This compares to coefficients from the individual studies ranging from 0.07 to 0.16, with a simple mean of about 0.12. The mother-distribution mean is statistically significant, with the 90 per cent confidence interval ranging between 0.03 per cent and 0.17 per cent.

Figure 4.3 graphically compares the various distributions. Steubenville, with the largest sample size, has both the smallest coefficient estimate and

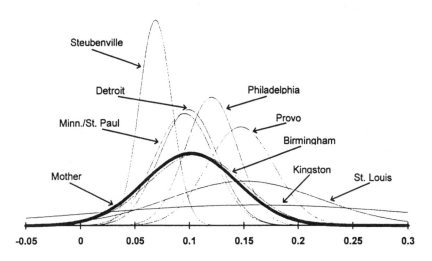

Figure 4.3   Estimates from eight studies and maximum likelihood estimate: percentage change in mortality for a 1 $\mu g/m^3$ increase in daily PM_{10}

the smallest standard error. The studies with the largest coefficient estimates, St Louis and Kingston, also have the largest dispersion. Consistent with its statistical insignificance, the Kingston distribution is nearly flat, and thus uninformative, contributing little to the mother-distribution estimate. The Birmingham distribution is almost identical to the mother distribution, with the Minneapolis/St Paul and Detroit distributions also having means near the mother-distribution estimate.

As noted above, the other three studies, performed in Santa Clara, California, Los Angeles, California and London (Fairley 1990; Shumway, Azari and Pawitan 1988; Schwartz and Marcus 1990), employed somewhat different estimation strategies and exposure measures. Table 4.2 shows the effect on the mother-distribution estimates of adding each one in turn, after converting coefficients to equivalent percentage changes in PM_{10}. Adding Santa Clara and Los Angeles leaves the mother-distribution mean nearly unchanged and increases its standard error only slightly. However, the London mean and standard error are much smaller than in the other studies. Including this study in the maximum-likelihood estimation reduces the mean effect from about 0.10 per cent to a little more than 0.09 per cent and slightly widens the 90 per cent confidence interval to between 0.02 per cent and 0.17 per cent. It may be appropriate to use an estimate that excludes the London study for transferring estimates to an area with relatively good ambient air quality.

So far, these meta-analyses have yielded only a single estimate that presumably would have to apply equally to all age groups. But as we have noted, evidence suggests that effects are greater for elderly and perhaps sick individuals. To the findings from these eleven studies, we can combine the evidence from the age-specific studies in Philadelphia and Santa Clara (Fairley 1990 and Schwartz and Dockery 1992a) to estimate the underlying mother distributions for age-specific effects. We assume that the estimated coefficients and standard errors for deaths of younger and older people in the two cities – b_{jy}, s_{jy}, b_{jo} and s_{jo} – are determined by the city-specific distributions with parameters b_{jy}, s_{jy}, b_{jo} and s_{jo}, where y and o stand for young and old, respectively, and j is an index for the two cities.[7] Again employing a random-effects approach, we assume that these parameters in turn are drawn from age-specific mother distributions with parameters β_y^*, σ_y^*, β_o^* and σ_o^*. The non-age-specific mother distribution is assumed to be determined by these underlying age-specific mother distributions according to

$$\beta^* = d_y\beta_y^* + d_o\beta_o^*$$
$$\sigma^{*2} = d_y^2\sigma_y^2\beta^* + \sigma_o^2 + \sigma_o^2\beta^*$$

(4.9)

Table 4.2   Meta-analysis of eleven epidemiological studies

Study	Location	Coefficient[a]	Standard error	Sample size	Mean exposure
Fairley (1990)	Santa Clara	0.0540	0.0241	549	37
Shumway, Azari and Pawitan (1988)	Los Angeles	0.1463	0.0305	508	35
Schwartz and Marcus (1990)	London	0.0299	0.0021	1680	174
Mother distribution, 8 Schwartz studies		0.1014	0.0424		
with Santa Clara		0.0999	0.0428		
with Santa Clara and Los Angeles		0.1013	0.0432		
with Santa Clara, Los Angeles and London		0.0950	0.0459		

Notes: [a] Percentage change in daily mortality for a 1 $\mu g/m^3$ increase in daily PM_{10}.

where d_y and d_o are the proportions of total deaths represented by individuals 65 or younger and individuals 65 older than, respectively.

The likelihood for the age-specific city parameters b_{jy} and s_{jy} is calculated as Equation (4.7). For the non-age-specific parameters, we replace β^* and σ^{*2} with the relationships shown in Equation (4.9). The model likelihood function is then

$$L^* = \prod_{j=1}^{2} \left[L\left(\frac{b_{jy}, s_{jy}^2}{\beta_y^*, \sigma_y^{*2}}\right) \cdot L\left(\frac{b_{jo}, s_{jo}^2}{\beta_o^*, \sigma_o^{*2}}\right) \right] \cdot \prod_{i=1}^{11} L\left(\frac{b_i, s_i^2}{\beta_y^*, \sigma_y^{*2}, \beta_o^*, \sigma_o^{*2}}\right)$$

$$(4.10)$$

Table 4.3 summarizes the results of maximizing Equation (4.10) with respect to the age-specific mother-distribution parameters. The table shows the two additional age-specific studies added to the eleven non-age-specific studies discussed previously. The all-ages mother-distribution parameters are repeated from Table 4.3 for comparison. The ≤ 65 estimate is statistically insignificant at the 90 per cent level, with the confidence interval ranging between -0.02 per cent and 0.11 per cent. The >65 estimate is significant, with the 90 per cent confidence interval ranging between 0.04 per cent and 0.23 per cent. Figure 4.4 graphically compares the age-specific distributions. The mother under-65 distribution is similar to the Philadelphia under-65 distribution. However, these two distributions and the Santa Clara under-70 distribution include large areas to the left of zero, indicating that their means are not statistically different from zero. The mean and the standard deviation of the over-65 mother distribution are 30 to 40 per cent larger than those of the all-ages mother distribution.

Estimating an underlying mother distribution assumes that the estimates of the concentration-response coefficient are constants, albeit with potentially different constants for different groups such as age groups. But the coefficients may instead be functions of (continuous) variables, such as the level of exposure. Regression analysis can test for such a relationship. Figure 4.5 plots actual and predicted coefficient values from regressions of study coefficients on mean exposure levels. The regressions include linear and log specifications for the ten estimates, with London, an outlier, now omitted. They also include ordinary least squares (OLS), generalized least squares (GLS), least trimmed squares (LTS) and local regression (LOESS) estimates. LTS is a robust regression estimator that minimizes the smallest half of the squared residuals. LOESS fits a piecewise linear regression.

Of these models, we would look for one that does the best job of predicting at relatively low ambient PM levels, because those are the levels

Table 4.3 Age-specific meta-analysis of epidemiological studies

Study	Age	Location	Coefficient[a]	Standard error	Sample size	Mean exposure
Schwartz and Dockery (1992a)	$\leq$65	Philadelphia, PA	0.0493	0.0375	2726	42
Schwartz and Dockery (1992a)	>65	Philadelphia, PA	0.1656	0.0293	2726	42
Fairley (1990)	<70	Santa Clara, CA	0.0331	0.0450	508	37
Fairley (1990)	$\geq$ 70	Santa Clara, CA	0.0762	0.0329	508	37
Mother distribution, 11 studies	all ages		0.0950	0.0459		
Mother distribution, 13 studies	$\leq$ 65		0.0432	0.0386		
Mother distribution, 13 studies	>65		0.1347	0.0591		

Notes: [a] Percentage change in daily mortality for a 1 $\mu g/m^3$ increase in daily PM_{10}.

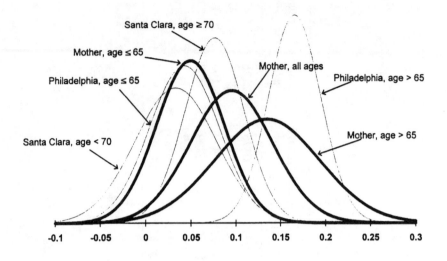

Figure 4.4   Age-specific meta-analysis of epidemiological studies: percentage change in mortality for a 1 μg/m³ increase in daily PM₁₀

observed in Minnesota and the rest of the study area. As reported above, the mean concentration pooled across receptors is 22 μg/m³ and the single highest annual average reported at any air-quality monitor in the region was 31 μg/m³. While all models predict similar coefficients at the mean exposure in the empirical studies of about 50 μg/m³, there are more significant differences at lower exposures, where LTS predicts the largest effects and GLS predicts the smallest.

Figure 4.6 compares the smoothed-residuals plots for the models shown in Figure 4.5. The LTS models' residuals indicate that they have the better fits, with the log model performing somewhat better than the linear model. The LTS models also tend to overstate effects throughout the range, whereas the other models have a strong tendency to understate effects, especially at low exposure levels. Multivariate models that include base mortality rates, an age dummy for age-specific estimates, and a dummy for Schwartz studies do not significantly improve explanatory power.

The log LTS model predicts the concentration-response coefficient β_i with its 90 per cent confidence interval to be:

$$\beta_i = \exp\{-1.00598 - 0.02682 \cdot x_i \pm [0.025 + 0.0004 \cdot (x_i - \bar{x})^2]\} \quad (4.11)$$

where x_i is the mean daily exposure at receptor i in μg/m³ and $\bar{x}$ is the

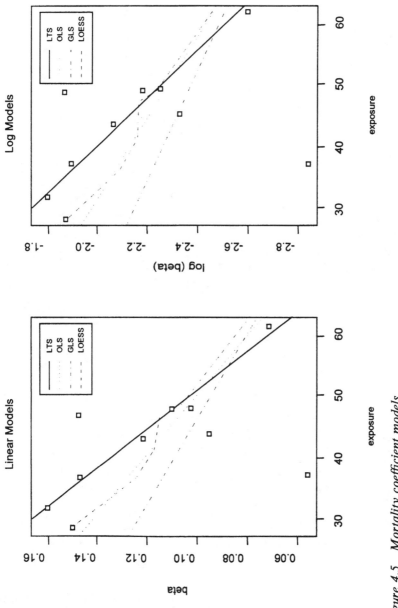

Figure 4.5 Mortality coefficient models

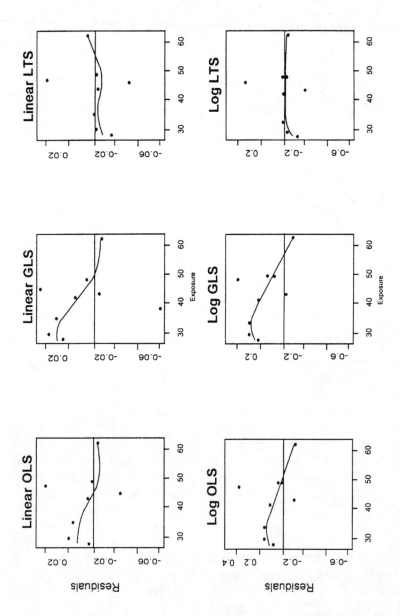

Figure 4.6   Smoothed-residuals plots for mortality models

overall mean daily exposure across studies (41.9 μg/m^3).[8] The negative sign of the x_i coefficient indicates that the percentage mortality increase for a one-unit increase in exposure is smaller at higher mean exposure levels. Figure 4.7 plots the shape of the corresponding total effect, which increases at a decreasing rate as average exposures rise. Schwartz and others have speculated that this fall in the coefficient at higher mean exposure levels is a result of an errors-in-variables problem.[9] Ambient exposures are only a proxy for actual human exposures, most of which occur indoors. If indoor exposures rise less than proportionally with ambient levels, then the estimated mortality coefficient will be smaller at higher compared to lower average ambient levels.

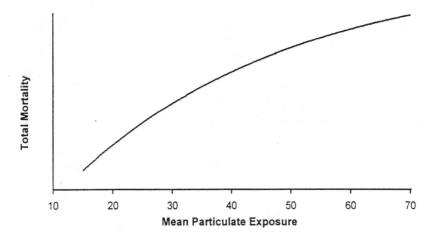

Figure 4.7   Total mortality from particulate exposure

At the overall mean daily exposure for all ten studies (again, excluding London) of 41.9 μg/m^3, the LTS model predicts a concentration-response coefficient of 0.1189 ± 0.0678, statistically indistinguishable from the mother-distribution estimate. However, the LTS model predicts higher marginal effects at the lower daily exposure levels of the study area. For example, rural exposures of about 15 μg/m^3 yield a predicted marginal effect of 0.2446 ± 0.0873, more than twice the mother-distribution estimate.

These meta-analyses illustrate both of the major steps of transferring information that we have highlighted in this book. First, they *summarize* the information from multiple studies. Second, they *adjust* for differences between the original contexts and the transfer context, in one case adjusting for the age compositions of various locations and in the other for differences in ambient pollution concentrations. Indeed, while we have noted that analysts can make *ad hoc* adjustments when transferring a single study's results, or even make statistical adjustments by transferring an entire equation from a single study, meta-analysis techniques often afford the analysts additional opportunities for such adjustments. More studies simply offer more opportunities for diversity to arise, creating a richer set of variables among which analysts can potentially make adjustments, including differences in the range of the data involved, institutional or geographic settings and methodological approaches in the original research.

These meta-analysis techniques offer three alternative ways to transfer information about the relationship between PM and mortality to the study area. First, there is an overall mother distribution that predicts a single effect in all age groups. As can be seen in Figure 4.3, this predicts mean effects similar to the Minneapolis/St Paul study by Schwartz (1991b), but still uses information from all eleven studies. Second, there is an age-specific mother distribution that takes into consideration important differences between health effects of PM on people over 65 and those under 65. Finally, there is a regression analysis that estimates a concentration-response function that is sensitive to differences in mean exposure. The results show that the latter function will lead to a much higher estimate of damages than will either of the mother distributions, predicting up to twice as many deaths. This disparity arises partly because the mean exposures at most of the receptors in the study area are far lower than in the studies used to estimate the function, requiring extrapolation outside the range of the available data. This fact gives us less confidence in the regression analysis than in the mother distributions.[10] The case study thus uses the mother-distribution analysis to transfer mortality risks using the age-specific distributions that control for important differences between age groups.

Chronic Health Effects

If exposure to PM is associated with mortality risks, it is not surprising that it would be associated with morbidity effects as well. In fact, exposure to PM appears to be related to emphysema, respiratory infections such as bronchitis, and the experience of minor respiratory symptoms. These effects can be divided up in many ways, depending on one's purposes, but we split them into two categories: chronic effects and acute effects. This distinction is motivated by the economic evaluation of the effects discussed in Chapter 5. Briefly, acute effects, easily measured in terms of *days* of cough, or *days* of headache, can be valued on a per day basis, whereas this would make little sense for long-lasting or permanent effects such as emphysema, which can even reduce an individual's life expectancy. We discuss chronic effects in this section, followed by a section discussing acute effects.

In one study, Portney and Mullahy (1990) found a significant concentration-response relationship between serious chronic respiratory illness in adults (comprising emphysema, chronic bronchitis and asthma) and annual TSP after controlling for such demographic variables as income, education and race. Average TSP exposure was 73 $\mu g/m^3$, ranging from 35 to 165 $\mu g/m^3$. While this study is a good candidate for a transfer, it included additional variables, such as temperature and percentage of smokers, that were either insignificant or unavailable in our study area. To circumvent this problem, we assumed that these variables take on the value of their mean from the original study and transfer them as a constant incorporated in the intercept term, with the standard error adjusted appropriately. After making this adjustment, converting TSP to PM, and adjusting for the influence of inflation in the income coefficient, we use the following concentration-response function based on Portney and Mullahy (1990) to estimate changes in the number of cases of emphysema, chronic bronchitis and asthma (standard errors in parentheses):

$$Ln\left(\frac{P}{1-P}\right) = -3.02 + 0.01093\,PM + 0.61\,RACE - 0.08\,INC + 5.78\,EDU$$
$$(1.22) \quad (6.96) \quad\quad (0.40) \quad\quad (0.06) \quad\quad (3.03)$$

$$(4.12)$$

where
  P   = the probability of having emphysema, chronic bronchitis or asthma;
  PM   = annual PM_{10} in $\mu g/m^3$,
  RACE = 1 if white, 0 otherwise,
  INC = annual household income divided by 10 000, and
  EDU = years of school completed divided by 100.

In addition to the illnesses discussed above, inhalation of PM and the consequent change in pulmonary and bronchial-clearance mechanisms is widely thought to affect host immune systems (US EPA 1982). These impacts, in turn, may contribute to increased susceptibility to infection. In one study, Dockery et al. (1989) studied a group of 10- to 12-year-old children from six communities in the eastern US. The authors collected time series of the children's illnesses and annual average pollution concentrations, including PM_{15}. Converting PM_{15} to PM_{10}, PM levels ranged from 20.1 to 88.2 $\mu g/m^3$ across the six cities. They found a strong association between PM_{15} concentrations and incidence of chronic cough. After controlling for maternal smoking, sex, age and the presence of a gas stove in the children's homes (a proxy for NO_2 exposure), Dockery et al. (1989) report the following concentration-response function with PM_{15} converted to PM_{10}:

$$Cases = \exp(0.052 \times \Delta PM_{10}) \times BC, \qquad (4.13)$$

where Cases is the number of cases of chronic cough in children, BC is the baseline number of cases, and PM_{10} is an annual average measured in $\mu g/m^3$. The baseline rate of chronic cough was 0.058 in the study. The 95 per cent confidence interval for the PM coefficient is between 0.0 and 0.103.

This function provides an opportunity to discuss the relevant population within the market area of the transfer. Dockery et al. studied 10- to 12-year-old children. In transferring Dockery et al.'s functions, then, should analysts limit the population to which they transfer it only to children of this age, or to all children or even to adults as well? Clearly, there is no single, correct answer to this question, and judgements will inevitably be at least somewhat arbitrary. Often, however, judgements can be informed by the results of other studies. For example, is there at least qualitative evidence that the effect may also exist in adults, or are there reasons to believe it does not? In this particular case, while we might apply the study to adults, we confine our transfer to children, though extending it to include children of any age.

Acute Health Effects

In a study of shorter-lasting respiratory infection, Schwartz et al. (1991) found a relationship between TSP and croup, a viral infection caused by influenza and other viruses. Although Schwartz et al. performed a logistic regression analysis, they do not report the entire model, leaving out important statistics needed to estimate effects. However, they do report a relative risk, from which we derive the following concentration-response function:

$$Cases = \exp(0.005 \times \Delta PM_{10}) \times BC, \qquad (4.14)$$

where Cases is the number of cases of croup in children daily, BC is the baseline number of cases, and PM_{10} is daily PM measured in $\mu g/m^3$.

The baseline rate is about three cases per one million people per day. Unfortunately confidence intervals are not reported for the relative risk. This study has the further disadvantage of using hospital visits as its dependent variable, which is likely to understate the true size of the effect throughout the population if some cases go unreported. Nevertheless, this is the only study that quantifies the effect of PM on the incidence of croup.

In addition to their research of chronic cough, Dockery et al. (1989) also found evidence of a relationship between PM and bronchitis. They found that

$$\text{Cases} = \exp(0.036 \times \Delta PM_{10}) \times BC, \qquad (4.15)$$

again after converting PM_{15} to PM_{10} and where Cases is the number of cases of bronchitis in children annually and BC is the baseline number of cases. The average annual rate of bronchitis in the study was about 6.5 per cent. The 95 per cent confidence interval for the PM coefficient is between 0.004 and 0.072.

Other morbidity effects may be less specific, or at least less severe, than croup or bronchitis, instead just being any of a number of mild symptoms, such as cough or runny nose. Some researchers group these into 'restricted activity days', or RADs, which simply indicate a day in which a person stays home from work or school because of such symptoms. In one such study, Ostro and Rothschild (1989) report a relationship in adults between respiratory restricted activity days (RRADs) and fine particles ($PM_{2.5}$) while controlling for ozone.[11] While this study is sound in its scientific and statistical aspects, it presents an example of a case where the health endpoint is not entirely consistent with the valuation linkage in the transfer. Using RRADs as the health endpoint, the study does not give information about the specific symptoms that keep people home. Yet these symptoms are likely to be a significant part of the reason people value their good health – and would pay to avoid ill health. People presumably care not only about the fact that they have to stay home, or that they are confined to bed, but about their experience of the symptoms (Desvousges et al. 1996). Accordingly, an RRAD caused by cough may have a different economic cost than an RRAD caused by headache, implying that a study quantifying RRADs, while giving part of the picture, must be incomplete. Still, if better information is not available, RRADs may be used for lack of a better alternative, and simplifications can be made to estimate the value of avoiding RADs. Krupnick and Kopp (1988), for example, valued RRADs as an average of the values for avoiding the likely underlying symptoms.

Fortunately for the case-study transfer, a major cross-sectional study has investigated the link between PM levels and specific respiratory symptoms, finding very similar coefficients. Braun-Fahrländer et al. (1992) studied pre-school children aged zero to five years in Basel, Zurich, and two other Swiss communities, testing the effect of both daily TSP and six-week averages. Controlling for temperature and seasonal dummy variables, they found that the previous day's TSP level had a significant relationship with the incidence of upper respiratory symptoms. Using mean values to replace temperature, season and a variable denoting a history of respiratory symptoms, and replacing TSP with PM, we derive the following concentration-response function from this study:

$$Ln\left(\frac{P(S)}{1 - P(S)}\right) = -4.600 + 0.00825 \text{ PM},$$
$$(0.531)\,(0.00316)$$

where $P(S)$ is the probability of having an upper respiratory symptom and standard errors are in parentheses.

In their study of six-week averages, Braun-Fahrländer et al. (1992) also found that TSP was significantly associated with coughing incidence, with a relative risk of 1.16 for a 20 $\mu g/m^3$ change and a 95 per cent confidence interval between 1.07 and 1.26. Converting to PM, this suggests the following concentration-response function:

$$\text{Number of cough episodes} = \exp(0.013 \times \Delta\text{PM}) \times \text{BC}, \qquad (4.17)$$

where BC is the number of base cases in the population. The 95 per cent confidence interval for the coefficient on PM is between 0.006 and 0.021. The average episode lasted 2.1 days.

Figure 4.8 depicts this concentration-response function up to a 1.0 $\mu g/m^3$ change in PM_{10}, well above the maximum change in this transfer. The function is non-linear, but is essentially linear within this range, suggesting that it could be linearized for some applications without losing too much information. For studies involving a greater range in changes, however, linearizing the function may oversimplify it. Such findings at this stage in the research are important, and could indicate a need to revise some decisions made at the study-design stage. As noted in Chapter 3, the approximate linearity within the relevant range of concentrations for this and other concentration-response functions suggests that we could have simplified our resolution, perhaps annualizing concentrations, without much loss of precision. In other cases, analysts may find non-linearities are too important to ignore.

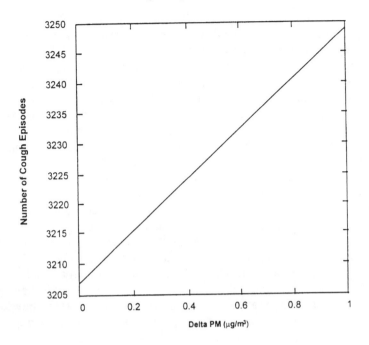

Source: Braun-Fahrländer et al. (1992).

Figure 4.8 Concentration-response function for cough episodes over relevant range of data

4.3 SULPHUR OXIDES

Sulphur oxides (SO_x) of concern include four compounds: sulphur monoxide, sulphur dioxide (SO_2), sulphur trioxide, and disulphur monoxide, but only SO_2 is present in the atmosphere in significant concentrations. Although natural sources of SO_2 exist, crude estimates attribute more than 95 per cent of atmospheric SO_2 to anthropogenic sources. The primary source is the burning of sulphur-containing fossil fuels, with electric utilities alone accounting for about 71 per cent of US emissions (US EPA 1995). SO_2 is removed from the atmosphere by a number of mechanisms, the most significant of which are dissolution in raindrops, dry deposition and inhalation by people and animals. SO_2 can also be transformed into sulphates (SO_4), which exist as particles and are discussed above.

The primary US NAAQS, which use SO_2 concentration as proxies for SO_x levels, are 0.03 ppm of SO_2 (annual average), 0.14 ppm of SO_2

(24-hour average), and 0.5 ppm of SO_2 (three-hour average). The World Health Organization standard is about 0.02 ppm (annual average). According to the AIRS, ambient daily concentrations of SO_2 in the study area are typically in the range of 0.002 ppm to 0.011 ppm. The 24-hour standard of 0.14 ppm was exceeded only once in 1991, the year modelled in the case study. The second or third highest 24-hour average at any site is typically less than half of the 24-hour standard. However, hourly SO_2 levels can be as high as 0.30 ppm in extreme cases. There has been and will continue to be a downward trend in SO_2 concentrations in the US as industry complies with the Title IV of the 1990 amendments to the US Clean Air Act. This law requires that, nationally, SO_2 emissions be reduced to ten million tons below 1980 levels by the year 2000.

Recent environmental regulation has focused on reducing SO_2 emissions, including the Clean Air Act and the Minnesota Acid Deposition Control Act. These laws are part of an effort to reduce dry deposition and acid rain, which can corrode materials and acidify surface water. However, the health effects of directly inhaling SO_2 are relatively modest.[12] As with PM, much of the inhaled SO_2 is filtered out by the nose, perhaps as much as 90 to 95 per cent at rest, though more SO_2 will bypass this filtering system during exercise. Once in the lungs, SO_2 begins a chain of physiological reactions that can be irritating to tissue.

The low levels of ambient SO_2 found in the study area suggest that health effects are likely to be minimal. In a review of the literature, the US EPA (1982) concluded that no respiratory effects occur in non-asthmatics below 5.0 ppm, and since then additional clinical and epidemiological studies, using both measures of airflow and symptomatic measurements, have confirmed this conclusion, at least for levels below 1.0 or 2.0 ppm, still well above those found in the study area (Bedi, Folinsbee and Horvath 1984; Folinsbee, Bedi and Horvath 1985; Shachter et al. 1984; Krupnick, Harrington and Ostro 1990).

Schwartz, Hasselblad and Pitcher (1988) studied the relationship between a broad range of symptoms and SO_2, which ranged from 0.01 to 0.22 ppm, somewhat higher than our study area overall, but with some overlap. Using three years of diary data kept by 110 student nurses in Los Angeles, they found that SO_2 was the only variable that was statistically related to chest discomfort. They found SO_2 to be unrelated to cough, eye irritation and headache when other pollutants were controlled. They used variables to account for autocorrelation in their model and an autoregressive variable to account for time trends. While these are reasonable judgements that improve the integrity of their study, it is not possible to reproduce these variables in the transfer study, making it impossible to transfer the whole equation. As with the Portney and Mullahy (1990) study of PM, therefore, it was necessary to simplify the equation, this time to the following form:[13]

$$\text{Cases} = 1.88 \ (\text{BC/Pop})(\text{Pop} - \text{BC})\Delta SO_2 \qquad (4.18)$$

where

BC = the number of base cases in the population,
Pop = the region's population, and
ΔSO_2 = the change in daily SO_2 measured in ppm.

This is the only quantifiable effect that seems to result from exposure to ambient levels of SO_2. Unfortunately, Schwartz et al. do not report the statistics necessary to calculate standard errors or confidence intervals around the SO_2 coefficient.

4.4 NITROGEN OXIDES

Of the several nitrogen oxides (NO_x), nitric oxide (NO) and nitrogen dioxide (NO_2) are the most prevalent in the atmosphere. Major anthropogenic sources of NO and NO_2 include transportation and other fuel combustion, with electric utilities accounting for about 29 per cent of all NO_2 emissions (US EPA 1995). NO_2 poses the more serious health risks of the NO_x and has consequently been the focus of most epidemiological studies. However, as noted in Chapter 3, we modelled NO_x concentrations when estimating the air-quality impacts of the case study's planning scenarios because of the difficulty in modelling NO_2, a reactive chemical. The use of NO_x as a proxy for NO_2 should lead to an overestimate of costs, because actual NO_2 concentrations are only a fraction of NO_x concentrations.

The US NAAQS for NO_2 are a maximum annual average of 0.05 ppm, with a one-hour alert level of 0.60 ppm. In the study area in 1991, data from AIRS indicate that annual average NO_2 concentrations ranged from 0.005 ppm to a high of 0.024 ppm in Minneapolis. The highest one-hour level was only 0.108 ppm. These data indicate that only health effects that can be quantified at very low levels of ambient NO_2 exposure are relevant.[14]

In their study of the effect of multiple pollutants in Los Angeles, Schwartz, Hasselblad and Pitcher (1988) found that NO_2 is statistically associated with eye irritation. The Los Angeles NO_2 levels range from about 0.1 to 0.45 ppm, with about half of the observations being above 0.11 ppm, the maximum level in our study area. They tested for the effects of weather and other covariates, but found that only total oxidants and the presence of a fever were significant in their logistic regressions. They also used the presence of eye irritation on the preceding day as a variable to predict the probability on the current day, and included variables to control for autocorrelation in their data. Again, however, lack of data on these variables for the study areas requires transferring the following simplified concentration-response function:

$$\Delta \text{ Cases} = 0.883 \frac{\text{BC}}{\text{Pop}} (\text{Pop} - \text{BC}) - \Delta \text{ NO}_2, \qquad (4.19)$$

where
   BC   = the number of base cases in the population,
   Pop   = the region's population, and
   $\Delta \text{ NO}_2$ = the change in daily maximum NO_2 levels measured in ppm.

NO_2 is a direct precursor of peroxyacetyl nitrate (PAN), a component of photochemical oxidants, which is accepted to be associated with eye irritation (Schwartz, Hasselblad and Pitcher 1988). Thus the eye irritation effects may actually be caused by PAN instead of NO_2. But so long as NO_2 is a precursor of PAN and so long as they are correlated in a consistent way, NO_2 may serve as a proxy for PAN in the case study.[15] NO_2 may also be a direct cause of the eye irritation, as it has itself been linked to eye effects such as reduced adaptation to darkness (Schwartz, Hasselblad and Pitcher 1988). To be conservative, the case study includes the effect of NO_2 on eye irritation. Although this effect has not been found in other studies, there is a plausible explanation for the effect and no contradictory evidence.

While this is the only study to examine the relationship to eye irritation, a number of studies have focused on the relationship between NO_2, especially indoor exposure (often indicated by the presence of a gas stove), and lower respiratory symptoms, especially in children. The studies have been equivocal, with about half showing a positive relationship. Many have the limitation of observing only the presence of a gas stove in the house and not actual NO_2 concentrations, and all measured only indoor air quality, which may affect people differently from outdoor air quality if people spend different amounts of time or engage in different activities indoors and outdoors.

Given these equivocal results, researchers have undertaken meta-analyses to evaluate where the weight of the evidence lies. Li, Powers and Roth (1994) performed a meta-analysis of fourteen studies using a linear regression model to control for differences in the age of the children, the location of the study (Europe versus the US) and the health endpoints examined. Using the best measure of the health endpoint, the reporting of 'one or more respiratory symptoms', they found no significant relationship between NO_2 and symptoms for children in five of the six age/location groups. When using a health endpoint that excluded asthma from the list of symptoms, Li, Powers and Roth found a significant relationship for half the groups. However, they suggest that the estimated odds ratios are biased in some of the studies and indicate that preliminary research shows that the effects of this bias may be significant. Given the questions that still surround this issue, certainly no reliable evidence proves that NO_2 has an effect on lower respiratory symptoms in children. As a result, the case study does not include this effect.

4.5 OZONE

Ozone (O_3) is both a naturally occurring compound and a pollutant attributable to man-made sources. It is present in both the stratosphere, or upper atmosphere, and the troposphere, or lower atmosphere, where it is associated with two distinct environmental problems. In the stratosphere, ozone occurs naturally and plays an essential role in screening out some solar radiation, but it may be eroding as a consequence of various industrial emissions. In the troposphere, ozone is itself a pollutant associated with respiratory effects when inhaled, and also is harmful to plants and materials at high concentrations. Volatile organic compounds (VOCs) and nitrogen oxides (NO_x) react with oxygen (O_2) to form ozone in the presence of sunlight and elevated temperatures. Thus ozone is known as a secondary pollutant. Automobiles, power plants and other industrial sources are primarily responsible for nitric oxide (NO) emissions; automobiles and chemical manufacturing are primarily responsible for VOC emissions (Consumer Energy Council of America 1990). According to AIRS, in 1991 hourly ambient ozone levels in our study area peaked at a one-hour high of 0.10 ppm, which is below the US NAAQS of 0.12 ppm. In 1997, the US added an 8-hour standard of 0.08 ppm based on a moving three-year average of the third highest eight-hour reading in each year.

Two studies have found that long-term ozone levels are statistically related to the number of cases of asthma in a population. In one of these, Abbey et al. (1993) studied the relationship between ozone and asthma and chronic bronchitis in a population of adults. Their results are equivocal, offering different conclusions depending on whether pollutants enter the analysis in terms of the number of days above a threshold or as mean exposure levels. But in another study, Dockery et al. (1989) found that ozone was statistically associated with asthma in children. They studied the effect of annual ozone levels in 10- to 12-year-old children in six cities, of which Portage, Wisconsin, a city just outside our study area, had the highest ozone levels. Like Abbey et al., they found that ozone was associated with asthma, but not with bronchitis, chronic cough or other respiratory illnesses. They control for several socioeconomic variables, but not for other pollutants, although they report that ozone is negatively correlated with the other pollutants. They report the following concentration-response function:

$$\text{Number of children with asthma} = \exp(32.4 \times \Delta O_3) \times BC \qquad (4.20)$$

where
ΔO_3 = the change in annual ozone measured in ppm, and
BC = the number of base cases of asthma in the population.

The 95 per cent confidence interval for the ΔO_3 coefficient is between 0.0 and 61.8.

In addition to such chronic effects, a large body of literature has also explored the effects of ozone and acute respiratory effects. This is a difficult literature to disentangle because of certain complications surrounding the nature of the effects, together with the wide range of different studies exploring them, but it raises a number of interesting transfer issues. Although the literature suggests that people resting probably do not suffer effects from the levels of ozone commonly found in the US (see US EPA 1986a), heavier breathing during exercise results in a larger effective dose, suggesting that people might suffer effects while exercising. The US EPA (1986a) and Hazucha (1987) analysed 24 related studies conducted between 1964 and 1985 in eight different laboratories. Hazucha's results suggest that people exposed to 0.2 ppm ozone will experience FEV_1 decrements of about 1.6 per cent to 4.7 per cent, depending on their level of exercise. Kinney, Ware and Spengler (1988) conducted an additional meta-analysis of four epidemiological studies and also found a relationship.

Although this research is based on a large number of studies, these short-term changes in peak expiratory flow and FEV may not be appropriate to include in a benefit–cost study. Such transient decrements do not necessarily pose a long-term health risk, leading some researchers to argue that they do not constitute an 'adverse health effect' for the purposes of regulation ('Guidelines ...' 1985). Furthermore, like RADs, FEV decrements are only ambiguously linked to the symptoms people notice and care about. Indeed, FEV decrements of less than 15 per cent are not generally perceptible (Hixson 1993). If people do not notice the effects of a small decrement in FEV, they are unlikely to change their behaviour and unlikely to be willing to pay to avoid the effect.

An alternative is to transfer health studies that use symptomatic measures – such as cough, wheezing and chest pain – to determine the effect of inhaling a pollutant. Such symptoms are not necessarily an additional effect of ozone inhalation, but rather may simply be a different way of measuring the same physiological effect on lung tissue that FEV decrements measure (Ostro, Lipsett and Jewell 1989).

But because they are more closely linked to discomfort and more likely to affect behaviour, symptomatic measures of pulmonary function can be linked more easily to valuation methods, making them more appropriate for benefit–cost analysis. Morton and Krupnick (1987) pooled data from four clinical studies of the symptomatic effects of exposure to ozone while exercising in healthy men. To synthesize the results of these studies, they used the presence of broadly defined 'upper respiratory symptoms' (sore throat, nasal congestion, and nose and throat irritation) and 'lower respiratory symptoms' (cough, sputum, wheeze, substernal irritation, dyspnoea, chest tightness, pain upon deep inhalation and shortness of breath) as their dependent variables. While this study uses all the available information from the toxicological studies, making it preferable to choosing any single one, it has the disadvantage of being based on toxicology studies, which poses some problems for the task of a transfer. First, it requires extrapolating from a small sample of mostly healthy adult males to the general population. Second, it requires the assumption that the exercise habits of people in our study area conform to those in the protocol of the toxicology studies, or at least that the effects are similar. Moreover, it does not allow for the fact that people may make behavioural adjustments to different ozone levels, perhaps foregoing exercise or exercising indoors. Thus, if available, epidemiologic studies would be preferable for a transfer.

Up to this point, our discussion has been limited to examining single two-hour exposures surrounded by periods of non-exposure. However, several studies have examined the effects of repeated exposure (Farrell et al. 1979; Horvath, Gliner and Folinsbee 1981; Folinsbee and Horvath 1986). These studies have generally found that pulmonary effects, whether measured by FEV decrements or subjective symptoms, are worse after a second exposure within 48 hours, but that the effects improve after subsequent daily exposures until at least the fifth day, when at some point symptoms worsen again. The importance of repeated exposures presents some complications for transferring the health effects from ozone exposures. All the studies we have reviewed so far treat exposure as discrete, one-time or multiple-time events, whereas in fact people are continuously exposed to varying degrees of ozone. To reflect this reality, a model would have to predict pulmonary effects based on current ozone levels and days of continuously lagged hourly ozone levels.

This problem suggests that epidemiological studies using longer averaging times would be more appropriate, because they explore effects under the real-world conditions of continuous exposure to varying levels of ozone. In addition, they study subjects under more realistic exercise conditions. Three additional epidemiological studies, Portney and Mullahy (1986), Ostro and Rothschild (1989) and Krupnick, Harrington and Ostro (1990), studied symptoms under longer averaging periods. The studies all found a significant relationship between exposure to ozone and symptom variables. Using real-world exposures instead of idealized, discrete exposures, these two studies provide potential concentration-response functions that would be consistent with the exposure data we have available in our transfer, and do so at ozone levels commonly found in the study area. However, they are not ideal, as they group symptoms into one indicator of symptoms (for example RADs) that does not differentiate among symptoms, and which therefore does not cleanly link to the valuation step of the overall transfer.

Re-analysing the Krupnick, Harrington and Ostro (1990) data, Ostro et al. (1993) separately examined the effects of ozone on upper and lower respiratory symptoms. They redefined the dependent variable to be a string of consecutive bad respiratory days rather than a single bad day, with the average string being 1.4 days long (Ostro et al. 1993). When controlling for temperature, sex, gas-stove use and the presence of a chronic respiratory disease, Ostro et al. report the following concentration-response functions:

$$
\begin{aligned}
LR &= \exp(1.04 \times \Delta O_3) \times BC \\
UR &= \exp(0.77 \times \Delta O_3) \times BC
\end{aligned}
\tag{4.21}
$$

where
    LR = the number of lower respiratory symptom events,
    UR = the number of upper respiratory symptoms events,
    ΔO_3 = change in the daily maximum O_3 levels measured in ppm, and
    BC = the number of base cases in the population.

The 95 per cent confidence interval for the coefficient on ΔO_3 is between −0.10 and 2.23 for lower respiratory symptoms and between 0.0 and 1.57 for upper respiratory symptoms.

This study has the advantages of using daily rather than hourly averaging times under conditions of continuous exposure, of accounting for the exercise habits of the population, and of using disaggregated symptom measurements. Thus it is the most appropriate study available to quantify respiratory symptoms in adults for the transfer case study. Although children and smokers are not included in the Ostro et al. population, studies indicate that these groups are less sensitive to ozone than non-smoking adults, with several studies finding no effect of ozone on the symptoms experienced by children.

In addition to these chronic and acute effects of ozone, some have suggested that, like PM, ozone may be associated with elevated mortality rates. In one recent study, Kinney and Özkaynak (1991) examined daily death counts in Los Angeles County and measures of total oxidants, SO_2, NO_2, CO and KM, a measure of particulate optical reflectance similar to coefficient of haze, over ten years. They performed an ordinary least squares regression using the number of daily deaths in the county (excluding accidents) as the dependent variable. When they included temperature and all the pollutants in the model, and transformed the data to remove seasonal cycles, only a one-day lag of oxidants and temperature were statistically related to mortality, although it was unclear how to sort out the relationships between NO_2, CO and KM. When any one of these three pollutants was used instead of all three it became significant, but total oxidants also remained highly significant.

Although the Kinney and Özkaynak study shows a strong relationship between oxidants and mortality, its results are controversial. At least two other epidemiological studies have failed to find any relationship between ozone and mortality. Dockery, Schwartz and Spengler (1992) found a significant relationship between mortality and PM, but a statistically insignificant one between mortality and ozone. However, this study differs from the Kinney and Özkaynak study in three other important ways. First, it used ozone and PM rather than total oxidants and KM as the pollution variables. This is an advantage over the Kinney and Özkaynak study because ozone is the actual pollutant of concern, whereas total oxidants are only a proxy. Second, it calculated exposure to ozone using daily means rather than daily maxima. Third, it used current ozone levels rather than one-day lags. This could be an especially important difference because Kinney and Özkaynak found that concurrent oxidant levels were not related to mortality, finding the relationship only with lagged oxidants. These methodological differences could account for the different results of the two studies, although this lack of robustness across measurements is itself a matter of concern.

In another study, Schwartz (1991a) found that mortality was

significantly related to TSP, but not ozone levels, whether with or without a lag, and whether using mean or daily maximum ozone levels. Because ozone levels and season were negatively correlated, Schwartz further tested for the effect of ozone in only the summer months and again found that ozone remained highly insignificant. These tests make it impossible to attribute the difference in results between this study and Kinney and Özkaynak (1991) to methodological differences.

Despite the discrepancies in the results of these three studies, the weight of the evidence tends to show that ozone is not related to mortality. Without further research confirming the results of Kinney and Özkaynak (1991), the case study does not include a transfer of the Kinney and Özkaynak results to the study area, where ozone levels are also much lower.

4.6 CARBON MONOXIDE

Of man-made sources, vehicles are the most significant source of anthropogenic carbon monoxide (CO), producing over 80 per cent of total CO produced in the US. Electric utilities contribute only about 0.4 per cent (US EPA 1995).

The US NAAQS for CO is a maximum of 9 ppm averaged over an eight-hour period, and 35 ppm averaged over a one-hour period. The state of Minnesota regulations use a stricter one-hour standard of 30 ppm. According to the AIRS, only one monitor in our study area (in St Paul) reported an exceedance of the eight-hour standard with a reading of 15.2 ppm and a second reading of 10.8 ppm. Most stations reported no readings above 9 ppm from 1985 to 1990. Over time, there has been a downward trend in CO levels in the US, generally attributed to smaller and cleaner-burning car engines.

CO reduces the ability of blood to carry and deliver oxygen. The effects of oxygen deficiency in the body have been linked to headaches at low levels, for example, as a symptom of altitude sickness. More recently, Schwartz, Hasselblad and Pitcher (1988) and Schwartz and Zeger (1990) found urban CO levels to be a significant predictor of headaches. Re-examining an older epidemiology study of student nurses in Los Angeles, the two studies used logistic regressions to estimate the effect of daily CO levels and other variables on the prevalence of headaches. Schwartz and Zeger controlled for allergies to pollen and found that daily CO was a significant predictor of headaches, reporting the following concentration-response function:

$$\text{Ln}\left[\frac{P(\text{Headache})}{(1 - P(\text{Headache}))}\right] = -2.163 + 0.0125 \text{ CO} + 0.328 \text{ Allergy} \quad (4.22)$$
$$(0.138) \ (0.0025) \qquad (0.0471)$$

where Allergy is a dummy variable for the presence or absence of allergies and standard errors are in parentheses. Seventeen per cent of the sample had pollen allergies. Note that the sample (student nurses; mostly females around 19 years old) is not representative of the population as a whole. Nevertheless, this is the best available study quantifying the effect of CO on headaches.

In addition to its relationship to headache, several studies have explored the link between ambient CO levels and the incidence and duration of angina pain in patients with ischaemic heart disease. This link seems probable because patients with ischaemic heart disease already have a compromised ability to deliver blood and oxygen to the heart muscle. Any failure to obtain oxygen can result in pain, an angina attack and/or cardiac arrhythmias in their heart's electrical patterns (measurable on an ECG). Allred et al. (1989a, 1989b) conducted a widely cited study to determine whether exposures to CO have a measurable effect on patients with ischaemic heart disease. Allred et al. (1989a) tested 63 men at both 2.4 per cent of haemoglobin occupied by CO (COHb) and 4.7 per cent COHb, achieved through one-hour exposures at varying CO levels. The study found statistically significant reductions in both the time to onset of angina pain and to the development of ECG readings indicating an angina attack. These two effects are noteworthy for two reasons. First, the pain is a noticeable and valued symptom to the patient. Second, the ECG change is evidence that the pain was caused by an angina attack and is generally agreed to be an objective measure of the same phenomenon. These results confirm those found in a majority of the other studies on CO and angina (Aronow and Isbell 1973; Aronow et al. 1972; Kleinman and Whittenberger 1985; Anderson et al. 1973; Sheps et al. 1987, Adams et al. 1988).

Unfortunately including the effect in the transfer study would be complicated by the need to quantify the relationship between air CO and COHb, although research by Coburn, Forster and Kane (1965) and Peterson and Stewart (1970) does make it possible to quantify this intermediate step. More importantly, all these studies are clinical studies that demonstrate only that CO *reduces the time* to onset of angina in exercising subjects. However, reduced exercise time is not an effect that can be readily valued. An effect for which a value could more readily be derived would be an increase in the *incidence* of angina. Although one could speculate from the studies reviewed here that CO exposure does indeed lead to an increase in the number of angina attacks in a population, it is not possible to quantify the effect at this time. Thus the case study does not include angina effects.

4.7   LEAD

Having a number of man-made sources that contribute to ambient levels, lead can enter the environment as a result of mining, smelting, processing and combustion of leaded gasoline, coal and oil, as well as from lead soldering in plumbing fixtures, lead shot, food packaging and leaded paint. Some of these sources emit lead into the atmosphere; some directly contaminate dusts, soils and water. In the mid-1980s, the primary source of atmospheric lead was gasoline combustion, which contributed 34 881 tons per year in the United States alone, or almost 90 per cent of the total (Battye 1983; US EPA 1986b). Since that time, however, the use of lead in gasoline has been eliminated in the US. Transportation now accounts for about one-third of man-made lead emissions, with industrial processes from smelters and battery plants accounting for about 60 per cent. Electric utilities contribute about 1 per cent of US emissions (US EPA 1995).

As a result of all these human activities, ambient levels of lead have increased over the centuries until very recently. In the US this trend has reversed in recent years, with national air-lead levels falling 80 per cent in conjunction with the fall in the use of leaded gasoline. Even in urban areas such as Minneapolis/St Paul, average quarterly air-lead levels had fallen to as low as $0.05 \, \mu g/m^3$ by 1991, well below the US NAAQS of $1.5 \, \mu g/m^3$ and the World Health Organization standard of 0.5 to $1.0 \, \mu g/m^3$. According to AIRS, the highest annual average in our study area was at Eagan, Minnesota, which reported a mean of $0.95 \, \mu g/m^3$ in 1991. World-wide, concentrations of air lead remain a significant health concern, especially in urban centres of developing countries where average concentrations of $70 \, \mu g/m^3$ have been reported.

There are many pathways for human exposure to lead. People can inhale lead directly or ingest lead from contaminated food and water and from mouthing contaminated objects and soils, a common activity in young children. Such contamination may be indirectly linked to air pollution as air lead settles into dusts, soils and surface water, or it may have independent sources. For example, food may be contaminated by canning and other processing activities, drinking water can be contaminated from solder and other lead sources in pipes, and soils can be contaminated from old paint chips. The US EPA (1986b) suggests that for two-year-old American children facing ambient air levels even as much as 50 per cent higher than the highest levels in our study region, only 8 per cent of the contribution to blood lead is attributable to inhalation, 50 per cent is from indirect air pollution, and the remainder is independent of air pollution.

In all cases, whether entering the body through inhalation or ingestion, some of the lead is absorbed by the bloodstream. From there, some is excreted, some enters into bones, and some enters into the body's soft tissues, with the concentrations in these tissues attaining equilibrium over time. In correlating health effects with lead exposure, most studies use blood lead as a measure of lead exposure, although some also use tooth lead. To complete the chain of linkages between changes in air quality and changes in health status, it is therefore necessary to quantify the relationship between air lead and these measures of exposure.[16] Because most concentration-response studies focus on blood lead, and because more is known about the effects of lead uptake on blood-lead levels than on tooth-lead levels, we use blood lead as the measure of exposure. In reviewing studies for this purpose, we use several criteria. We consider the quality of the measurements of air lead and blood lead, the size of the study's sample, and the level of lead exposure, with preference given to those studies that explore the effects of ambient exposures. This last issue is also partly a question of functional form in the statistical analysis. Colombo (1985) and the US EPA (1986b) have argued that linear models are best at exposures below $10 \, \mu g/m^3$, but that absorption into the bloodstream begins to diminish at higher levels.

Two broad categories of epidemiological studies have evaluated the effects of air lead (Pb-A) on blood lead (Pb-B). Disaggregate studies use statistical analyses to control for confounding variables such as soil lead. To the extent that air lead and other lead pathways are positively correlated but not causally linked (for example, because urban environments have more air pollution and more lead paint), these confounders should be controlled. On the other hand, to the extent that they are correlated because air lead settles into soils and dusts, these indirect effects of lead through other pathways should be included in the coefficient on air lead. Although the links are indirect, air emissions are still ultimately the source of this lead. Thus some authors, such as Brunekreef (1984), have advocated using aggregate analysis in which air lead is the only exposure variable. Such studies would also capture other components of the correlation, however, and, to the extent that they attribute lead from other sources (such as paint) to the air, the estimates they produce should thus be considered an upper bound. We review both kinds of studies and consider each of their merits in our sensitivity analysis. Desvousges et al. (1995a,b) reports a review of this literature using the above criteria. Based on this analysis, the case study uses the following concentration-response function for adults:

$$\frac{\partial \text{Pb-B}}{\partial \text{Pb-A}} = 1.64 \pm 0.22 \qquad (4.23)$$

And for children:

$$\frac{\partial \text{ Pb-B}}{\partial \text{ Pb-A}} = 2.54 \pm 0.84 \qquad (4.24)$$

The 90 per cent interval for this function spans the existing estimates from both an aggregate and a disaggregate analysis of lead exposure.

Increasing blood-lead levels can have a broad range of effects, of which at least three are quantifiable at common levels: neurotoxic effects, cardio-vascular effects and effects on foetal development. The neurotoxic effects of lead have long been known and are well established. Lead's effects are also apparent on symptomatic measures of health, with very high blood-lead levels (100–120 μg/dl for adults and 80–100 μg/dl for children) causing severe brain damage or mental retardation and even death, and levels above 45μg/m^3 showing signs of damage to the central and peripheral nervous system in both adults and children. These severe effects occur at blood-lead levels that are much too high to justify including them in our study. However some (but not all) studies have also found mild symptomatic effects at ambient blood-lead levels in children, whose developing nervous systems are more sensitive to toxic exposures.

These studies have explored lead's effects on intelligence (IQ) and cognitive abilities, on behaviour (such as hyperactivity), and on minor hearing impairment. Of these effects, we focus on lead's effect on IQ as the most tangible and measurable of all of lead's potential neurotoxic effects, the same judgement made in a US EPA risk assessment (Whitfield and Wallsten 1988). In a simple meta-analysis of IQ studies, Needleman and Gatsonis (1990) began with a pool of 24 studies and selected twelve that employed multiple regression analysis – seven that used blood lead as a descriptive variable, and five that used tooth lead. Using regression techniques, with a linear functional form for these seven blood-lead studies, they found an average weighted coefficient -0.152 on blood as an explanatory variable for full-scale IQ scores, with a 95 per cent confidence interval ranging between -0.1 and -0.2. The case study uses this concentration-response relationship to quantify the IQ effects in children of a change in blood lead at ambient levels. This function has the advantage of applying to a wide range of ages, applying to the relevant range of lead exposure, and utilizing the results from all the best available studies.

Although the transfer study includes this effect, we should note that questions remain about how to interpret the link between exposure and IQ effects. Some researchers have found that the effects of lead on IQ are reversible when exposure returns to lower levels. Others, however, have found that blood-lead levels at a young age continue to explain lower test scores at older ages (Needleman et al. 1990; Bellinger, Stiles and Needleman 1992), suggesting that exposure is most important at some critical stage of development. The interpretation matters because it influences the choice of the affected population – that is, the population to which to transfer the concentration-response information. If adopting the former interpretation, one should include the effect in all children for as long as that change in exposure lasts. If adopting the latter interpretation, one should include the effect only among children who reach the critical age during the period of exposure and then allow the effect to be permanent for those cohorts. In our case study we assume that the changes in air quality associated with the scenario are permanent, making the effects *de facto* permanent, regardless of the hypothetical possibility of reversing them. To be conservative, we further assume that the scenarios have an immediate effect on all children.

Researchers have also explored the possibility that lead may affect the body's cardiovascular system in several ways. In particular, studies show that elevated blood-lead levels may also cause hypertension, either by affecting the release of hormones that regulate blood pressure (Vander 1988), affecting vascular reactivity (Chai and Webb 1988), or causing morphological, biological and functional changes in the heart (Kopp, Barron and Tow 1988). Moreover, other studies have shown that lead can damage the kidney as well, which can contribute to hypertension. Among men, Pocock et al. (1984, US 1985), Parkinson et al. (1987), Schwartz (1986a,b, cited in US EPA 1990) and Schwartz (1991c) have all found a positive relationship between blood lead and blood pressure. Of these, the Schwartz (1991c) study has several advantages for the case study. It uses a large sample size, uses data from the general population instead of the workplace, which over-represents relatively healthy people, and examines diastolic blood pressure as the dependent variable instead of systolic pressure, making it consistent with the available valuation studies (see Chapter 5). The case study therefore used the Schwartz (1991c) concentration-response function, applying it to men aged 20 years and older. The function is

$$\frac{\partial \text{ diastolic blood pressure}}{\partial \text{ Pb-B}} = \frac{2.928}{\text{Pb-B}} \quad (4.25)$$

$$(1.002)$$

(Standard error is in parentheses.)

Schwartz (1991c) and Grandjean et al. (1989) are the only studies of the effects of lead on women's blood pressure, with contradictory findings. Although the effect in women is less clearly established, the results of the Schwartz (1991c) study – coupled with the toxicological evidence and strong evidence of an effect in men – warrant including this health effect in our damage-cost study. Schwartz (1991c) finds that

$$\frac{\partial \text{ diastolic blood pressure}}{\partial \text{ Pb-B}} = \frac{1.640}{\text{Pb-B}} \qquad (4.26)$$
$$(0.6963)$$

with the standard error again in parentheses.

Not surprisingly, perhaps, the foetus is also at great risk from lead exposure, and pregnant women may be particularly susceptible to lead poisoning because of the iron and calcium deficiencies common during pregnancy. Indeed, people have long known about the effect of lead on the foetus. Lead was once taken to induce abortion, and early studies observed higher rates of spontaneous abortions, miscarriages, stillborn births and neonatal deaths to women with high exposures to lead (US EPA 1990). Studies of animals have also found repeatedly that lead can affect litter size, birth weight and survival rates of offspring. These effects arise both directly from intrauterine lead exposure to the foetus and indirectly through effects on maternal nutrition or hormonal state.

Recent epidemiological studies provide dose-response functions relating maternal lead exposure to the outcome of pregnancies. McMichael et al. (1986) found that the incidence of pre-term deliveries increased greatly with maternal blood lead. In particular, using multiple logistic regression analysis, they found that the relative risk for a 1 μg increase in blood lead after controlling for age, social status, occupation and smoking, was 1.11. However, they did not find any relationship with birth weight, a result confirmed by Graziano et al. (1989), but contradicted by Bornschein et al. (1989). While the question of a relationship between lead and birth weight is inconclusive, McMichael et al. provide evidence of a relationship with pre-term delivery, and their study is used to quantify the effect:

Number of pre-term deliveries $= \exp(0.104 \times \Delta \text{ Pb-B}) \times \text{BC}, \quad (4.27)$

where BC is the number of pre-term births already in the population. Unfortunately, McMichael et al. do not report confidence intervals on the blood-lead coefficient.

Although pre-term deliveries are not an important health effect *per se*, they are indirectly related to a continuum of children's health risks. While it is not possible to quantify all of these, the most significant is probably the contribution of pre-term delivery to the risk of infant mortality. To quantify this effect, it is necessary to capture the effects of a shorter gestation period while controlling for birth weight, another important risk factor for infant mortality. Williams et al. (1982) used data on 2.3 million births from the California Department of Health Services to study neonatal mortality rates in different birth-weight and gestational-age groups. Assuming a marginal change in gestation length from 38 or 39 weeks to 36 or 37 weeks and assuming the median birth weight at 38 or 39 weeks, their data show neonatal mortality rates increase from 0.0019 to 0.0025, an increase of 0.0006. In other words, these assumptions indicate that for 1667 pre-term deliveries caused by an increase in ambient lead levels, there will be one additional neonatal death. This conclusion is not overly sensitive to the assumptions; looking at likely alternative birth-weight and gestation-length groupings, we can be fairly confident that the true increase in neonatal mortality rates is between 0.0005 and 0.0014.

4.8   ILLUSTRATIVE CHANGES IN HEALTH EFFECTS

This chapter concludes with some illustrative calculations demonstrating this linkage in the transfer. The calculations use data on the predicted change in air quality for the urban scenario and demographic data for the sample urban receptor from Chapter 3. With relatively high impacts and dense population, these data involve relatively large effects. Three examples include mortality effects, morbidity effects and acute morbidity effects, demonstrating a variety of functional forms, averaging times and demographic data. Although they use only the most likely values for each variable and parameter in the calculations, recall that actual calculations employ Monte Carlo simulations to draw these values from various distributions.

First, consider a calculation of mortality effects. For adults over 65 years of age, the concentration-response function from the meta-analysis gives the most likely percentage change in mortality as $0.13 \cdot \Delta PM$ (see Table 4.3). Although it is estimated with daily data, the concentration-response function is linear, and can thus be simplified by using annual data. As reported in Table 3.3, at the sample urban receptor we estimated that the urban scenario would lead to a $0.0228 \ \mu g/m^3$ increase in annual average PM. Applying this to the concentration-response function gives a 0.00307 per cent change in mortality. With an estimated 127 baseline deaths per year in this receptor among adults aged 65 or more,[17] this implies that the urban scenarios would lead to 0.388 expected deaths in the receptor. Similarly, it yields an expected increase of 0.251 deaths among people under 65, for a total of 0.639.

Next, consider a calculation of chronic respiratory disease (emphysema, chronic bronchitis or asthma) from PM. Portney and Mullahy (1990) report the following concentration-response function (Equation 4.12):

$$\text{Ln}\left(\frac{P}{1-P}\right) = -3.02 + 0.01093\,\text{PM} + 0.61\,\text{RACE} - 0.08\,\text{INC} + 5.78\,\text{EDU}$$

or

$$P = \frac{1}{1 + \exp(3.02 - 0.01093\,\text{PM} - 0.61\,\text{RACE} + 0.08\,\text{INC} - 5.78\,\text{EDU})}$$

where

P   = the probability of having emphysema, chronic bronchitis, or asthma,

PM   = annual PM_{10} in $\mu g/m^3$,

RACE = 1 if white, 0 otherwise,

INC   = annual household income divided by 10 000, and

EDU   = years of school completed divided by 100.

To calculate the change in the probability of having respiratory disease, substitute values for annual average PM levels with and without the urban scenario, as well as for the demographic variables at each receptor. The ambient annual PM level without the scenario is $26.6\,\mu g/m^3$. The values for RACE, INC and EDU are 0.926, 2.43 and 0.120 respectively.

Thus, substituting these values into the equation gives:

$$P = \frac{1}{\begin{array}{l}1 + \exp(3.02 - 0.01093 \cdot 26.6 - 0.61 \cdot 0.926 + 0.08 \cdot 2.43 \\ -5.78 \cdot 0.120)\end{array}}$$

$$= 0.15902$$

This is the probability of having chronic respiratory disease before the scenario. Again, the estimated average annual change in PM concentrations at the receptor is about $0.0228\,\mu g/m^3$. Thus, after the scenario, the probability of having chronic respiratory disease would involve all the same data except for a 0.0228 increase in PM:

$$P' = \frac{1}{1 + \exp[3.02 - 0.01093 \cdot (26.6 + 0.0228) - 0.61 \cdot 0.926}$$
$$+ 0.08 \cdot 2.43 - 5.78 \cdot 0.120]$$
$$= 0.15905$$

The change in the probability of having one of these chronic respiratory diseases at this receptor is thus 3×10^{-5} for the urban scenario. With 51 179 people over the age of 18 (the affected population) in the receptor, this is an expected increase of about 0.170 cases of emphysema, chronic bronchitis or asthma in the receptor for the scenario.

As the third example, consider the Braun-Fahrländer et al. (1992) concentration-response function for cough episodes among young children (aged five years or less). They estimate (Equation 4.17):

$$\text{Number of cough episodes} = \exp(0.013 \times \Delta PM) \times BC$$

using a six-week averaging time. Recall from Chapter 3 that for this averaging time we estimated deltas for nine six-week averages at each receptor and then represented these deltas with step functions. At the sample receptor the median change in six-week average PM for the urban scenario fell in a bin represented by a $0.014449\,\mu g/m^3$ increase in PM. The BC rate of cough days per six-week period among this age group is 3207.[18] Thus the change in cough episodes for the period is $\exp(0.013 \times 0.014449) \times 3207 - 3207 = 0.602$. Repeating these calculations at the receptor for each of nine six-week periods in the year gives an expected annual change in cough days of 9.37.

The first two linkages of the transfer study provided the change in air quality necessary for transferring concentration-response functions in this third linkage of the analysis. Combining air-quality changes with relevant background data, it is now possible to calculate the effects on health services at all 618 receptors in the study. In the next chapter, we turn to the fourth linkage in the transfer process: transferring economic values for these services.

NOTES

1. The discussion should be regarded as illustrative because it does not include more recent studies that may have become available since the case study was undertaken in 1994.
2. If $P(S)$ is not small or if $P(S)_1$ is considerably different from $P(S)_0$, then the predicted prevalence will be biased.
3. AIRS is a database with regularly updated information from air-quality monitors throughout the US. Because we model air emissions using 1991 weather data, we

gathered extensive data on 1991 air quality in the study area, collecting hourly observations from all available monitors. We also collected less extensive information from past years.

4. These simple conversions neglect the fact that the different measures are often not simply different units of the same entity, but rather measures of different, though related, entities. This is especially true of BS and COH relative to PM_{10} and TSP (US EPA 1982).

5. This subsection has benefited from discussions with Tom Grahame, US Department of Energy.

6. Ironically, the Minneapolis data from Schwartz (1991b) would not be the most appropriate, as they were obtained from a time (1973–82) when concentrations were higher than they are today.

7. The interpretation of young and old is different in the two studies. Fairley divided his population at age 70, whereas Schwartz and Dockery divided theirs at age 65. We treat the studies as if they had both split their samples at age 65.

8. To simplify externality-cost calculations, the 90 per cent confidence-interval formula was derived by regressing the usual prediction error on the squared exposure deviation. The R-squared was 0.99.

9. US EPA Critical Evaluation Workshop on Particulate Matter–Mortality Epidemiology Studies, Raleigh, North Carolina, 9–11 November, 1994.

10. One solution to this problem might be to use the results from each quantile as a separate data point for those studies that report results by quantile. This could be explored in future research.

11. This contrasts with the results of Portney and Mullahy (1986), who found no relationship between RRADs and SO_4 in their data of adults from the 1979 National Health Interview Survey, even after controlling for O_3 and for sociodemographic variables such as income and smoking habits.

12. See *National Acid Precipitation Assessment Program* (US Council on Environmental Quality 1991) for a good discussion on SO_2 within the context of other pollution concerns.

13. The original study uses a logistic function such as that shown in Equation (4.1). Taking the partial derivative of P with respect to x_i, and rearranging terms leads to the function shown. Note ΔCases is interpreted as the change in the probability of experiencing the symptom times the size of the population.

14. In most regions of the US, total personal exposure to elevated NO_2 concentrations appears to be dominated by indoor sources of NO_2 such as gas stoves, kerosene heaters, and unvented gas space heaters. In a study conducted in Wisconsin, Quackenboss et al. (1986) compared outdoor versus indoor weekly average concentrations of NO_x during the winter. Their results showed that indoor concentrations in gas-stove homes were 3.2 times higher than outdoor levels, while indoor concentrations in electric-stove homes were actually 0.6 times lower during the same period. Nevertheless, any increase in outdoor NO_2 levels would increase people's total exposure, and therefore could potentially lead to unwanted health effects. However, as we will see below, the available concentration-response functions do not utilize information about ambient NO_2 levels, using instead the level of base cases to implicitly account for varying ambient pollution levels (including indoor pollution). Thus there is no need to make a separate adjustment for indoor exposures when transferring the concentration-response functions.

15. NO_2 and PAN are also related in complex ways to the formation of ozone. See Chapter 3 for a discussion of the role of NO_2 in ozone formation.

16. We also had to determine the baseline distribution of lead exposure. The most famous study of blood-lead levels is the second National Health and Nutrition Examination Study (NHANES II). Conducted from 1976 through 1980, this study found that the overall mean blood-lead level in the US was 13.9 μg/dl; that about 1.9 per cent of the sample had levels above 30 μg/dl, the US EPA maximum safe level; and that about 0.3 per cent had blood lead over 40 μg/dl (US EPA 1990). Although this study is useful, its findings are now dated because blood-lead levels have dropped considerably since the 1970s due to increased regulation of gasoline and other lead sources. More recent

evidence in Crocetti, Mushak and Schwartz (1990) and US Department of Health and Human Services (1988) confirms that lead levels have fallen in children and young women. Using the proportional changes found in these sub-populations as a guide, we adjusted the NHANES II results for all populations.

17. Using the *Monthly Report of Vital Statistics*, we estimate this using a death rate of 0.028 times the population of people 65 or over in the receptor.

18. The National Health Information Survey reports 3.239 RADs for children under seven years of age. Multiplying by 6/52 to adjust from annual to six-week numbers, assuming all RADs involve cough as a symptom, and assuming the incidence of the condition is the same among children under age five (the affected population), we estimate BC to be 0.3737 times the number of children in the receptor under age five.

5.   Health effects measured as monetary costs

Air quality affects other services besides those of health reviewed in the previous chapter. Before turning to these effects, however, we proceed to the next step in the disaggregate transfer methodology: namely, estimating the economic value of effects on a per unit basis. Specifically, this chapter discusses estimating the costs of the health effects just reviewed. For example, if a scenario will increase the number of cough-days in a receptor by nine days, we next want to know the cost of these nine cough-days. Thus we shall explore the quantification of these costs before turning to the other effects of air quality on services, to better illustrate the continuity and flow of the linkages involved for each effect.

Transferring economic values from one context to another involves the same basic considerations discussed previously. When choosing among valuation studies to transfer, analysts should look for studies that have been conducted according to the best scientific practices, and for studies that match the new policy context as well as possible. On the other hand, they should try to summarize as much information as possible from all available studies. In addition, they must, as always, ensure that the units of measurement match the previous link.[1] For example, if analysts have estimated effects in terms of the number of cases of bronchitis, they must transfer the economic value of bronchitis cases, avoiding unknown quantities or different – albeit related – constructs, such as restricted activity days (RADs).

This chapter begins with a conceptual model of health valuation. Section 5.2 assesses some of the empirical valuation methods as applied to valuing health. Section 5.3 reviews the available studies and discusses our approach to summarizing and transferring them. Finally, Section 5.4 continues the illustrative example with an estimate of costs based on estimated effects and valuation information.

5.1   A CONCEPTUAL MODEL OF HEALTH VALUATION

Concentration-response functions that quantify the relationship between air quality and health often use health *risks* as their dependent variable.

These functions indicate that if people are exposed to poorer air quality, they face a greater risk of experiencing some health effect, whether temporary (such as a cough) or permanent (such as emphysema). In the most extreme instances, people face a risk of premature death. A unit of risk is defined as the probability of an event, such as a probability of contracting bronchitis equal to 1 in 10 000 in a given time period. Cumulative risk is defined as the sum of risks for a group of people. For example, if 500 000 people face this 1 in 10 000 risk of bronchitis, the cumulative risk for the group would be 50 cases – the expected number of cases in the population as a whole. In the case of mortality risks, these sums are called 'statistical lives'.

Valuing statistical lives or 'statistical bronchitis cases' raises many concerns. Ethical considerations, for example, arise when it comes to discussing the value of life. While there are genuine considerations here, note that the question as it relates to benefit–cost analysis does not require us to value a *specific* person's health or life but only health or mortality *risks*. Such risks are present in everyday life, whenever people make choices about whether to wear safety belts, work at a risky job, or live in cities with air pollution. In making these choices, people implicitly make trade-offs between health risks and benefits – such as mobility in a car, a good salary, and the social and cultural benefits of life in the city – thereby exhibiting behaviour that reflects how they perceive and value risks. From this choice-making behaviour, economists can infer the values people place on health risks for use in benefit–cost analyses.

This distinction is directly related to the distinction between *ex ante* and *ex post* perspectives. From an *ex post* perspective, analysts would determine health effects by counting observed changes in bronchitis cases and deaths after a given policy has been implemented. Similarly, even when evaluating a policy before implementing it, they could predict the expected number of health effects in a population and value them at people's *ex post* WTP. However, they would never be able to identify which specific individuals a scenario would affect: all they would really know is that a population faces an expected number of adverse events. From the *ex ante* perspective, in contrast, air pollution imposes a negative externality – the risk of experiencing an undesirable health effect – on all exposed people rather than imposing realized health effects on an identifiable subset of the exposed population. In other words, from this perspective air pollution is valued before health risks are experienced rather than after they are experienced.

From this point of view, the *ex ante* approach is more appealing. It is consistent with the timing of benefit–cost analysis relative to the effects of the policy and avoids some of the most difficult ethical questions about the value of an individual's life or health. However, viewed another way, the distinction is arbitrary. From the perspective of Graham (1981), the two approaches are simply two points of a set of payment pairs contingent on two outcomes – one where the health effect occurs and one where it does not – that leave expected utility constant. In particular, the *ex ante* payment, or option price, is a payment that is the same for either outcome, and the *ex post* measure is a payment that is made only if the health effect occurs. But other combinations of payments contingent on the two outcomes are also conceivable.

Ex ante valuation studies have been conducted for mortality risks and are available for a transfer. However, it is usually easier to measure WTP for morbidity from an *ex post* perspective, and most empirical valuation studies have used this approach.[2] Accordingly, we transfer *ex post* values to quantify the costs of the morbidity effects estimated in Chapter 4. For most effects this is probably an acceptable approximation, but differences may be larger for more severe effects. Thus, assuming that the *ex ante* perspective provides the preferable welfare measure, this is another place where the transfer process adds bias and uncertainty to the benefit–cost estimates. When they cannot avoid these problems, transfer analysts should at least attempt to assess what they imply for their welfare estimates.

The difference between *ex ante* WTP, or option price, and the expected *ex post* WTP (that is, the *ex post* WTP to avoid an effect times the probability of experiencing the effect) has come to be known as option value. Schmalensee (1972) was the first to show that option value may be either positive or negative. Unfortunately, the sign is indeterminant without information about preferences. It also depends on the interpretation of the effects of the policy being evaluated. In particular, suppose we model people as having a given probability of being sick (for example, having a cough) and model a change in air quality as affecting the severity of that illness. With this interpretation, the sign of option value depends on the relative values of the marginal utility of income in the healthy and sick states (Bohm 1975; Freeman 1989). For a marginal change, option value will be positive if the marginal utility of income is higher in a sick state than in a healthy state, and negative if it is higher in the healthy state. Most likely, the marginal utility of money is approximately constant for small changes in health status, making the difference between the measures small. For larger changes, however, evidence suggests that the marginal utility of income is lower in the worse health state (Viscusi and Evans 1990), so that option value is negative and *ex post* values overstate *ex ante* ones. On this interpretation, then, we probably introduce an upward bias in our estimates of damage by using *ex post* values.

On another interpretation, however, air quality affects the probability of experiencing some illness of a given severity. This interpretation is more consistent with the concentration-response functions, which predict the change in probabilities of some health effect.[3] Freeman (1989) computes the difference between *ex ante* and *ex post* WTP under a number of assumptions about preferences and finds that the difference can be positive or negative, and can sometimes be large. However, for small effects with *ex post* values of less than 1 per cent of income – the majority of effects estimated in this transfer – the relative difference between *ex ante* and *ex post* values is always less than 1 per cent in his examples. This suggests that the error is greatest in the severe morbidity effects such as emphysema. For example, using the utility functions estimated by Viscusi and Evans (1990), *ex post* values for a marginal change in probabilities understate *ex ante* values by 12 per cent to 40 per cent for the severe morbidity effects their data are based on.

A conceptual model for valuing health risks from an *ex post* perspective will help identify necessary assumptions and interpret transfer values (see Berger et al. 1987 for a model from an *ex ante* perspective). This is more than a formal exercise. Rather, by elucidating the different reasons why people care about health, and how they relate to one another, the model serves as a guide for appraising empirical valuation studies. Other things equal, original studies that are more consistent with the model, capturing all the relevant aspects of the value of health in the appropriate ways, are better candidates for a transfer. In this way, conceptual models such as the following can play an important role in the transfer process. Putting it simply, analysts must have a thorough understanding of what they want to transfer before attempting to do so.

We can model the different behavioural effects of a change in air quality with a form of the household production approach first applied to health outcomes by Grossman (1972) and to the health effects of air pollution specifically by Cropper (1981). In particular, we adapt a model presented by Harrington and Portney (1987).[4] Recall from Chapter 1 that household production models follow from the notion that households act like firms, combining market goods with time, behaviour patterns and skills to 'produce' final consumption goods. For example, a household could purchase exercise equipment, nutritious food, vitamins and medicines, and professional medical services and use them in combination with leisure time, sleeping habits, safety precautions, and a clean environment to produce health, the final commodity.

In this model, people can be in different health conditions that fall along a univariate scale of 'health state', h.[5] On this index, a health state of zero represents death and a health state of one represents perfect health, although states worse than death might also be conceivable. As will become clear in Section 5.3, using a health-state index allows more flexibility for actually assigning values to the specific health effects. A person's health state is a function:

$$h = h(q, b; a, m) \qquad (5.1)$$

where q is ambient air quality, b is the individual's genetic and biological endowment, a is expenditures on averting-behaviour commodities or activities to avoid exposure to pollution (for example, purchasing air filters) and m is expenditures on mitigation to reduce the effects of pollution after exposure, such as taking medicine.

Utility u is a function of health state h, the level of leisure l, and expenditures on consumption goods z:

$$u = u(h, l, z) \qquad (5.2)$$

Moreover, the amount of leisure that a person enjoys is a function of health-state and other characteristics w:

$$l = l(h, w) \qquad (5.3)$$

Thus ill health can affect u directly because of pain and discomfort, and indirectly by reducing time available for leisure or, viewed another way, by restricting the leisure activities available to the individual.

Ill health can also reduce the time available for work or diminish work productivity, thereby affecting income:

$$y = y(h, \mathrm{k}), \qquad (5.4)$$

where y is income and k is an index of non-health forms of human capital, such as physical strength, education or experience. As a result of this last effect, health state also enters the budget constraint, where income must cover total expenditures:

$$y \geqq z + a + m \qquad (5.5)$$

The individual's problem is to maximize utility, Equation (5.2), subject to Equations (5.1), (5.3) and (5.5). This problem can be written as the Lagrangian:

$$\mathrm{Max}_{\{x,a,m\}} \mathscr{L} = u(z, l(h, w), h(q, b;\ a, m)) + \lambda(y - z - a - m) \qquad (5.6)$$

The first-order conditions for a welfare maximum are

$$z: u_z - \lambda = 0 \tag{5.7}$$

$$a: u_h h_a + u_l l_h h_a + \lambda y_h h_a - \lambda = 0 \tag{5.8}$$

$$m: u_h h_m + u_l l_h h_m + \lambda y_h h_m - \lambda = 0 \tag{5.9}$$

$$\lambda: y - z - a - m = 0 \tag{5.10}$$

By writing Equation (5.6) as the indirect utility function v, totally differentiating it with respect to q, and setting it equal to zero, we can identify the change in y that must take place for utility to remain unchanged after an exogenous shift in q. In this way, we can solve for the *WTP* for a change in q.

$$v_y(dy^*/dq) + v_q = 0 \tag{5.11}$$

$$WTP \equiv -(dy^*/dq) = v_q/v_y \tag{5.12}$$

Taking the derivatives of v, putting $v_y = \lambda$, and substituting the first-order conditions (5.8) or (5.9) for λ, this simplifies to

$$WTP = h_q/h_a = h_q/h_m \tag{5.13}$$

which is the basis of the averting-behaviour valuation approach. Some authors have interpreted this to mean that *WTP* is a function only of the technical parameters of the health production function, Equation (5.1). But as Harrington and Portney (1987) point out, since a and m are choice variables, the value of the ratios in Equation (5.13) depend on the parameters of the individual's utility function.

In fact, Equation (5.13) is not immediately helpful because the partial derivative of health status with respect to air quality, h_q, is not observed. Instead, as we noted in Chapter 4, epidemiological concentration-response functions measure the total effect of air quality on health, which includes the behaviour adjustments for different levels of averting behaviour and mitigation. That is, they measure

$$dh/dq = h_a a_q + h_m m_q + h_q \tag{5.14}$$

Now, from rearranging the terms in equation (5.8), we have

$$y_h = \frac{\lambda - u_h h_a - u_l l_h h_a}{\lambda h_a} \tag{5.15}$$

Multiplying both sides of Equation (5.15) by dh/dq and substituting Equation (5.14) where appropriate gives

$$y_h(dh/dq) = -(1/\lambda)u_h(dh/dq) - (1/\lambda)u_l l_h(dh/dq) + m_q + a_q + h_q/h_a$$
$$(5.15a)$$

Or, using Equation (5.13),

$$WTP = y_h(dh/dq) + (1/\lambda)u_h(dh/dq) + (1/\lambda)u_l l_h(dh/dq) - m_q - a_q$$
$$(5.16)$$

This equation shows that the total value[6] for air quality consists of several components, including increased earnings (the first term), the decrease in pain or discomfort of the health effect (the second term), improved leisure (the third term), and savings on mitigating or avoiding the health effect (the fourth and fifth terms). Notice here the important distinction between the total *ex post* WTP for air-quality improvements and *ex post* WTP for the health effects. The former includes all five terms in Equation (5.16), but the latter includes only the first four terms. While mitigation costs are best considered part of the WTP for health because they are a consequence of experienced health effects, averting-behaviour costs are a response to changes in air quality, and will be incurred regardless of the health outcome. Thus, averting-behaviour costs are not part of *ex post* WTP for health.

A look at the behaviour of a representative individual will help make these components more concrete. In Figure 5.1, the individual may or may not be exposed to air pollution. If she is not exposed, her health state is unchanged and *ex post* damages are zero. If she is subject to exposure, she has a choice partially to avert the potential exposure. To the extent that she does avert, the costs of averting behaviour become one component of the realized damages of air pollution. But suppose that, whether because of the limited availability of averting technology or her willingness to pay for them, her averting strategies do not completely eliminate the effect of the air pollution on her health. Then she still faces a decrease in her health status from h^0 to h', but it is not as severe a decrease as the shift to h'' that would have taken place if she had not averted.

Having experienced the health effects, however, the individual still has an opportunity to mitigate these effects or symptoms, for example, by seeking treatment. As with averting behaviour, the costs of mitigation become part of the total cost of the air pollution, including both treatment that she purchases out of her own pocket and, from society's perspective, subsidized medical costs as well. Also, as with averting behaviour, we

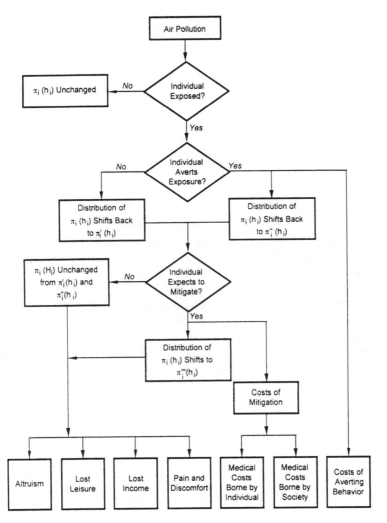

Figure 5.1   *Schematic of the different components of the total health-related social costs of air pollution*

assume that the mitigation she takes does not restore her health to h^0, either because of symptoms experienced before mitigation, or because the mitigation is not fully successful, or because it causes side effects. Still, mitigation does improve her health status to a level h''', higher than either h' or h''.

The boxes at the bottom of Figure 5.1 represent the different components of the value of air quality, and correspond to the terms in Equation (5.16) – with two exceptions. Equation (5.16) refers only to the affected individual's WTP. However, the appropriate measure in cost–benefit analysis is the sum of social costs and benefits and should include the value that other people may hold for the individual's health. Other people in society may hold values for two possible reasons, both shown in Figure 5.1. First, they may have an altruistic concern for the person's health. Although altruistic values are important in principle, they are difficult to measure and are usually excluded from cost–benefit studies. We are not aware of any studies that have measured altruistic values for health effects.

A second reason others may be willing to pay for a person's health is their third-party payments for health care. Medical expenses take two forms: those that the affected individual bears (m^I) and those that the rest of society bears (m^S) through insurance or taxes. To the extent that a decline in the affected individual's health state would lead to an increase in m^S, other people will also be affected by that individual's health through an increase in insurance rates, an increase in taxes or a decline in government services. Accordingly, others too will be willing to pay some amount to prevent an increase in the probability of the individual experiencing a health effect. But the individual's WTP will be affected only by the private costs of the illness (dm^1/dq) instead of by the full social costs and will consequently understate the total benefits of avoiding the illness.

On the other hand, expected medical expenses (m_Q) may *over*state the social costs of mitigating behaviour because of inefficiencies in the health-care system. If medical care is priced higher than marginal costs because of a lack of competition, mitigating expenses do not accurately represent social opportunity costs, but rather reflect transfers of consumer surplus from patients, insurance purchasers and taxpayers to the suppliers of health-care services. Such transfers are not social costs because they do not deplete resources but only transfer them from one party to another. This further observation suggests that m_Q would overstate social costs and that WTP in Equation (5.16) contains an upward bias in addition to the downward biases discussed above.

In practice, no available studies have attempted to include all of these effects because of intractable measurement problems. Therefore we shall continue to use the WTP estimate shown in Equation (5.16) as our basis for discussion, but shall not ignore some of these potentially important concerns. However, we consider them only in a qualitative manner, recognizing that the WTP estimate in Equation (5.16) does not include the values of others that involve either altruism or third-party payments (a downward bias in our measure), and that the equation includes medical costs, which are in part a transfer of surplus from one party to another (an upward bias in our measure). Although these biases may offset each other to a degree, their relative magnitudes are unknown. Thus the ultimate usefulness of an analysis based primarily on WTP requires that the net effect of omitted cost factors be small relative to WTP.

Having identified the components of the private and social costs of air pollution, this model provides a tool for guiding the transfer process and the discussion throughout this chapter. We also use it to gain two more general insights. First, we are now in a better position to understand some of the discussion in Section 4.1 on the differences between toxicology and epidemiology. Recall that epidemiology studies observe health effects after people have undertaken averting behaviour, and thus, in terms of Figure 5.1, quantify effects as h' rather than h'' (ignoring mitigation for the present). But by quantifying these health effects and multiplying by the WTP to avoid them, we omit the averting-behaviour portion of the figure (or the a_q term in Equation 5.16). To capture the total costs of a change in air quality, we would ideally want to quantify the increased expenditures on averting behaviour from a change in air quality as well, which we could then add to WTP to avoid the health effects, an approach taken by Harrington, Krupnick and Spofford (1989) in their study of water quality. This would be an additional part of the disaggregate transfer, but it is one we have not quantified. On the other hand, toxicology studies do not allow people to undertake averting behaviour, and thus quantify effects as h''. This solves the problem of having to quantify this term, but it does so by creating an opposite problem. Multiplying h'' by WTP to avoid health effects overstates total costs because the costs of averting behaviour are presumably less than or equal to the value of the health effects averted.

While this first insight of the conceptual model involves the relationship between the WTP for air quality and for health effects, the second insight involves the appropriate way to value these health effects. In the above paragraph we ignored the effects of mitigation, but the question now arises as to whether an epidemiology study measures health without or with mitigation. That is, in terms of Figure 5.1, whether it measures health as h' or h''. When epidemiology studies quantify cases of symptoms, and if mitigation only reduces the duration or severity of a case, the distinction does not affect the transfer. In other cases, we assume that epidemiology studies measure health status after mitigation. Because most people record their symptoms in some kind of diary or report them to a doctor, they can only report what they experience, which includes the effects of mitigation.

This is reasonable enough, but it has consequences for the appropriate way to value health effects. For example, contingent-valuation studies that value people's WTP to avoid a health effect should do so in a context in which people understand that the health effect they are valuing can be mitigated (at the market price of mitigation). Unfortunately, some studies may have instead included the consumer surplus of mitigation in their values. The lesson here is that, in the words of Krupnick and Kopp (1988), the costs of contracting an illness should measure the entire 'experience' of the illness.

5.2   EMPIRICAL METHODS FOR VALUING HEALTH

Among the non-market valuation methods, economists have used contingent-valuation (CV), hedonic, and averting-behaviour methods to estimate the WTP to avoid health effects, as well as the cost-of-illness (COI) approach. Having introduced these methods in Chapter 1, here we evaluate the potential of each type of study to be transferred in the case study, discussing certain concerns specifically related to health valuation using the lens of the conceptual model just presented. Tolley, Kenkel and Fabian (1994) and Johannesson (1996) provide more comprehensive treatments of health valuation.

In addition to some of the general concerns mentioned in Chapter 1, such as the cognitive difficulties respondents may have in constructing values on a survey, there are also some specific theoretical and institutional concerns that arise when applying CV to health. Theoretically, the analysis in the previous section suggests that, to be properly interpreted, CV studies must clearly specify that mitigation opportunities are available for the health effects being valued. In addition, because marginal WTP probably diminishes with increasing health status, CV studies must specify whether respondents are purchasing health improvements or avoiding further illness. Unfortunately, as we shall see below, they have not always done so. Institutionally, health insurance and subsidized health care may cause respondents to reject any scenario that requires them to pay the full cost of drugs or health care, or to overstate WTP on the presumption of a subsidy (Desvousges et al. 1996). Alternatively, respondents may reject the efficacy of the scenario for achieving health benefits if they mistrust drugs and doctors, causing them to understate their true WTP. Moreover, respondents may have difficulty valuing effects they have never personally experienced or have not known close friends and family to experience.

CV, if it overcomes these implementation and other well-documented problems with expressed preference, can potentially measure WTP. By valuing effects instead of environmental quality, it cannot capture the costs of averting behaviour. But so long as respondents understand the effect they are valuing, CV can yield values that include the effects of health on leisure, income, discomfort and medical expenses.

Hedonic methods are capable of measuring marginal WTP and, at a minimum, bounds on WTP for non-marginal changes. To value health, researchers have applied the hedonic method to wages, estimating wages as a function of on-the-job health risks and other factors (see Viscusi 1992, 1993). However, there are some concerns about the transferability of hedonic wage studies to environmental health risks. As Kask (1992) notes, such differences amount to differences in the commodity being valued in the original study and in the transfer study. Transferring WTP information from one context to the other or from one commodity to another may be inappropriate if people value these kinds of risks very differently. Slovic, Fischhoff and Lichtenstein (1979) have identified several ways in which people may distinguish risks. These include the following:

1. *Voluntariness*: Do people face this risk voluntarily?
2. *Control*: If exposed, to what extent can the individual avoid death?
3. *Knowledge*: How well do those exposed to the risk understand what the risk is?
4. *Newness*: Is the risk new and novel or old and familiar?
5. *Common/dread*: Have people learned to live with the risk or is it one people dread?
6. *Possible disaster*: Does the risk kill one at a time or large numbers at a time?
7. *Suffering*: Will risk cause suffering before death or will death come quickly?
8. *Timing*: Is the risk of death immediate or likely to occur at some later time?

One major difference between workplace and environmental risks is the degree of voluntariness individuals face. People often believe they choose to face some risks (for example, automobile accidents), whereas other risks appear to be beyond their control (for example, the risk of getting cancer from an unknown contaminant). The risks associated with the wage-risk studies are more voluntary than the risks caused by pollution. To the extent that people fear involuntary risks more, transferring WTP from hedonic wage studies may underestimate WTP in the environmental-policy context.

Another important dimension is the suffering the individual experiences before death. Will exposure to the risk cause the individual to go through a period of mental or physical anguish before death, or will death be quick and painless? Because of the nature of reported deaths in the workplace (most are accidents, not prolonged and disease-related), job risks are assumed to cause quick deaths with little suffering. On the other hand, deaths resulting from exposure to pollution usually follow a period of suffering from disease or discomfort. Individuals' WTP is thus likely to be less for the workplace risk scenarios, resulting in further understatement of the value of pollution-related risk.

An additional concern is that individuals' risk perceptions are not necessarily the same as their actual risk exposures. Misperception may lead to inaccurate compensation for the risks they face. The availability of risk data and the overconfidence that individuals place in their perceptions are factors that may cause inaccurately perceived risks (Slovic, Fischhoff and Lichtenstein 1979). In addition to errors associated with inaccurate perceptions, background risk levels also may introduce bias. It is generally expected that people at higher baseline risk value a risk reduction more than people at a lower baseline value the same reduction (see, for example, Sussman 1984). If so, the fact that workplace risks are generally higher than environmental risks may be another important difference. Empirical studies have found mixed results for this hypothesis, however, and Miller (1990) found no relationship when looking across studies, a finding we confirm below.

Of related concern to the difference in risks between the original context and transfer context are the differences in the affected population. Because of self-selection bias, people in high-risk workplace contexts may be less averse to health risks than the general population. Moreover, they also tend to be younger and healthier than the elderly or sick population affected by air pollution. Although the bias is not known with certainty, differences in expected quality-adjusted life years suggest that this sample bias tends to overstate externality costs.

Based on a theoretical foundation like the conceptual model presented earlier, in principle the averting-behaviour method can capture all the various aspects of people's WTP for air quality and health. Comparing it with the conceptual model is instructive. Recall from Equation (1.2) that the averting behaviour measures marginal WTP for a change in air quality as

$$WTP(dq) = p_a \frac{\phi_q}{\phi_a} = -p_a \cdot a_q$$

Note that this partial change in averting expenditures is not the change that is actually observed, because observed changes will also reflect behavioural adjustments to a different health status. But as one component of total value in the conceptual model, these observed changes provide a lower bound on WTP so long as people's behavioural adjustments do not compensate so much that air quality improvements actually lead to health decreases, that is so long as the dh/dq terms in Equation (5.16) are positive (Harrington and Portney 1987; Bartik 1988a). Bartik (1988a) further shows that even for the non-marginal case the change in averting expenditures needed to keep health status constant provides a tighter lower bound on WTP for air quality improvements. (A similar result applies to the case of air quality decreases.)

A final method used to estimate health effects is cost-of-illness (COI) studies. COI studies add up foregone income and the costs of medical treatment to calculate the out-of-pocket expenses of an illness from an *ex post* perspective. In some cases COI studies measure treatment costs including third-party payments; in others they do not. Unfortunately, the COI method ignores several important components of the total value of health effects as outlined in Section 5.1, including such non-monetary costs as pain and discomfort and, in most cases, foregone leisure time. Thus, according to most interpretations, COI studies underestimate WTP. However, given accurate measurements, they may at least provide reliable lower bounds (Chestnut and Violette 1984; Harrington and Portney 1987; Cropper and Freeman 1991).

In fact, this lower-bound interpretation depends both on whether or not the COI studies include third-party payments and on whether they are said to be bounding an individual's WTP or society's aggregate WTP. Because affected individuals will only be willing to pay to avoid the costs that they must bear, COI studies can provide a lower bound on the individual's WTP if they measure medical expenses excluding third-party payments, a result that has been confirmed in empirical studies (Rowe and Chestnut 1985; Berger et al. 1987). When COI studies measure total costs of treatment they may overstate the individual's value for the treatment because third-party payments may induce the individual to purchase more treatment than he or she would have purchased in the absence of such subsidies. Consequently, in these cases COI studies do not provide an unambiguous lower bound on the individual's WTP. However, they can still provide a lower bound on the total social costs if medical care is competitively priced. As noted above, even this bound may not hold if some medical expenses represent transfers of surplus.

Figure 5.2 illustrates the difference between the private and the social costs of mitigation. The figure shows individuals' compensated demand for medical services (mitigation) after a decrease in health. Assuming it is competitively priced, medical care has a cost to society of P_M^*. Individuals face a lower cost, P_M^S, after third-party payment by insurance coverage, entitlement programmes or both. Were they facing the social cost of the medical care, individuals would consume M*. But because they do not bear the full social cost, individuals purchase additional medical care, up to M^S. Note that individuals' marginal expenditure does not exceed marginal WTP, but that the total marginal social cost of these services does. Individuals pay price times quantity, the area given by $P_M^S AM^S O$, and this is the COI measure exclusive of third-party payments. Still assuming that medical care providers price their goods and services at their opportunity cost, the area $P_M^* BM^S O$ represents the actual social cost of the mitigation. This is the area measured by COI studies that include third-party payments.

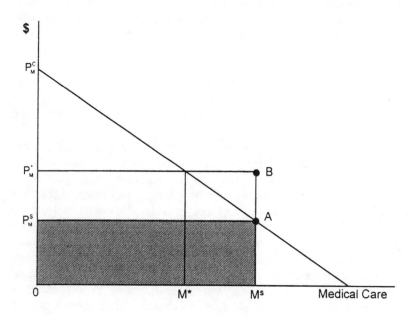

Figure 5.2   Individual demand for medical services

Figure 5.3 shows individuals' marginal WTP for health MWTP(H), rather than for medical care. Abstracting from the costs of such other inputs as averting behaviour, the figure also shows the costs individuals must pay to 'produce' better health through medical care. MC^0 is the marginal cost curve under the original state of air quality; MC' is the marginal cost of maintaining health after a decrease in air quality. Because

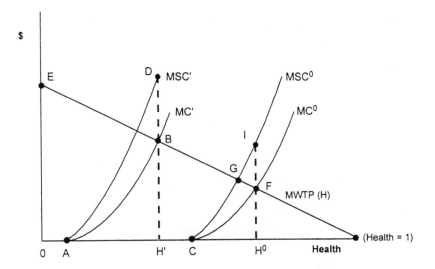

Figure 5.3   WTP for health

of subsidies, MC^0 and MC' are lower than the corresponding social cost curves, MSC^0 and MSC'.

Under the original level of air quality, individuals will 'purchase' health up to H^0, with a total private medical cost equal to the area under MC^0 up to H^0, or CFH^0. Thus total surplus is equal to EFCO. With the change in air quality, and the corresponding shift of the cost curves, surplus falls from the full area EFCO to the smaller area EBAO. First, individuals will purchase less health, and health state falls from H^0 to H' while surplus falls by the area $BFCH'$, a cost of air pollution that COI studies cannot capture. They will also now have to pay more to maintain even the lower health state H', which is measured by the area under MC', or ABH'. This is the private cost of mitigation, and it corresponds to the area $P_M^S AM^S O$ in Figure 5.2. Society, however, will pay more than the individuals do, paying the amount under MSC', or the amount ADH'. This is the social cost of mitigation, and it corresponds to the area $P_M^* BM^S O$ in Figure 5.2.

We now can return to our discussion of using COI studies as a lower bound. In terms of Figure 5.3, WTP to avoid the drop in air quality is equal to the loss of surplus that would be experienced with that drop, or the area ABFC. COI studies that measure costs net of third-party payments capture a portion of this area ($ABH' - CFH^0$) but not all of it, thereby providing a lower bound on WTP. The total social costs of a decrease in air quality equal the loss of surplus plus the costs that other people must bear for medical care (or the area ADB − CIF), leading to the total area (ADBFC − CIF). COI studies that measure costs gross of third-party payments capture a portion of this area as well, specifically (ADH′ − CIH^0), providing a lower bound for that social measure (but not for the individual measure).

For the purpose of public policy decisions, *total* social costs should be measured and not just the sum of the private costs of affected individuals. As noted in the previous section, other people are also affected indirectly if they must bear some of the costs of treatment through taxes or insurance costs. In effect, they too have a small WTP for the individual's health. Accordingly, from a benefits perspective the relevant benefit of improved air quality is the change in total medical costs, a class of benefits known in benefit–cost analysis as 'cost-difference' or 'cost-savings' benefits.[7] Thus COI studies are more useful when they include third-party payments. Because they can capture these costs as well as foregone income, such COI studies can be very useful. However, they cannot capture the value of any remaining decline in the individual's health or various other components of total value, and can therefore provide only a lower bound on social costs. COI studies, although not actual measures of WTP in the strictest sense, do have a relationship to our conceptual model. They capture the costs of foregone income, the medical costs borne by individuals and, in some cases, those borne by society. Less frequently, COI studies capture the costs of foregone leisure time. In our conceptual model these costs appear as:

$$COI = y_h h_q + m_q \tag{5.17}$$

In the few studies that include foregone leisure, $(1/\lambda)u_L h h_q$ would be measured as well.

An additional problem with some COI studies is that they look only at people who are actually treated for health effects, for example, by surveying hospital records. In doing so, they look at a biased sample because not all people who experience the effect seek treatment. Suppose for example that roughly half the population is willing to pay for an expensive treatment and half is not. A COI estimate surveying hospital cost would identify the treatment costs, but transferring this cost to the entire number of estimated cases would overstate social costs because not all people have a WTP this high. In this respect, COI studies can sometimes resemble cost-of-replacement measures by assuming that people value their health as much as the cost of restoring it. Though it may sometimes be more difficult, especially when a doctor's diagnosis is required to do it properly, a more proper approach would be to identify all the people experiencing an effect and then observe the average medical expenditure.

5.3 REVIEW OF VALUATION STUDIES AND SELECTED VALUES FOR TRANSFER

The above methods have all been used at various times to estimate the cost of ill health, and all could potentially be transferred in our case study. In this section, we review specific valuation studies for the health effects quantified in Chapter 4, again classifying them as short-term morbidity effects, chronic morbidity effects, and effects on mortality risks.

Short-term Morbidity

A number of studies have valued the types of short-term morbidity effects transferred in the case study. Some of these are less useful for this application than others because they measure the effects in a way that does not cleanly match the units from available concentration-response functions. For example, Reardon and Pathak (1989) find people's WTP to avoid a typical year of allergy symptoms. Although these symptoms are related to many of the respiratory symptoms caused by air pollution, making this a potentially useful study, this study does not provide the WTP for a single day or episode of symptoms as required by the concentration-response functions.

Nevertheless, a number of CV, averting-behaviour, and COI studies have estimated people's WTP to avoid a specified number of days of common symptoms, including Loehman et al. (1979); Rowe and Chestnut (1985); Krupnick (1986); Tolley et al. (1986a); Berger et al. (1987); Dickie et al. (1986, 1987, 1988); Chestnut et al. (1988); and Alberini et al. (1994). Collectively, these studies provide estimates for a wide range of common, often overlapping, minor symptoms, including cough, headache and eye irritation. At the same time, each estimate taken individually ought to give analysts pause before transferring it. For example, Krupnick (1986) and one set of estimates in Rowe and Chestnut (1985) are COI studies that do not accurately capture the full components of WTP, while the averting-behaviour study by Dickie et al. (1986, 1987) certainly involved the common problem of joint production in the averting behaviours. The CV studies by Loehman et al., Rowe and Chestnut, Tolley et al., Dickie et al. (1987, 1988), and Alberini et al.,[8] which comprise the majority of the estimates, also have some limitations. Some used elicitation formats such as bidding games and payment cards that may induce bias. In particular, Dickie et al. (1987, 1988) used a revision procedure that has been criticized (for example, Cropper and Freeman, 1991; Krupnick and Kopp, 1988). Several also had small sample sizes and/or low response rates. In addition, because most of the CV health studies asked respondents WTP questions about several different conditions, the results from these studies may be affected by intra-study anchoring or sequence effects. Finally, Alberini et al. conducted their study in Taiwan, suggesting that the results may not transfer well to the US.[9]

Both of these factors – the rich quantity of data taken collectively and the limitations of any individual study – seem to suggest an excellent opportunity for a meta-analysis. But it would have to be a different kind of meta-analysis from what we have envisioned so far: rather than combining different measures of the same entity (outcome, commodity, and so on), it would have to combine results that are not only from different studies, but are also of different, though closely related, entities. The key to resolving this difficulty is to make a transition from thinking of a 'cough day' or 'headache day' as individual commodities to thinking of a single composite commodity, 'health', involving different attributes, including the presence or absence of specific symptoms such as cough or headache. Thinking of it in this way, health is like the differentiated commodities, houses or cars for example, that economists have analysed with hedonic methods. This approach is in fact used in one CV study (Alberini et al. 1994) that predicts WTP for sick days partly as a function of the number of symptoms experienced.

To formalize the approach for a meta-analysis, we employ a health-state index used in the literature to quantify health along a univariate scale. Specifically, we employ the Quality of Well-Being (QWB) index of Fanshel and Bush (1970) and Kaplan, Anderson and Ganiats (1993), which rates health status on a scale from 0 to 1, where 0 represents death and 1 represents perfect health. With this index, we can assign an index score to each of the health effects valued in the CV studies. This provides the information needed for the meta-analysis. Data on the willingness to pay for health effects, provided by the CV studies, can be regressed on the severity of the health effect, as provided by the QWB score, the duration of the effect, and potentially other variables, such as individuals' demographic characteristics.

To do this, we use estimates of WTP for short-term health effects from five CV studies (Rowe and Chestnut, Chestnut et al., Dickie et al., Loehman et al., and Tolley et al.) valuing 21 conditions as the dependent variable (53 data points in all). The data are given in Table 5.1. These observations exclude those from COI studies, from averting-behaviour

Table 5.1 WTP values for various health conditions

Study	Health condition	Number of days	1993 $ WTP	1993 $ WTP/day	Standard error	Sample size	QWB
Chestnut et al. (1988)	Angina	2	$216.00	$108.00	–	22	0.641
Chestnut et al. (1988)	Angina	1	$131.00	$131.00	–	22	0.641
Dickie et al. (1988)	Throat congestion	1	$21.75	$21.75	7.77	25	0.830
Dickie et al. (1988)	Cough	1	$15.01	$15.01	4.44	26	0.743
Dickie et al. (1988)	Sinus congestion	1	$17.23	$17.23	4.13	41	0.830
Dickie et al. (1988)	Wheezing	1	$15.07	$15.07	9.08	8	0.743
Dickie et al. (1988)	Shortness of breath	1	$9.05	$9.05	5.84	11	0.743
Dickie et al. (1988)	Pain on deep inspiration	1	$34.98	$34.98	13.72	10	0.701
Dickie et al. (1988)	Chest tightness	1	$25.68	$25.68	6.79	15	0.701
Dickie et al. (1988)	Cannot breathe deeply	1	$19.31	$19.31	7.98	19	0.743
Dickie et al. (1988)	Headache	1	$24.63	$24.63	6.02	49	0.756
Dickie et al. (1988)	Eye irritation	1	$19.86	$19.86	8.38	34	0.770
Dickie et al. (1988)	Runny nose	1	$12.80	$12.80	6.53	13	0.830
Dickie et al. (1988)	Chest congestion	1	$3.14	$3.14	1.70	10	0.701
Loehman et al. (1979)	Cough/sneeze (mild)	1	$12.11	$12.11	22.39	356	0.743
Loehman et al. (1979)	Cough/sneeze (severe)	1	$33.43	$33.43	55.75	356	0.682
Loehman et al. (1979)	Cough/sneeze (mild)	7	$39.92	$5.70	65.80	356	0.743
Loehman et al. (1979)	Cough/sneeze (severe)	7	$87.35	$12.48	134.12	356	0.682
Loehman et al. (1979)	Cough/sneeze (mild)	90	$106.29	$1.18	146.61	356	0.743
Loehman et al. (1979)	Cough/sneeze (severe)	90	$237.51	$2.64	411.84	356	0.682

(continued)

Table 5.1 Continued

Study	Health condition	Number of days	1993 $		Standard error	Sample size	QWB
			WTP	WTP/day			
Loehman et al. (1979)	Shortness of breath (mild)	1	$34.86	$34.86	79.01	356	0.743
Loehman et al. (1979)	Shortness of breath (severe)	1	$70.16	$70.16	173.96	356	0.622
Loehman et al. (1979)	Shortness of breath (mild)	7	$85.72	$12.25	142.07	356	0.743
Loehman et al. (1979)	Shortness of breath (severe)	7	$209.72	$29.96	415.76	356	0.622
Loehman et al. (1979)	Shortness of breath (mild)	90	$233.72	$2.60	483.36	356	0.743
Loehman et al. (1979)	Shortness of breath (severe)	90	$493.16	$5.48	735.09	356	0.622
Loehman et al. (1979)	Head congestion (mild)	1	$19.84	$19.84	39.53	356	0.756
Loehman et al. (1979)	Head congestion (severe)	1	$46.66	$46.66	86.14	356	0.695
Loehman et al. (1979)	Head congestion (mild)	7	$41.90	$5.99	64.21	356	0.756
Loehman et al. (1979)	Head congestion (severe)	7	$90.48	$12.93	134.48	356	0.695
Loehman et al. (1979)	Head congestion (mild)	90	$115.12	$1.28	163.50	356	0.756
Loehman et al. (1979)	Head congestion (severe)	90	$317.02	$3.52	554.16	356	0.695
Rowe and Chestnut (1985)	Asthma day	9.5	$578.33	$60.88	122.57	65	0.683
Tolley et al. (1986a)	Throat congestion	1	$40.04	$40.04	4.41	176	0.830
Tolley et al. (1986a)	Throat congestion	30	$285.05	$9.50	29.68	176	0.830
Tolley et al. (1986a)	Drowsiness	1	$43.41	$43.41	4.76	176	0.680
Tolley et al. (1986a)	Drowsiness	30	$439.45	$14.65	61.77	176	0.680
Tolley et al. (1986a)	Angina (mild)	1	$88.22	$88.22	74.33	176	0.701
Tolley et al. (1986a)	Angina (mild)	10	$206.07	$20.61	220.56	176	0.701
Tolley et al. (1986a)	Angina (severe)	1	$164.99	$164.99	135.68	176	0.580

Tolley et al. (1986a)	Angina (severe)	10	$349.56	$34.96	326.81	176	0.580
Tolley et al. (1986a)	Angina (severe)	20	$1127.25	$56.36	2149.27	176	0.580
Tolley et al. (1986a)	Cough	1	$34.83	$34.83	4.03	176	0.743
Tolley et al. (1986a)	Cough	30	$230.10	$7.67	23.99	176	0.743
Tolley et al. (1986a)	Nausea	1	$69.49	$69.49	10.67	176	0.649
Tolley et al. (1986a)	Nausea	30	$257.08	$8.57	26.67	176	0.649
Tolley et al. (1986a)	Headache	1	$55.42	$55.42	6.38	176	0.695
Tolley et al. (1986a)	Headache	30	$674.69	$22.49	86.80	176	0.695
Tolley et al. (1986a)	Eye irritation	1	$38.32	$38.32	3.44	176	0.770
Tolley et al. (1986a)	Eye irritation	30	$325.50	$10.85	47.81	176	0.770
Tolley et al. (1986a)	Sinus congestion	1	$48.44	$48.44	4.41	176	0.769
Tolley et al. (1986a)	Sinus congestion	30	$367.09	$12.24	37.48	176	0.769

Notes: Each health condition was assigned a QWB score based on how the condition was described in its study. Note, then, that the same condition may have several different QWB scores in the table. Both Loehman and Tolley arbitrarily assign the categories mild and severe to health conditions. In cases where condition descriptions were not included, we consulted several health professionals and reviewed several medical guides to aid our classification of a moderate case. Loehman's original sample was trimmed by 5 per cent at each end of the distribution to account for outliers and protest bids.

studies, (because of problems of joint estimation), and from the Alberini et al. study in Taiwan. In principle, the observations need not be limited to those for health effects related to air quality; observations for any short-term health effects could help define the relationship between WTP and the QWB index. In fact, these were the only studies we found that valued short-term effects, with other health-valuation studies valuing long-term or chronic conditions (Thompson, Read and Liang 1984; Thompson 1986; Harrington, Krupnick and Spofford 1989).

The independent variables are the duration of the health effect valued, measured in days, and the severity as measured by the QWB index. This index comes from a large body of literature based on a model first proposed by Fanshel and Bush in 1970. Over the last two decades, the index has been operationalized, updated and revised several times, with the most recent weights used in this analysis coming from Kaplan, Anderson and Ganiats (1993).[10] The QWB index measures health in four dimensions: three 'function states' – mobility, physical activity and social activity – and the most severe symptom/problem complex. Because it includes dimensions for both function levels and symptom/problem complexes, the index incorporates both illness and dysfunction into one index score.

In applying the QWB index to the health effects measured in the CV studies, we categorize each condition based on the descriptions in each CV study. In cases where respondents received no description of the health condition, we assumed a moderate case and calculated QWB scores based on a review of major medical guides and the expert opinion of several health professionals.[11] These QWB scores are also given in Table 5.1.[12]

Although health-state indexes offer the most conceptually appealing approach for evaluating policies that have an impact on human health, some researchers are concerned about their reliability, stability and validity (Mehrez and Gafni 1989; Torrance 1986). While recognizing these concerns, we note that the QWB index has been extensively evaluated by health researchers. (See Kaplan, Bush and Berry 1978; Froberg and Kane 1989; and Kaplan and Ernst 1983 for a discussion of these issues.) Although some criticisms of health-state indexes may limit their usefulness in certain contexts, our analysis indicates that the QWB index is a useful construct for rating the short-term conditions with which we are concerned.

Before turning to the empirical results, consider several expectations about the relationship between WTP and the dependent variables. First, of course, WTP should increase with both severity and duration of the symptoms. Second, if the marginal utility of income is constant over this small range of moderate health effects, and if there is diminishing marginal utility for health, WTP should increase at an increasing rate with severity. However, the interpretation of the movement of WTP with increasing duration is not as clear. Diminishing marginal utility of health implies that WTP should increase at an accelerating rate for avoiding additional sick days, but likewise that it should increase at a decreasing rate for reductions in currently experienced sick days. Unfortunately, the data mix WTP estimates for increases and decreases in health effects, meaning that the WTP is in some cases a compensating surplus measure and in other cases an equivalent surplus measure. While this is one limitation with this work, such second-order differences may be minor for the range of effects considered here. For further discussion of this issue, as well as other aspects of the meta-analysis, including more details about the data and the health-state index literature, see Desvousges et al. (1995a) and Johnson, Fries and Banzhaf (1997).

In later revisions, this meta-analysis was conducted using fixed-effects and random-effects models to account for the panel nature of the data set (Johnson, Fries and Banzhaf 1997). Preliminary regressions used for purposes of this transfer used generalized least squares to regress WTP on QWB, the number of days of the illness occurring (DAYS), and a dummy variable to control for a handful of observations measuring WTP for 90 days of a symptom from the Loehman et al. study (NINETY). The GLS regressions weighted all observations by the sample size in the CV survey to allow larger studies to have greater influence on the regression line. This procedure makes sense intuitively – larger studies should have more precise WTP values. Alternatively, we could have used regression weights based on the inverse of each observation's standard error. Although this weighting variable is preferred in theory, the standard errors of Dickie et al. (1987, 1988) were several orders of magnitude less than those of other observations, despite the extremely small sample sizes in the Dickie study (see Table 5.1), so that these observations largely controlled the regressions. Because of this, sample-size weights were used instead of the variance.

The final model was:

$$Ln(WTP + 1) = 12.00(1 - QWB) + 0.6752 \, Ln(DAYS)$$

$$-1.170 \, NINETY \qquad (5.18)$$

All explanatory variables are highly significant and possess the expected signs. The adjusted R^2 is 0.72. The logarithmic form of the WTP variable indicates that as QWB scores decrease and individuals move farther from perfect health, they will be willing to pay more and more for the same absolute change in health status. In addition, it implies that WTP increases with duration at a decreasing rate.

This regression equation is used to predict the WTP to avoid the short-term health effects to be transferred, identified in the previous chapter. Table 5.2 presents the WTP predictions for these effects. The values are a function of both the QWB score associated with the effect and the number of days the effect lasts. For purposes of comparison, Table 5.3 presents the WTP estimates along with the estimates from Tolley et al. (1986a), Loehman et al. (1979) and Dickie et al. (1987, 1988). Almost all of the WTP estimates from the valuation studies lie within the range of the confidence intervals.[13]

Table 5.2   Predicted WTP values for reductions in short-term health effects included in our damage estimates

Health effect	1-QWB	Average number of days	Mean (1993 $)	90% confidence interval (1993 $)
Acute bronchitis	0.378	2	$148.07	$48–$347
Chest discomfort	0.299	1	$35.17	$12–$82
Cough	0.318	2.2	$76.38	$25–$179
Croup	0.378	3	$195.02	$64–$457
Eye irritation	0.230	1	$14.80	$5–$35
Headache	0.305	1	$37.87	$12–$89
Lower respiratory effects	0.318	1.4	$56.03	$18–$131
Upper respiratory effects	0.231	1.4	$19.07	$6–$45

Chronic Morbidity

Several of the health effects in the case study are long-term, chronic conditions. Although the QWB function does control for the duration of illness, it is best at detecting small differences, such as the difference between one day and seven. Effects that may last for years must be valued outside of the daily health-valuation function. Unfortunately, there are few valuation studies available for these effects – probably an insufficient number to conduct a meta-analysis – and most are COI studies. Such problems with the quality of available information arise frequently in transfer studies, and analysts must simply do what they can with what is available. In this case it is necessary to transfer specific studies for those effects that were identified in Chapter 4. In particular, exposure to particulate matter can result in chronic cough in children and chronic

Table 5.3 WTP values for reductions in various health effects

Health effect	Predicted WTP[a]	Tolley et al. (1986)	Loehman et al. (1979)	Dickie et al. (1987, 1988)
Cough (mild)	$21($7–$49)	$34.83	$12.11	$15.01
Cough (severe)	$44($15–$104)	–	$33.43	–
Headache (mild)	$18($6–$41)	–	–	$24.63
Headache (severe)	$38($12–$89)	$55.42	–	–
Shortness of breath (mild)	$21($7–$49)	–	$34.86	$9.05
Shortness of breath (severe)	$92($30–$216)	–	$70.16	–
Eye irritation	$15($5–$35)	$38.32	–	$19.86

Notes: [a] 90 per cent confidence intervals are listed in parentheses.

bronchitis, emphysema and asthma in adults; exposure to ozone can increase the likelihood of asthma in children; and exposure to lead can result in hypertension in adults and anaemia and IQ decrements in children.

Viscusi, Magat and Huber (1991) used a computerized conjoint-analysis survey to estimate WTP to avoid a 1 in 100 000 risk of chronic bronchitis. They estimate annual payments to be about $8.83, or about $883 000 per statistical case. In addition, Krupnick et al. (1989) and Cropper and Krupnick (1989) employed a COI study to measure the costs of chronic bronchitis, as well as the costs of emphysema, hypertension and other diseases. Cropper and Krupnick report that the mean annual medical expenses (in 1993 dollars) are $229.27 (SE =61.44) for chronic bronchitis, $1499.64 (SE =100.65) for emphysema, and $511.42 (SE = 55.34) for hypertension. Hypertension did not have a statistically significant effect on earned income, but chronic bronchitis did, affecting the probability of a person participating in the labour force, but not their income levels conditional on participation. Depending on their age, people with chronic bronchitis lost between $2100 and $11 500 annually, with an average of $5200. Emphysema affected both the probability of people participating in the labour force and their income levels conditional on participation. The effects on income are a function of both age of onset and the present age of the affected person, and range between $4700 and $36 000 annually, with an average of $19 500.

Johannesson, Jönsson and Borgquist (1991) used CV to measure the

WTP of hypertensive Swedes for drug treatment that would reduce their diastolic blood pressure. Johannesson et al. (1993) followed up these earlier results using a model that included people's perceived health improvement from the therapy measured on a health-status index. They predicted mean WTP to be $1712 (SE = 856) per year in US 1993 dollars for the treatment. Unfortunately, the authors give only the standard deviation of the predicted bids, which does not take into consideration the uncertainty of their model.

In a benefit–cost analysis of EPA regulation of lead in drinking water, Levin (1987) performed a COI study of hypertension, which can also result from exposure to atmospheric lead. She reports an average annual cost of $316 per case for doctor visits, medicine, hospital-bed days and time spent away from work valued at the wage rate. The weakest aspect of this calculation is the cost of medicine ($85), which she calculated using the average cost of all drugs, an amount which may be higher or lower than the cost of those prescribed for hypertension. This COI amount reflects the average cost for both detected and undetected cases of hypertension, one possible reason why it is lower than the Cropper and Krupnick (1989) results.

Levin also provides a COI study of IQ points, noting that several studies have examined the relationship between IQ and earnings. Summarizing these studies, she suggests that a one-point decrement in IQ can cause a 0.20 to 0.75 per cent change in lifetime earnings directly and a 0.18 to 0.56 per cent change indirectly (for example, because of more limited educational opportunities). Levin concludes that, overall, a one-point decrement can cause a 0.90 per cent reduction in lifetime earnings. Using 1986 census data, she suggests that the present value of lifetime earnings, deferred 20 years at a 5 per cent discount rate, is $345 700 in 1993 dollars. Nine-tenths of 1 per cent of this amount is about $3100 per IQ point. This translates to an annual WTP of $160.00. Although this amount does not include other costs of lost IQ, such as the simple enjoyment of increased intellectual aptitude, as in other COI studies, it can provide a lower bound on the total value. Lacking any information about the error bounds of this estimate, we assume that the 90 per cent confidence interval is between $0 and $320.

These studies must provide the valuation estimates for the chronic effects identified in Chapter 4. One chronic effect is the number of asthmatics in populations of children, an effect linked to exposure to ozone. This is a chronic effect because it increases the actual number of asthmatics instead of the number of attacks each asthmatic faces. Unfortunately, no study values asthma as such. However, Krupnick and Kopp (1988) have examined the health literature and estimate that asthmatics experience an average of about ten attacks per year. Using the WTP value for an asthma attack predicted by the QWB model, $43.90, an estimate of the annual WTP for asthma is about $439. This estimate is conservative because it does not control for DAYS, which would have reduced it to $212.

Another effect identified in Chapter 4 is a combination of emphysema, chronic bronchitis and asthma. The value of this aggregate effect is the average of the individual valuations for each effect weighted by its share of the effect. Unfortunately, we do not know the relative share of each of these effects in the concentration-response function. Thus it is necessary to use the simple average values for asthma, chronic bronchitis and emphysema. Although Viscusi, Magat and Huber (1991) probably provide the better estimate of chronic bronchitis risks, the estimates for the other chronic diseases are *ex post* COI values. Thus, for consistency, we use the COI estimate from Cropper and Krupnick (1989) for chronic bronchitis, about $5400 dollars per year after combining treatment costs and lost earnings. To quantify the uncertainty of this estimate, we use a standard error for this value that encompasses the range of income effects that the authors identify, or about $2800. The COI estimate for emphysema, when adding medical expenses to lost earnings, is about $21 000, with a range of $6200 to $37 500 (or a standard error of about $9400). Averaging the three and combining the standard errors, the estimate for this aggregate effect is $8900 (SE =3300) per year.

A third effect is chronic cough. Cropper and Krupnick (1989) did not include chronic cough in their list of chronic diseases, but other chronic respiratory effects can be seen as providing a range of the possible values for this effect. Using the range provided by the above values for chronic bronchitis and asthma, we assume that chronic cough has a mean value of $2900 with a standard error of $1500.

To value hypertension, we can use either the Cropper and Krupnick (1989) or the Levin (1987) COI studies or the CV work by Johannesson et al. (1993). The first two studies have the limitation of being only COI studies. The Johannesson study is difficult to transfer because it measures the values of Swedes, who may have different preferences and may face substantially different relative prices. However, the study has the important distinction of valuing a specific reduction of six points of diastolic blood pressure. Because the concentration-response function quantifies the effect of exposure to lead on diastolic blood pressure, rather than on the probability of having hypertension as such, this study is much more consistent with the required health endpoint. Because the drug treatment would reduce diastolic blood pressure by an average of six points (Johannesson, 1992), a one-point change in the diastolic blood pressure of hypertensive people has a value of $285 per year, which is one-sixth the WTP found in Johannesson et al. (1993). Lacking useful information about the confidence around this estimate, we assume the 90 per cent confidence interval is between zero and 570 (SE = 171).

Finally, to value a small change in IQ decrements, we transfer the study by Levin (1987) that estimates the annual cost of income from a one-point drop in the IQ at $1600. These judgements are summarized in Table 5.4.

Table 5.4   Selected WTP values for chronic health effects (1993 $)

Chronic effects	WTP value (annual $)	Standard error
Asthma	$439	5.62[a]
Emphysema, chronic bronchitis and asthma	$8900	3300
Chronic cough	$2900	1500
Diastolic blood pressure (1 point)	$285	171
IQ score (1 point)	$160	97

Notes: [a] The asthma standard error is for LN(WTP + 1). The 90 per cent confidence interval is between $68 and $489.

From the earlier discussion, we can interpret the values transferred from these COI studies as a lower bound on WTP. Being based on COI estimates, and in some cases on COI estimates of different but related effects, these values for chronic morbidity represent one of the weakest links in the transfer study. Having in most cases only one available study to transfer, there is no possibility of making judgements about which is the 'best' study, or about how to summarize the results of several. This is one of the most frustrating problems for transfer analysts, because there is really no solution. In such cases, analysts are simply constrained by the limited studies available for transfer.

One additional transfer concern may offset the bias from using COI studies. The concentration-response functions for chronic conditions use cross-sectional data to estimate static differences in the steady-state incidence of each effect. Thus they do not provide dynamic information about the effects of an increase in pollution or incidence over time. Presumably, incidence would gradually increase to a new steady-state level. In this transfer, we assume that the full effect occurs in the first year following the scenarios, leading to an overstatement of damages.

Mortality

Economists have devoted considerable attention to determining people's WTP for reducing their risk of death. Like the large number of epidemiological studies estimating mortality risks of exposure to particulates, the large number of studies valuing mortality-risk reductions provides another example of a potential embarrassment of riches for transfer analysts. Which of the many studies should the analysts choose in such a case? Here, again, analysts should use as much of the information as possible. In most transfers, analysts have taken a step in this direction, transferring a qualitative judgement of the central tendency of the various studies rather than just a 'best study'. For example, in other analyses of the externalities of electricity generation, Harrison et al. (1993), Thayer et al. (1994) and Rowe et al. (1994) transfer what seems to be a consensus value per statistical life (VSL) of $4 million[14] based on several literature reviews of hedonic wage studies, with different lower and upper bounds to represent the uncertainty of this estimate. In estimating an upper bound, Harrison et al. simply add 50 per cent to the value of their most likely estimate, a move that Thayer et al. comment is 'characteristic of the frustration of applied researchers in attempting to fairly represent the scientific literature' (p. X-6). Indeed, all of these moves reflect a struggle to summarize adequately and adjust original estimates for use in transfer.[15] As with any research, they also reflect judgement on the part of the transfer analyst, but the judgements are often not apparent, and the criteria for making them are even less so. Such situations, where there is a large volume of literature to summarize, and where the final estimates will be especially sensitive to the function transferred, call for a meta-analysis. The meta-analysis can provide both a more explicit basis for choosing a most likely estimate to transfer and a standard error to quantify its uncertainty. In this case, we offer a simple regression analysis of WTP estimates as a function of risk levels and the source of the original data.

Before turning to this analysis, however, we first briefly review the studies involved.[16] Of the approaches to valuing mortality, hedonic-wage studies are the most numerous. Early examples are Thaler and Rosen (1976), Brown (1980) and Arnould and Nichols (1983). These studies used actuarial risk estimates from the Society of Actuaries on total mortality risk, of which the relevant workplace risks are only one portion. The studies yield relatively low estimates for VSL, ranging from $860 000 in Thaler and Rosen to $1.6 million in Brown. (All estimates are in 1993 dollars.) Other early studies relied instead on the US Department of Labor's Bureau of Labor Statistics (BLS) data, the most prominent including Dillingham (1979, 1985), V.K. Smith (1983), Viscusi (1978,

1981), Olson (1981) and Leigh and Folsom (1984). These studies yield values that are considerably higher than those that use actuarial data, ranging from an average value of $1.05 million in Dillingham (1979) to $11 million in Leigh and Folsom.

Later wage-risk studies sought to provide more complete information, resolve some of the concerns that emerged in earlier studies, and use more relevant data (Marin and Psacharopoulos 1982; Low and McPheters 1983). The most recent wage-risk studies have abandoned BLS data altogether. Moore and Viscusi (1988a) estimated two VSLs, one using data from the National Institute of Occupational Safety and Health (NIOSH) and one using BLS data, to see how the newer NIOSH data affected the labour market estimates. The results are substantially different: $2.7 million from BLS data and $6.9 million from NIOSH data. Other studies using NIOSH data report higher estimates as well, including Viscusi and Moore's (1989) $8.6 million and Moore and Viscusi's (1990) $17.8 million. In one study, however, Kniesner and Leeth (1991) report a VSL of only $645 000 using NIOSH data.

Two major CV studies have also explored mortality risks. Gerking, de Hann and Schulze (1988) use a survey to elicit the value of avoiding a work-related fatality. They asked respondents to place themselves on a ladder representing risk levels with illustrative occupations, and asked them how much of a decrease in wages they would accept for a one-step decrease on the risk ladder. They estimated a VSL of $3.68 million. In the other major CV study, Jones-Lee, Hammerton and Philips (1985) estimated the value of avoiding death in an automobile accident. From a nation-wide survey of WTP values, they estimated VSL at $3.9 million. However, we do not include this second CV study in our meta-analysis because it does not measure the value of work-related fatalities as the other studies in our analysis do. The difference in the two types of risk is such that they are perceived differently and should be treated separately.

Two final studies, Blomquist (1979) and Dardis (1980), used the averting-behaviour approach to estimate the value of mortality risks. Blomquist (1979) estimated the premium that people are willing to pay to avoid death by using a seat belt in an automobile. His calculations included the amount of time required to find, untangle, and buckle a seat belt, and the number of trips taken in the car based on annual number of miles driven and distance to the workplace. The slightest difference in his estimation of eight seconds to buckle a seat belt and the actual time an individual takes to buckle a seat belt may result in a large difference in the estimated value of the individual's life. Differences in the number of trips taken in the car could also result in significantly higher or lower estimates of the value of life. Dardis (1980) estimated the value individuals place on life through the purchase of smoke detectors, basing her estimates on the annual cost of buying the smoke detector and replacing the batteries. Her estimates imply a VSL of $660 000. Again, this estimate is based on a small dollar amount – the cost of maintaining a smoke detector – a small change which could greatly influence the VSL estimate. We do not use these studies in the meta-analysis because of the problem of extrapolating from these small numbers.

The meta-analysis uses these 29 VSL studies, of which 28 are wage-risk studies and one is a CV study. The appropriate transfer value is the WTP for marginal changes in risk, rather than simply a VSL which may be a function of risk levels. The reported VSL estimates were converted into WTP estimates by

$$WTP = VSL \cdot RISK \qquad (5.19)$$

whenever risk information was available. These values, as well as RISK and the source of risk, for the 29 studies included in the analysis appear in Table 5.5.

We regress WTP as a function of RISK and other variables. The first step of the meta-analysis involved estimating a variety of model specifications to evaluate the fits of various functional forms and the robustness of predicted WTP with ordinary least squares (OLS).[17] Most models have adjusted R^2 values between 0.3 and 0.5. As expected, the coefficient on RISK is positive and significant in all models, suggesting that people require more compensation for greater risks. However, in non-linear models designed to explore the possibility of increasing *marginal* WTP for greater risk levels, the models often do not predict reasonable WTP values for relatively low levels of risk. To determine if predicted WTP values were 'reasonable', we convert them back into VSL estimates, finding the implied VSL to be much larger than the range of $3 million and $10 million found in the studies. This is a consequence of extrapolating to low risk levels that lie outside the range of data from the studies. Specifically, the transfer context requires transferring estimates for mortality risk levels from particulates of about one in ten million, whereas the original studies generally have a mean risk level around three deaths per 10 000. Accordingly, transferring these estimates may be inappropriate.

Moreover, the WTP values for the lowest risk exposures appear to be approximately linear in risk, and these models had the best fit. Because these low levels of risk are of most interest, we linearized the functional form between risk and WTP. The specification also includes a dummy variable for all data sources other than BLS data. Algebraically, the

Table 5.5 Mortality studies used in meta-analysis

Study	Value of a statistical life (1993 $)	Risk level[a]	Source of sample[b]	Basis for calculating risk[c]	WTP (CD) (1993 $)	Type of study[d]
Dillingham (1979)	$1 050 000	1.7	QES	BLS	$178.50	WR
Dillingham (1985)	$7 604 316	0.83	QES	BLS	$631.16	WR
Gegax, Gerking and Schulze (1985)	$2 155 200	10.1	n/a	BLS	$2176.75	WR
Gegax, Gerking and Schulze (1985)	$8 625 000	4.56	n/a	BLS	$3933.00	WR
Gegax, Gerking and Schulze (1985)	$2 527 800	8.23	n/a	BLS	$2080.38	WR
Leigh and Folsom (1984)	$10 190 058	1.42	PSID	BLS	$1446.99	WR
Leigh and Folsom (1984)	$11 056 874	1.26	QES	BLS	$1393.17	WR
Moore and Viscusi (1988a)	$2 703 840	0.52	PSID	BLS	$140.60	WR
Moore and Viscusi (1988b)	$8 253 000	0.589	QES	BLS	$486.10	WR
Olson (1981)	$10 672 200	0.9508	CPS	BLS	$1014.71	WR
R.S. Smith (1974)	$7 900 000	1.25	Industry/census	BLS	$987.50	WR
R.S. Smith (1976)	$5 100 000	1.25	CPS	BLS	$637.50	WR
V.K. Smith (1983)	$5 043 500	3.1	n/a	BLS	$1563.49	WR
Viscusi (1978)	$5 249 290	1.182	SWC	BLS	$620.47	WR
Viscusi (1981)	$7 100 000	1.04	PSID	BLS	$738.40	WR
Kniesner and Leeth (1991) – US	$645 186	4.36	CPS	NIOSH	$281.30	WR
Moore and Viscusi (1988a)	$6 857 850	0.79	PSID	NIOSH	$541.77	WR
Moore and Viscusi (1990)	$17 800 000	1.0	PSID	NIOSH	$1780.00	WR
Viscusi and Moore (1989)	$8 600 000	0.783	PSID	NIOSH	$673.38	WR
Arnould and Nichols (1983)	$946 708	10.0	US Census	Actuarial	$946.71	WR

Brown (1980)	$1 600 000	20.0	NLSYM	Actuarial	$3200.00	WR
Thaler and Rosen (1976)	$859 800	10.0	SEO	Actuarial	$859.80	WR
Consineau, Lacroix and Girard (1988)	$4 243 067	0.764	Canada	Foreign	$324.17	WR
Kneisner and Leeth (1991) – Australia	$3 583 723	1.4	Australia Mfg	Foreign	$501.72	WR
Kniesner and Leeth (1991) – Japan	$6 333 850	0.32	Japan Mfg	Foreign	$202.68	WR
Marin and Psacharopoulos (1982)	$3 100 000	2.0	UK Census	Foreign	$620.00	WR
Low and McPheters (1982)	$1 157 158	3.27	n/a	FBI	$378.39	WR
Butler (1983)	$1 200 000	0.5	SC WC	SC WC	$60.00	WR
Gerking, de Haan and Schulze (1988)	$3 676 100	2.5	Work fatality	Perceived risk	$919.03	CV

Notes: [a] Deaths per 10 000

[b] KEY:
QES = Quality of Employment Survey
CPS = Current Population Survey
NLSYM = National Longitudinal Survey of Young Men
PSID = Panel Study of Income Dynamics
SC WC = South Carolina workers' compensation data
SWC = Survey of Working Conditions
SEO = Survey of Economic Opportunity

[c] KEY:
BLS = Bureau of Labor Statistics
NIOSH = National Institute of Occupational Safety and Health
Actuarial = Society of Actuaries
SC WC = South Carolina workers' compensation data

[d] KEY:
WR = wage risk
CV = contingent valuation

Source: Viscusi (1993); Fisher, Chestnut and Violette (1989).

model is

$$\text{WTA} = \beta_1(\text{RISK}) + \beta_2(\text{RISK} * \text{NON-BLS}) \qquad (5.20)$$

where RISK equals the number of deaths per 10 000 people. It is important to control data sources for several reasons. Although one non-BLS data source, NIOSH data, has become widely accepted in recent years, NIOSH data seem to show inconsistent relationships between risk levels and VSL values. Furthermore, studies using BLS data generally predict higher CD values than studies using non-BLS data.

Note the significance of assuming a linear functional form in risk. The assumption is consistent with the conclusions of Miller (1990) that there seems to be no relationship between marginal WTP and risk levels. Accordingly, our estimates essentially reduce to a simple VSL that is invariant to risk levels. Algebraically, note that after dividing both sides by RISK, Equation (5.20) becomes

$$\text{WTP/RISK} \equiv \text{VSL} = \beta_1 + \beta_2(\text{NON-BLS}) \qquad (5.21)$$

Thus, from an OLS perspective, the only thing differentiating this analysis from a simple mean is the fact that we are controlling for the data source of the original studies.

Because of the sensitivity of the OLS results to outliers, however, we also employ a robust regression technique known as least trimmed squares (LTS). Least trimmed squares uses a genetic algorithm to systematically remove outlying observations from the model. Through a complex process of random sampling, LTS removes observations in order to minimize the sum of the m smallest squared residuals:

$$m = \left(\frac{n}{2}\right) + \left(\frac{p+1}{2}\right) \qquad (5.22)$$

where n equals the number of observations and p equals the number of independent variables (Rousseeuw and Leroy 1987). Compared to the OLS model, the LTS model provides a better fit and more reasonable predicted WTP values at low levels of risk.

Table 5.6 presents regression results for the linear models estimated using OLS and LTS. By removing outliers, LTS provides an excellent fit of the data, with an adjusted R^2 of 0.98. Figure 5.4 presents the regression results graphically. All models reflect the linear form of Equation (5.24). We show regression lines for NON-BLS = 0 and NON-BLS = 1. The OLS regression that sets NON-BLS equal to 0 is almost identical to the LTS regression in which NON-BLS equals 1, providing some central tendency in the models to use as a basis for a transfer.

Table 5.6   *Regression results of risk-valuation models*

	OLS	LTS
β_1	332.86	880.92
	(52.32)	(34.59)
β_2	−190.48	−517.38
	(60.39)	(73.44)
$\beta_1 + \beta_2$	142.38	363.54
	(30.16)	(64.79)
Number of observations	29	
Adjusted R^2	0.287	

Note: Standard errors are shown in parentheses.

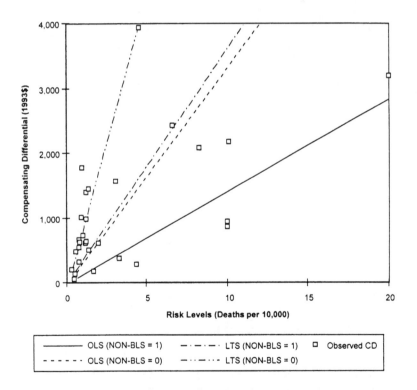

Figure 5.4   Risk-valuation functions

An examination of the linear OLS and LTS models' residuals also provides information on how well each predicts WTP. The residuals reflect the difference between the observed CD values and the estimated regression line. Figure 5.5 shows smoothed fits of the residuals for risk levels less than 2 (per 10 000 people) associated with the linear OLS and LTS models. The residuals of the LTS model are almost perfectly symmetric around zero at low risks, whereas the OLS residuals are biased upward. It appears then that the LTS model is more appropriate for low levels of risk. We thus use the LTS model for this transfer. With the NON-BLS variable set to 1 – one of the central models in Figure 5.5 – the VSL estimate is then about \$3.6 million, with a 90 per cent confidence interval between \$0.4 and \$6.8 million.

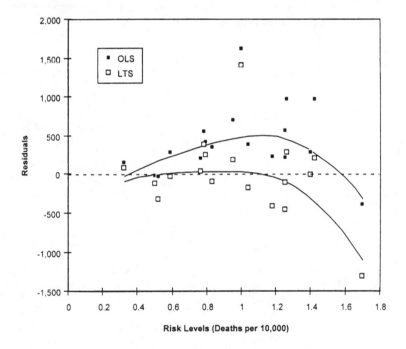

Figure 5.5   Residuals for OLS and its models

Transferring this value requires two caveats. First, it is based on the workplace risk studies that, as noted in Section 5.2, may not be appropriate for environmental risks. Second, and also noted previously, transferring a single VSL estimate neglects likely differences between WTP of young, healthy workers and the elderly, who are more at risk from air pollution. Moore and Viscusi (1988b) find that WTP is higher if more expected life years would be lost, and Desvousges et al. (1996) and Johnson et al. (1998) offer preliminary evidence that it is lower for people experiencing limitations on their activity and ability to care for themselves.[18] The first caveat probably creates a downward bias in the transfer, the second an upward one. Still, these wage-risk studies offer the best evidence at present for inferring the value of mortality risk.

5.4   ILLUSTRATIVE CALCULATIONS OF WTP

Actually calculating the WTP for the different effects is a relatively simple matter of multiplying the magnitude of predicted effects times the per unit willingness to pay. The previous chapter indicated that the sample receptor would experience an annual increase of 9.37 cough episodes; 0.170 cases of emphysema, chronic bronchitis or asthma; and 0.639 expected deaths as a result of the urban scenario. As shown in Table 5.2, the predicted cough episodes last an average of 2.2 days and are associated with a 0.318 index score, giving a central value of $76.38 per case, using the estimated function. Multiplying this value by 9.37 episodes yields a cost of $716 at the sample receptor from the urban scenario. Similarly, the central value of avoiding a case of emphysema, chronic bronchitis or asthma was estimated to be $8900 from the COI studies, for a cost of $1513 at the sample receptor, and the central value of a statistical life is $3.6 million, for a cost of $2.323 million. These reflect the most likely values, but again, actual calculations employ Monte Carlo simulations that draw the per case values from a statistical distribution.

NOTES

1. The previous step involved both looking backward to match the previous link and looking forward to match the next link. Because valuation is generally the last step in a benefit–cost analysis, we may now concentrate only on the backward-looking direction.
2. To the best of our knowledge, only Magat, Viscusi and Huber (1988), Viscusi, Magat and Huber (1991), and Krupnick and Cropper (1992) have actually measured people's values for morbidity risks. These studies use conjoint analysis, employing iterative questions that present respondents with a series of pairwise comparisons to test their marginal rate of substitution between morbidity risks and either money or other risks. Magat, Viscusi and Huber (1988) studied people's WTP for household cleaners that are less likely to cause burns, create chlorine gas or poison children. Viscusi, Magat and Huber (1991) and Krupnick and Cropper (1992) studied people's marginal rate of substitution for risks of contracting chronic bronchitis relative to both dollars and another risk, the risk of dying in an automobile accident. But these studies are not

adequate for valuing the many health effects that can result from air pollution, nor are they suitable for estimating the health-state utility function that we use to quantify the relationship between health state and WTP (Section 5.3).

3. In actuality, both interpretations are right. Air quality probably changes the entire density over potential future health states.

4. See also Gerking and Stanley (1986) and Berger et al. (1987). For overviews, see Smith (1991), Cropper and Freeman (1991) and Freeman (1993).

5. This approach differs from other models, including Harrington and Portney, which quantify health in terms of the number of sick days of an unspecified severity.

6. Although we say this is the 'total value' of air quality, the model focuses solely on an analysis of health. Air quality may have value for other reasons as well.

7. It is important to distinguish between the role of COI studies when used to measure the value of something such as air quality, as we are doing, and when used to value medical care itself. The value of air quality is partly related to the medical costs that air pollution incurs, something that COI studies can measure well. The total value of medical care is the consumer surplus or, in Figure 5.2, the triangle between the demand curve and the price, $P_m^c AP_m^s$, something that COI studies cannot measure, regardless of whether they net out third-party payments.

8. The study by Berger et al. is based on the Tolley et al. work.

9. See Desvousges et al. (1995a,b) for a more extensive review of these studies.

10. Studies also include Bush, Fanshel and Chen (1972); Bush et al. (1973); Patrick, Bush and Chen (1973); Kaplan, Bush and Berry (1976, 1978); Kaplan and Bush (1982); Kaplan and Ernst (1983); Kaplan and Anderson (1988, 1990); Oregon Health Services Commission (1991); Kaplan et al. (1995).

11. We would like to thank Dev Pathak, Zafar Hakim and Josephine Mauskopf for their help with this task.

12. Because we cannot construct QWB scores with complete accuracy, the use of QWB score as an independent variable in our regression model may introduce an errors-in-variables problem. This would cause attenuation in the estimate for the QWB coefficient.

13. Because the functional form assumes proportional exponential errors, the standard confidence-interval calculations produced very large upper-bound estimates that were inconsistent with the data. To compute confidence intervals, we bootstrapped the error distribution for each observation. Specifically, we resampled the sample errors 1000 times for each observation to approximate the error distributions. We then removed the 5th and 95th percentile values from each distribution and averaged these values across all observation to obtain a mean lower and upper bound. The mean lower bound adjustment equals 0.33 times $\hat{y}$, and the mean upper bound adjustment equals 2.34 times $\hat{y}$, where $\hat{y}$ = the dependent variable.

14. In 1990 or 1992 dollars, depending on the study.

15. See also Miller (1990) for an example of an attempt to make systematic adjustments to the original estimates before finding an average value. Miller argues that after certain adjustments, the original estimates for VSL converge to about \$2.4 million.

16. For more thorough treatments, see Viscusi (1993) and Fisher, Chestnut and Violette (1989).

17. Regressions weighted by sample size were also estimated. The weighting had little effect on parameter estimates and predicted WTP values.

18. These studies are based on a stated-preferences survey of Canadian respondents. The commodity was described as a relatively small increase (six months to two years) in expected longevity. Preliminary estimates indicate much smaller values than labour-market studies. Respondents were also willing to pay very little for life extensions with severe physical limitations.

6. Other effects: agriculture, materials and visibility*

In this chapter, we turn to transfers of three additional kinds of welfare losses: agriculture, materials and visibility. Just as we did for the analysis of health damages, for each of these effects we start where the analysis left off at the end of Chapter 3, having estimated the change in environmental quality for the scenarios. Following the linkages in the transfer methodology, the next steps involve estimating the changes in services and then the value of these changes. Section 6.1 discusses the agricultural damages (or benefits) of a decrease (or increase) in air quality. Estimating these damages is complicated by the relationship between available concentration-response data and the optimizing behaviour of farmers, as influenced by government farm policy. Section 6.2 discusses materials damages, which include both the corrosion of materials and the soiling of surfaces. Finally, Section 6.3 discusses visibility damages. Because of the limited available information, the last two sections receive considerably shorter treatment than that given to either health or agricultural benefits and costs.

6.1 AGRICULTURAL EFFECTS

Any defensible estimate of the external effects of electricity generation on welfare must include the cost of damage to agriculture. As we demonstrate in this section, agriculture is a key industry in our study area, and agricultural productivity is sensitive to changes in air quality.

In this section, we present a conceptual model for measuring the welfare impacts of agricultural losses due to air pollutants and discuss the modelling choices for our transfer. We provide some background on agriculture in our study area and explain our choice of crops. Then we present the concentration-response functions we used to link air pollution to crop yields. Finally, we examine how changes in crop yields caused by air pollution might affect the behaviour of farmers, further affecting economic welfare.

* This chapter was written with Sheila A. Martin.

Conceptual Approach

At first, it may seem that valuing agricultural losses from changes in the level of air quality involves a relatively straightforward two-step application of the disaggregate transfer methodology: estimate changes in agricultural production from transferred concentration-response functions and multiply by market price.[1] This approach has been employed by Heck et al. (1984), Adams, Crocker and Thanavibulchai (1982), and in other previous transfer studies. However, this two-step approach neglects the potential behavioural changes of farmers that can accompany changes in environmental quality and the corresponding changes in agricultural productivity. Farmers may change the mix of inputs of agricultural production (for example, fertilizers) or substitute among crops with different responses to environmental quality. Furthermore, farmers' decisions are complicated by government farm programmes. Thus, like health effects, the linkage between air quality and crop yields has both physical and behavioural dimensions. While crops have a natural, biological response to air quality, the behaviour of farmers who plant and tend crops also determines the ultimate impact of changes in environmental quality on agriculture. This is similar to the distinction between epidemiological and toxicological studies of health effects. The available studies quantifying the linkages between air quality and crop yields are analogous to toxicological studies; they measure yield changes in controlled chambers or experimental fields rather than statistically across real farms.

To incorporate these considerations, we perform a transfer in three conceptual steps. First, we transfer available dose-response functions to estimate the change in agricultural productivity. However, actual output is not likely to fall by the same proportion because farmers may switch to new crops or respond to incentives of farm programmes. To capture these effects, we next transfer a crop-supply model based on the domestic crop models developed by the Food and Agricultural Policy Research Institute (FAPRI). This model has been used to assess the potential impact of a number of agriculture-related policies, including an analysis of changes in the secondary ambient standards for ozone (Kopp and Krupnick 1987). The model includes a crop-supply specification that is based on maximization of the farmer's expected net returns per acre, given forecasted changes in technology, available government crop programmes and variable costs of production per acre. While allowing farmers to switch to new crops and react optimally to the incentives of farm programmes, the model does not allow for the possibility that farmers may also change the mix of inputs in the production process (for example, adding more fertilizer or labour).

In the third step, we estimate the economic value of these supply changes. We assume that agricultural demand is perfectly elastic, so that prices do not change as a result of changes in air quality. That is, we assume farmers are price takers. This assumption allows us to quantify costs and benefits completely on the supply side. Figure 6.1 provides a conceptual overview of the supply-side welfare effects of changes in yield of a single crop due to air pollution. As declines in air quality affect agricultural productivity, the supply curve shifts from S to S'. Both supply curves incorporate the effects of government farm programmes on farmers' optimizing behaviour. Thus the area of welfare loss is the shaded area between the two supply curves, which is the change in the farmers' producers' surplus.

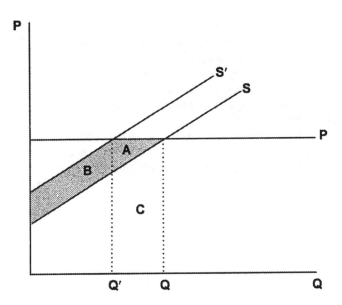

Figure 6.1   Changes in producers' surplus from declines in agricultural productivity

For national or large regional effects, the price-taking assumption would be unrealistic, with the price elasticity of demand for most food products estimated to be between −0.039 and −1.39 (Huang 1985) and several studies showing that changes in consumer welfare may account for a large portion of total welfare changes (Adams, Glyer and McCarl 1988). However, the assumption is more realistic for our study area. Farm products are relatively homogeneous, and a single producer, or even an area's entire group of producers, do not usually produce enough of the total product to influence the stocks available, and, therefore, national price. This assumption is probably the most unrealistic when considering hay, whose price can sometimes vary significantly among regions. In assuming price-taking behaviour, even for hay, we may underestimate the magnitude of benefits or costs from air pollution levels.

Background to Agriculture in the Study Area

Agriculture is one of the most important industries in our study area (Minnesota, western Wisconsin, and south-eastern South Dakota). According to the US Department of Agriculture (USDA), Minnesota ranked sixth in the nation in 1991 in cash receipts from farming for all commodities, with total receipts of $6.9 billion. Wisconsin ranked ninth, with total receipts of $5.3 billion. South Dakota contributes a significant percentage of the nation's supply of oats, wheat, corn and hay. Because agriculture is so important to these states' economies, and because agricultural production is sensitive to air quality, the cost of damages to agriculture are an important component of external effects of electricity generation.

Our assessment of the agricultural damages caused by air pollution focuses on damages to field crops. Although a significant amount of the revenue from agriculture in Minnesota, Wisconsin and South Dakota comes from dairy farming, very few studies have evaluated the effect of air pollution on livestock, and concentration-response functions are not available for cattle and milk production. Decisions about which crops to model were based on information about the importance of each crop to the regional economy and the sensitivity of crops to changes in air pollution. Choosing the crops that are most important to the economy and most sensitive to air pollution ensures capturing the majority of the agricultural welfare losses.

Table 6.1 shows that corn, soybeans and hay are the three most significant crops in all three states. In Minnesota and South Dakota, we estimate damages for corn, soybeans, hay and wheat. These four crops represented about 87 per cent of the total value of field crops in Minnesota, and about 90 per cent of the field crops in South Dakota in 1991. While the value of sugar beet production in Minnesota is greater than wheat, there is no concentration-response information available for sugar beets. Wisconsin damages include corn, soybeans, hay and potatoes. These four crops represented about 94 per cent of the total value of field crops in 1991 and about 80 per cent of total crop value. The next three highest-ranked crops in 1991 were cranberries, sweet corn and snap beans.

Table 6.1   Value of production and relative rankings: primary field crops in Minnesota, Wisconsin and South Dakota, 1991

Crop	Value of production ($1000)			Rank		
	Minnesota	Wisconsin	S. Dakota	Minnesota	Wisconsin	S. Dakota
Corn for grain	1 620 000	875 840	519 480	1	1	1
Corn for silage	—[a]	103 740	—[a]	—[a]	4	—[a]
Soybeans	1 064 249	122 430	310 846	2	3	3
Hay (including alfalfa)	529 895	508 200	349 958	3	2	2
Sugar beet	248 074	N/A	N/A	4	N/A	N/A
Wheat	214 752	16 825	96 175	5	13	4
Potatoes	78 875	103 574	7 565	6	5	9
Sunflowers	47 370	N/A	43 301	8	N/A	6
Barley	76 563	4 968	31 216	7	20	7
Oats	26 220	31 800	45 815	10	9	5

Notes: [a] No price available.

Sources: Minnesota Agricultural Statistics Service (1992); South Dakota Agricultural Statistics Service (1993); Wisconsin Department of Agriculture, Trade, and Consumer Protection (1992).

However, no concentration-response functions for cranberries or snap beans are available.

Estimating the Physical Linkages between Air Quality and Crop Yields

In our discussion of the agricultural effects of air quality, we focus on the three pollutants that have documented effects on agriculture: ozone (O_3), sulphur dioxide (SO_2) and nitrogen dioxide (NO_2). Previous research has shown that 90 per cent of crop damage from air pollution is caused by ozone alone or in conjunction with SO_2 or NO_2 (Heck et al. 1982). The most significant source of concentration-response functions for these crops and pollutants is the National Crop Loss Assessment Network (NCLAN). NCLAN was formed in 1980 to examine the impact of ozone and SO_2 on major agricultural crops. NCLAN researchers conducted 41 studies on 14 crops between 1980 and 1986. After the 41 studies had been completed, the data were combined by statisticians who developed an average dose-response function for each pollutant and crop by pooling the data from the relevant studies. These pooled data are good candidates for a transfer because they do not require assumptions about the specific variety of seed that will be planted in the study area. Thus we transferred these pooled NCLAN-based dose-response functions to quantify the effects of air pollutants on yield for all crops except potatoes, which were not covered by the NCLAN studies.

A small number of other studies have also quantified dose-response functions for some crops (Pratt 1982; Brewer and Ashcroft 1982; Oshima et al. 1976; Leung, Reed and Geng 1982; Klein et al. 1978; Krupa and Nosal 1989; Krupa 1987). Transferring only the NCLAN studies means using the 'best-study' approach to transfer in this instance. The NCLAN results are based on the pooled samples of many studies that followed a consistent methodology. Incorporating one or two additional studies for each crop, based on different methodologies, would provide only a marginal amount of additional information. Thus the 'best-study' approach appears more appropriate than meta-analysis in transferring agricultural dose-response information.

To transfer the NCLAN data, two options are available. Both Kopp, Vaughan and Hazilla (1984) and Sommerville et al. (1989) analysed NCLAN data and estimated dose-response functions. While the former research has some notable strengths, the latter uses the entire set of 41 studies rather than a subset of the data, and offers an 'average' function for all cultivar varieties instead of separate functions for different cultivars, which would be difficult to transfer. Accordingly, the Sommerville et al. analysis is used for the transfer.

Sommerville et al. used a Weibull response model to fit the pooled data to dose-response functions. The Weibull distribution, or a binomial logistic, accurately captures the plateau-type responses typical of dose-response data compared with other functional forms. Taking the example of a function used to quantify the effects of ozone, the dose-response function can be represented as

$$Y = \alpha \exp\left\{-\left[\left(\frac{O_3}{\omega}\right)\lambda\right]\right\} + \varepsilon \tag{6.1}$$

where
  Y = yield (in kg/ha);
  O_3 = the seasonal ozone mean (in ppm/hour)
  α = intercept, or hypothetical yield when $O_3 = 0$;
  ω = parameter that represents the O_3 dose at which yield is reduced to 0.37α;
  λ = dimensionless parameter controlling the shape of the O_3 response curve; and
  ε = model error.

In some cases, the α parameter was estimated as a function of other variables that might influence yield, including the level of SO_2. In this case, the equation was fitted to the model as shown above, with a more specific specification for the intercept:

$$\alpha = a + b(SO_2) \tag{6.2}$$

where
  a = intercept, or the yield level when SO_2 and O_3 are equal to 0; and
  SO_2 = the four-hour seasonal mean, in ppm/hour.

Note that with this specification, the relative yield from a change in the O_3 level is independent of a. Thus the impact of O_3 on yield is not affected by changes in the level of SO_2.

Table 6.2 summarizes the Sommerville et al. (1989) dose-response functions for the different crops. The table indicates the number of NCLAN studies (not data points) upon which the dose-response function was based and the parameter estimates. The model intercepts (the value of production when SO_2 and $O_3 = 0$) vary by cultivar, and sometimes by moisture and stress. While actual yield estimates are sensitive to this intercept, the relative yield, which we used as an input to the agricultural-supply model, is not affected by the intercept.

In each of the NCLAN studies except wheat, the crops were exposed to a range of ozone concentrations for twelve-hour periods during each day

Table 6.2 *Concentration-response functions from Sommerville et al. (1989)*

Effect	No. of NCLAN studies		Concentration-response function (Sommerville et al. 1989)
	Ozone	SO$_2$	
Corn	2	1	$Y = [12\,530 - (251 * SO_2)] * \exp\left\{-\left[\left(\dfrac{O_3}{0.124}\right)^{2.83}\right]\right\}$
Wheat	4	1	$Y = [5010 - (57 * SO_2)] * \exp\left\{-\left[\left(\dfrac{O_3}{0.136}\right)^{2.56}\right]\right\}$
Soybeans	14	4	$Y = [4311 - (1964 * SO_2)] * \exp\left\{-\left[\left(\dfrac{O_3}{0.107}\right)^{1.58}\right]\right\}$
Alfalfa hay	3	1	$Y = [15\,521 + (7.5 * SUMSO_2)] * \exp\left\{-\left[\left(\dfrac{O_3}{0.178}\right)^{2.07}\right]\right\}$

Notes: *Y* is yield; SO$_2$ is four-hour seasonal mean in ppm/hour; SUMSO$_2$ is the seasonal exposure sum in ppm/hour; and O$_3$ is the twelve-hour seasonal mean in ppm/hour.

during the growing season. For wheat, the plants were exposed to ozone concentrations for seven hours each day. For the SO_2 experiments, the plants were exposed to a range of SO_2 concentration for four hours each day. In each of these experiments, and in the equations reported in Table 6.2, ozone and SO_2 concentrations are measured as the mean twelve-hour, seven-hour or four-hour exposures, in ppm per hour, except for SO_2 exposure to hay, which was measured as the seasonal cumulative exposure in ppm per hour.

In the functions reported, the sensitivity of yield to ozone increases with higher ozone levels, although it is slightly less sensitive to ozone at higher levels of SO_2. The sensitivity of yield to SO_2 is linear in SO_2, but similarly diminishes at higher ozone levels. The functions also indicate that crops are likely to be far more sensitive to ozone than to SO_2, with soybeans being the most sensitive. Note finally that Sommerville et al. predict that alfalfa yields will *increase* with increasing SO_2 levels. While some other studies support this finding (Krupa and Nosal 1989 and Krupa 1987), others do not (Brewer and Ashcroft 1982). Given these ambivalent findings, it is prudent to take a more cautious approach and not transfer alfalfa effects for SO_2.

NCLAN did not study the effect of pollution on potatoes. However, Foster et al. (1983) estimated the following linear regression model based on a sample size of 16 potato plants:

$$Y = 1530 - 15.8 * O_3 \qquad (6.3)$$

where Y is yield and O_3 is the sum of all hourly ozone concentrations over a 91-day growing season. The authors also tested for the effects of SO_2 and for an interaction term between ozone and SO_2 and found that they did not significantly affect yields. In other research, Rowe and Chestnut (1985) found a negative but statistically insignificant relationship, but Clarke, Henninger and Brennan (1983) support the finding that potatoes are sensitive to ozone concentrations, although their use of an anti-oxidant for the control group may not be ideal for a transfer study. The transfer uses the Foster et al. study to quantify an effect of ozone on potatoes and assumes there is no effect of SO_2.

Evidence of a relationship between NO_2 and crop yields is far weaker than that of ozone and SO_2. Although some studies have found a relationship, they examine only very high levels of exposure such as above 0.5 ppm for durations longer than one hour. For comparison, the annual average NO_2 levels in our policy area range from 0.005 to 0.024 ppm, with the highest one-hour urban concentration being 0.108 ppm. In a study of exposures closer to ambient levels, Irving,

Miller and Xerikos (1982) evaluated the effect of NO_2 on soybeans, exposing them to concentrations from 0.12 to 0.37 ppm, but found no significant effect on yield. Heck and Tingey (1979) found that corn is tolerant of NO_2-induced foliar injury, and Elkiey, Ormrod and Marie (1988) found no effect on potatoes exposed to 0.1 ppm of NO_2 for 15 days. While Sinn and Pell (1984) do report an effect on potatoes, they use concentrations twice as high as those found in the transfer context and do not report a concentration-response function. Given the findings of most of these studies, there appears to be insufficient basis for quantifying agricultural externalities from NO_2 pollution in the case study.

Estimating Behavioural Responses to Air Quality Changes and Economic Benefits and Costs

As noted above, the next two steps of the transfer process for agriculture are to estimate the final changes in output after allowing farmers to adjust their behaviour and then to estimate the welfare losses of this change. These two steps were estimated together in spreadsheets supplied to us by FAPRI, thereby taking into account the market distortions caused by agricultural policy as of 1994, when the case study was conducted.[2] Commodity programmes affect incentives for producing each crop and therefore alter the relationship between changes in yield and changes in supply. Kopp and Krupnick (1987) point out that this policy-driven market distortion has largely been ignored by previous analyses of the economic impact of ozone control. To explain how these programmes affect the supply of commodities, a brief description of the commodity programmes – as of 1994 – is provided in the following paragraphs.

Of the five crops considered in this analysis, only corn and wheat are directly affected by commodity programmes. However, the supply of other crops can be affected by these policies because a farmer's allocation of acreage among crops depends on the profitability of all crops, including the programme crops. Furthermore, participation in these programmes is voluntary, and farmers decide how to allocate acres based on the profitability of participating in each programme.[3]

The target price is a key factor in determining the impact of the corn and wheat programmes. Regardless of how they choose between the programme options of selling on the market or forfeiting their crop to the government, farmers receive a deficiency payment equal to the target price minus the price they receive. However, farmers may only enrol specific parcels of land, called base acres, in these commodity programmes. Similarly, farmers have a limited amount of production that is eligible under the programme.

To control expenditures, the US government established the Acreage Reduction Program (ARP). Under the ARP, the government forecasts supply and price to decide how much of the base acreage must be 'set aside'. Farmers must comply with the ARP in return for single participation in the programme. Similarly, in an effort to control the oversupply of corn, the '0–92' plan pays volunteers to keep their eligible acres out of production. The volunteers are paid 92 per cent of the deficiency payments to which they are entitled on their eligible acres.

The soybean programme is somewhat simpler than the corn and wheat programmes. A marketing loan programme provides soybean farmers with credit at planting time. If the market price is lower than the loan rate farmers pay back at the market price and pocket the difference between the loan rate and the market price. There is no deficiency payment, and there are no payment limitations on these marketing loan payments.

While not strictly a commodity programme, the US Conservation Reserve Program (CRP) affects the supply of commodities by altering farmers' incentives for planting crops. Landowners participating in the CRP agree not to produce on highly erodable land in return for an annual rental payment. Aside from the obvious opportunity cost of lost production, participation in the CRP carries an additional cost: each acre of land in the CRP reduces the farm's aggregate acreage base over the ten years of the CRP contract.

Within the context of these government programmes, the FAPRI modelling system estimates the economic impact of simulated changes in the ambient air levels of the pollutants under study. The model establishes a baseline value of production for each crop by county for 1993 through 2006, the year the scenarios are assumed to be implemented. After the baseline is established, the model is estimated again under the conditions of the simulations. The simulated changes in ambient air quality for the year 2006 lead to changes in the projected yield, which affect the other equations in the model. The model calculates the value of production and deficiency payments by county under the simulated conditions and calculates the changes from the baseline projections.

The FAPRI US crops model is a simultaneous system of equations that determines the supply, demand and prices of 11 commodities.[4] The US crops model is linked to the other models in the FAPRI system by several key variables appearing in more than one model. Using these relationships, a simultaneous solution of the FAPRI modelling system is obtained by iteration.

On the supply side, the US crops model assumes that farmers base their planting decisions on a comparison of the net returns they expect to receive under various alternatives. These alternatives include planting acres in various crops and participating in government programmes that require acres to be idled. Acres are divided among various categories, including production and idling under the various programmes. All the policy variables relevant to the expected net return from programme participation are included in the model. Once the number of acres in each category is determined, crop yield per acre is determined as a function of government policy parameters such as target prices, idled acreage, a time trend to denote technological progress, and other factors.

The demand side of the US crops model includes all major categories of domestic demand, including feed use, exports, food use, ending stocks and seed use. Feed use is determined by livestock numbers and prices and by the prices of alternative feeds. Export demand is determined by other crop prices and by hundreds of other factors included in the FAPRI world trade model. Food use is determined by commodity prices, consumer expenditures and population. Seed use is linked to area planted. Equilibrium prices in the US crops model are determined by equating total supply and total demand in an iterative process.

As explained earlier, the conceptually correct measure of changes in welfare due to changes in environmental quality would be the change in producers' surplus. As previously shown in Figure 6.1, the shift in the supply curve from S to S' leads to a reduction in quantity supplied from Q to Q'. This reduction incorporates behavioural responses of farmers to changes in yield, as well as supply responses due to government crops programmes. The sum of Areas A and B is conceptually the appropriate measure of the change in welfare in a single crop market following from a change in yield.

However, the FAPRI CLAIMS model calculates changes in the value of production, which is equal to the sum of Areas A and C. Thus, although the model incorporates appropriate assumptions about changes in resource allocation to estimate changes in the production of each crop and its value, it does not take the next appropriate step by correcting for differences in the cost of producing the alternative combinations of crops.

The divergence between the value of production and producers' surplus (difference between Areas B and C in Figure 6.1) depends, in part, on the elasticity of the supply curve. Change in the value of production would be the appropriate welfare measure if farmers have no behavioural response to the change in agricultural productivity – that is, if farmers did not switch to new crops as a result of the yield change. In that case, the farmers' lost welfare would be equal to changes in the value of the crops that farmers can produce, *given a fixed allocation of inputs*.

The magnitude of the difference between the change in producers' surplus and the change in the value of production also depends on the relative costs of the farmers' different production choices. If the mix of crops chosen prior to the supply shift costs the same as the mix of crops chosen after the supply shift, then the sum over all crops of changes in the value of production will equal the total change in producers' surplus.

To arrive at a more defensible estimate of the welfare impact of the changes in production, it may be appropriate to apply a portion of FAPRI's US Farm Income model. This model calculates net farm income by subtracting farm expenses from the value of production. However, these expenses are calibrated on a national level and may need substantial adjustment to be applicable to a small region such as our study area.

Because the yield effects may lead to a change in deficiency payments, the total change in the value of production is not borne by farmers, and the FAPRI modelling system is capable of estimating the actual change in farmer income after adjusting for such payments. However, government deficiency payments may be considered transfers of welfare from tax-payers to farmers. A larger view of welfare should include all US taxpayers, not just farmers.[5] Using this perspective, it is not appropriate to subtract government deficiency payments from total damages. In principle, this tends to make estimates of agricultural damages slightly larger than if they were strictly limited to changes in farm income. In practice, deficiency payments are a small fraction of damages.

Illustrative Calculations

Estimated background concentrations and deltas for ozone and SO_2 are used to predict the ratio of yields after the change in concentrations to those before. An example calculation for corn yields may help to illustrate the concentration-response functions. Suppose a rural receptor has an ambient ozone level of 0.025 ppm (averaged over the peak 12 hours of each day during the corn-growing season). Suppose further that the change in ozone levels at the receptor for this averaging period is 0.001 ppm. Using the equation from the first line of Table 6.2, and cancelling the constant terms, the relative yield is:

$$\text{Relative yield} = \frac{\exp\left[-\left(\dfrac{0.025 + 0.001}{0.124}\right)^{2.83}\right]}{\exp\left[-\left(\dfrac{0.025}{0.124}\right)^{2.83}\right]} = 0.998738 \qquad (6.4)$$

This relative yield is then entered in the FAPRI model to predict the change in participation in farm programmes and the final change in the value of production.

6.2 MATERIALS EFFECTS

Materials effects can be divided into two types: the accumulation of dirt, ash and dust on surfaces, generally described as soiling; and the corrosive effects on the materials. Although the effects of PM on soiling and dirtying surfaces are a straightforward physical process, the effect of sulphur dioxide (SO_2) and other pollutants on materials can be more complex. SO_2, ozone and nitrogen oxides (NO_x) all contribute to the deterioration of structural materials, probably in that order of importance. However, synergistic effects among them and other factors such as climate can make isolating the partial effects difficult. For example, NO_x can exacerbate the effects of SO_2 on such materials as steel (Acres International Limited 1991) and limestone (Lindquist et al. 1988). Despite these difficulties, researchers have estimated the effects of pollution on materials in chambers or under ambient conditions, and have done so for a variety of materials, including paint, metal, stone, brick, cement, fabrics and glass.

As in other cases, the work done at the link between air quality and effects on materials services must match up with the link between materials services and willingness to pay. To think about these relationships, it is useful to employ a household production model as we did with health effects. Specifically, households combine air quality with detergents and other products to produce cleanliness (Courant and Porter 1981; Watson and Jaksch 1982; Harford 1984). As with the conceptual model for health valuation, willingness to pay (WTP) for air quality in the context of materials involves the cost of averting behaviour and increased cleaning costs used to maintain service levels plus the disutility from any decline in materials services remaining after these adjustments.[6] Unfortunately, most studies have used a replacement- or restoration-cost approach to valuing materials effects, which assumes that damaged materials are fully replaced or restored at their full cost. This measure bears little relationship to WTP. On the one hand, it may be lower than WTP in so far as it neglects the disutility of temporarily lower service levels before the materials are replaced. If these temporary effects are small, relative to the time horizon of service flows, this consideration is likely to be small. On the other hand, the cost-of-replacement measure probably overstates WTP if people prefer to accept lower materials services than pay the price of replacement. Figure 6.2 illustrates this point. The figure shows the demand for materials services, D, and the supply of materials services both before the scenarios, S, and after the associated decrease in air quality, S', under the assumption of constant marginal cost. The appropriate measure of the change in welfare is the change in consumer surplus, or the trapezoid P'ACP. This loss includes both the decline in materials services and the increased cost of maintaining existing services. But the cost-of-replacement measure assumes that there is no decline in services, but that people pay the higher price to maintain the old level of services, for the larger rectangle P'BCP. Perhaps even more importantly, households and firms may have technologies that can maintain service levels at lower cost than replacement or other assumptions made in the studies.

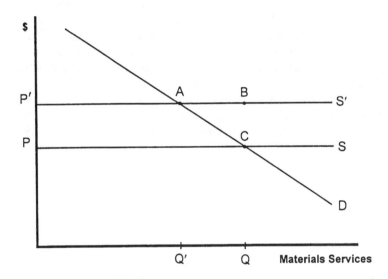

Figure 6.2   Welfare measures of materials damages

In an early application of this replacement-cost approach, Salmon (1970) estimated damages to structural materials using two methods. In the first method, he estimated the percentage of the material that was injured and then estimated costs to be proportional to the rate of physical injury, with 100 per cent implying material replacement. In the second method, cost-of-prevention, he estimated costs from the averting behaviour required to maintain service levels, such as the cost of applying a zinc-rich protective coating to galvanized steel. Salmon chose whichever method seemed more suited for a particular material. To compute actual dollar losses, Salmon multiplied the change in a given material's deterioration rate due to air pollution by the economic value of the exposed stock of materials. He computed this value as the annual production volume of a given material in dollars times the average economic life of the material times the percentage of the material that is exposed. The value also reflects the labour time of, for example, actually applying paint to a surface. Salmon concludes that SO_2 and ozone are responsible for the most materials damage, and that paint incurs the highest damages from an increase in pollution.

TRC Environmental Consultants, Inc. (1984) examined damage caused to painted surfaces and zinc, used extensively in buildings, from SO_2 in greater metropolitan Boston. They surveyed the metropolitan area to estimate the stock of these materials and transferred existing dose-response functions to estimate their deterioration. They then valued the effect on paint at the average cost of commercial painting contractors in the area and the cost of the effect on zinc as the price of a zinc-rich paint that would be applied to damaged stocks.

Acres International Limited (1991) evaluated both materials and soiling damages for Ontario Hydro for three different scenarios – low, medium and high production of fossil-fired electricity – for the period 1991 to 2006. They calculated total materials damages as the sum of damages to individual materials, which are given by the following:

$$\text{damage}_{ij} = (S_j * P_i) * (I_j * E_i) \qquad (6.5)$$

where

damage_{ij} = the damage estimate for material j at receptor I,
S_j = the value (\$) of the exposed stock of material j,
P_i = the ratio of the region's population to the total population,
I_j = a measure of the fraction of material j that is lost in the presence of $1\ \mu g/m^3$ of SO_2 in one year and
E_i = the concentration of SO_2 in the region attributable to a certain source of pollution.

The variable S_j from Equation (6.5) in turn is calculated as

$$S_j = (C_{jk} * L_j) * (X_j * V_j) \qquad (6.6)$$

where

C_{jk} = the total value (\$) of material j consumed in year k,
L_j = the economic life of material j in years k (this variable is a

measure of how long a material lasts, given natural weathering and no pollution),

X_j = exposure factor of material j and

V_j = labour factor of material j, from Salmon (1970).

Acres likewise computes estimates for soiling caused by particulate matter. Acres assumes that the economic value of soiling is equal to the cost of cleaning that would be incurred if consumers always chose to clean soiled materials. Specifically, damages from particulate matter are calculated as:

$$S_{ik} = R_{ik} \cdot (C_h \cdot F_h \cdot P_{ik}) + R_{ik} \cdot (C_w \cdot F_w \cdot P_{ik}) + N_{ik} \cdot B \cdot (C_b \cdot F_h \cdot P_{ik})$$
$$+ N_{ik} \cdot S \cdot (C_s \cdot F_w \cdot P_{ik}) \tag{6.7}$$

where

R_{ik} = number of residential dwellings in region i in year k,

N_{ik} = exposed wall area (ft^2) of non-residential buildings in region i in year k,

B = non-glass portion of total exposed wall area,

S = glass portion of total exposed wall area,

C_h = cost of cleaning exterior walls of an average residential dwelling,

C_b = cost of cleaning non-residential building exterior, non-glass walls (per ft^2),

F_h = factor measuring the change in exterior wall cleaning frequency (per μg/m^3)

C_w = cost of cleaning exterior windows per average residential dwelling,

C_s = cost of cleaning exterior windows on non-residential buildings (per ft^2),

F_w = factor measuring the change in window cleaning frequency (per μg/m^3) and

P_{ik} = concentration of particulates (μg/m^3) in region i in year k.

Acres surveys companies in Ontario that specialize in cleaning glass and other exterior surfaces to determine cleaning costs per square foot, and bases the incremental change in cleaning frequency on Salmon (1970).[7]

In the only study to use a methodology consistent with our conceptual model, Manuel et al. (1982) of Mathtech Inc. assessed the benefits of reduced materials and soiling damage from decreasing SO$_2$ and total suspended particulates (TSP) concentrations. They based their model on the household-production approach, with goods such as cleaning products and air quality being intermediate goods that households use to produce cleanliness. Conceptually, the model employs a two-stage process. First, consumers determine how much of their income to allocate to broad categories of aggregate goods, such as food, clothing, recreation and cleanliness. Next, within each category, they allocate money to different inputs that produce the aggregate good; in the case of cleanliness, this could include detergents, furniture polish, dry-cleaning services and so on. Empirically, the model works in the opposite direction. First the demand functions for the various disaggregate goods are estimated, with air quality affecting expenditures on these goods. This in turn affects the 'price' of an aggregate good like cleanliness, and under certain specified conditions a demand for cleanliness can be estimated.

This approach is one of the greatest strengths of the Manuel et al. study. Consistent with economic principles, it estimates the demand for cleanliness and the change in consumer surplus from changes in the price of cleanliness. This allows it to capture two important aspects of economic welfare: the increased cost of maintaining cleanliness at higher pollution levels, and the losses from accepting a lower level of cleanliness as a consequence of these higher costs. As noted above, the replacement-cost approach does not distinguish between these different types of welfare loss.

To employ their model, Manuel et al. used price and expenditure data for household products from the 1972–73 *Consumer Expenditure Survey* conducted for the Bureau of Labor Statistics. They matched this to air-quality data from the same years. The age of these data is now probably the greatest weakness in the Manuel et al. study, as relative prices and preferences may have changed considerably over the past 25 years.

Manuel et al. estimated the benefits of improvements in air quality, and reported these benefits on a per household, per unit of air pollution basis. Using the average of each day's second highest TSP and SO_2 concentration as their pollution variable,[8] they estimate per household benefits for a $1 \mu g/m^3$ decrease as \$0.35 and \$0.30 for TSP (soiling damage) and SO_2 (materials damage), respectively (as usual, all estimates are in 1993 dollars).

For their own transfer study of the externalities of electricity generation, Harrison et al. (1993) asked Dr Horst of Mathtech to re-estimate these benefits based on an annual average of the pollutants. According to Horst (1995), the two averaging times are comparable from a statistical point of view, with neither having a much better fit. However, an annual average has a theoretical advantage because processes such as corrosion and soiling are probably a function of cumulative exposure rather than daily peaks. According to Harrison et al. (1993), at ambient conditions per household materials and soiling damages for a $1 \mu g/m^3$ increase in annual average PM_{10} and SO_2 are about \$3.21 and \$0.93, respectively. Low estimates were \$0.61 and \$0.20 for PM_{10} and SO_2, respectively; high estimates were \$5.89 and \$1.67.

Because it is the only study that measures welfare benefits in a manner consistent with economic principles, the Manuel et al. results for soiling damages were transferred to the study area, transferring the revised per household damages reported in Harrison et al. (1993). To quantify the uncertainty of the estimate, we use a 90 per cent confidence interval that brackets the high and low values reported by Harrison et al., or a standard error of \$1.58.

Although these per household damages are a reliable way to transfer soiling damages, relying on the household sector may not be sufficient for quantifying materials damages, which can greatly affect the public and industrial sectors. On the other hand, the Acres study, which would account for these additional sectors, does not use the correct welfare measurement, using a cost-of-replacement approach to valuing materials losses. This represents a common dilemma facing transfer analysts. Should one transfer an estimate that represents the better welfare measure but a poorer definition of the commodity, or vice versa? As we have stressed throughout this book, returning to the requirements of the policy context and having a clear conceptual understanding of the issues involved can help guide the transfer strategy. From the above discussion, transferring the Manuel et al. study, with the proper welfare measure but limited only to the household sector, would understate damages. In contrast, as noted in the discussion surrounding Figure 6.2, transferring the Acres study, with a better definition of the commodity that includes all sectors of the economy, but with a cost-of-replacement estimate of values, would overstate damages. A conservative strategy is to transfer the Acres study for materials damages from SO_2. The case study includes damage calculations for eight materials that past studies have shown to have the largest costs: aluminium, cement, copper, stone, zinc, paint, carbon steel and brick. Table 6.1 provides the values for the variables in Equations (6.5) and (6.6) used in the calculations. The latest *Census of Manufacturers* published by the Bureau of the Census and recent data from *Mineral Commodity Summaries* (US DOI 1993) provides information on the exposed stock.[9]

Consider an illustrative calculation for paint damages at the sample receptor. At that site, annual SO_2 is predicted to increase $0.345 \mu g/m^3$ under the urban scenario. The receptor, with over 70 000 people (very large comparatively), has a population ratio of approximately 0.000287. Substituting these for P and E in Equation (6.5) and values for paint for S

Table 6.3 *Variables for materials damages*

	C_{jk} Consumption (1993 \$)	L_j Economic life	X_j Exposure factor	V_j Labour factor	S_j Value of the exposed stock	I_j Materials lost[a]
Aluminium	7 325 621 248	16	0.67	2.0	1.57061 E + 11	0.0000178
Cement	4 169 850 675	40	0.67	2.6	2.90555 E + 11	0.0000084
Copper	5 555 733 094	22	0.67	2.4	1.9654 E + 11	0.0000214
Stone	545 792 000	50	0.93	2.3	58 372 454 400	0.0000195
Zinc	1 283 981 615	36	0.8	2.3	85 050 942 178	0.000428
Paint	12 543 431 680	4	1.0	3.3	1.65573 E + 11	0.000221
Carbon steel	68 382 400	18	0.03	2.3	84 930 941	0.0000424
Brick	288 471 200	40	0.93	2.3	24 681 595 872	0.0000084

Source: Kalvins (1985).

[a]

and I from Table 6.3, paint damages are estimated to be:

$$\$1.656 * 0.000221 * 0.345 * 0.000287 = \$3610$$

in 1993 dollars.

6.3   VISIBILITY EFFECTS

Electric utilities emissions also can lead to increased concentrations of sulphates, nitrates and particulates that may reduce visibility, giving a cloudy or hazy appearance to the atmosphere. While primarily a matter of aesthetics, poor visibility may also have other side effects, such as delaying air travel. Visibility levels in the study region, while not as high as in the western plain states, are also not as low as in regions where visibility has gained much attention. In the study region visibility is typically about 15 miles (US EPA 1979).

In principle, transferring visibility damages (or benefits) for a decrease (or increase) in air quality is a relatively straightforward application of the disaggregate transfer methodology. First the physical linkages between air quality and visibility are estimated. While these linkages are complicated and difficult to calculate, and options for transfer are limited, the linkages are straightforward in the sense of being uncomplicated by behavioural considerations. Whereas human health effects, agricultural output and even materials effects all involve both physical and behavioural responses to a change in air quality, visibility is purely physical.[10] The second step after calculating these physical linkages is to value the visibility effects with WTP.

In practice, modelling the physical effect of marginal changes in pollution on visibility levels is a complicated task because visibility is a regional problem that cannot readily be linked to individual pollution sources (National Research Council 1993). Moreover, many of the needed parameters for some models (visual range, sulphate levels, nitrate levels, carbon levels and ammonia levels) are not available over parts of the study area. As a result, it is not possible to model visibility impacts with any certainty. Yet simple models are available that estimate 'extinction coefficients', a measure of the amount of light scattered by pollutants. The change in extinction can then be used to estimate the change in visual range. For example, Trijonis and Yuan (1978) estimated extinction coefficients for nitrates and sulphates when controlling for relative humidity. They used 25 years of airport visibility data (with days of precipitation deleted) and 10 years of particulate measurements in six US cities: Chicago, Newark, Cleveland, Lexington, Charlotte and Columbus.

In a previous transfer study, Harrison et al. (1993) used the following extinction coefficients for various pollutants:

1. Sulphates: $4.06 \text{ m}^2/\text{g}$
2. Nitrates: $2.90 \text{ m}^2/\text{g}$
3. PM_{10}: $2.30 \text{ m}^2/\text{g}$
4. NO_2: $0.28 \text{ m}^2/\text{g}$

The coefficients assume an average humidity of 50 per cent. Visual range is then given by:

$$\text{Visual range} = 3000/B \qquad (6.8)$$

where visual range is in kilometres and B is the total extinction.

The transfer case study also uses these coefficients to calculate the change in B (and then visibility) from changes in the annual average of pollution concentrations. Since Equation (6.8) is non-linear, we need information about the background value for B. Given a background visual range of about 15 miles (or about 25 kilometres) in the study area, the baseline value of B is approximately 3000 divided by 25, or 120.

The second step of the process monetizes the potential damages from changes in visibility. Here we review some of the more prominent and reliable studies on visibility, all of which use contingent valuation (CV) to measure the WTP for improved visibility. The review considers only studies of residential visibility, as opposed to scenic vistas with large visual ranges like the Grand Canyon. The estimates from these studies of scenic areas prove to be relatively small per visual mile (often around $0.10 compared to about $12.00 for residential areas). Visibility values are likely to be negligible for parks in the Minnesota area because they are of less significance than the Grand Canyon.

Irwin et al. (1989) conducted a study that measured the value of urban visibility in Denver. Respondents were asked to rank various photographs of the city in terms of visibility and then place a monetary value on a one-step change. The average respondent offered to pay $157 in taxes and/or fees for combined visibility and health benefits, with the value of health benefits significantly exceeding visibility values. Although respondents were not asked to value visibility separately, the average respondent stated that 33 per cent of the combined value measured the value of visibility alone. Using the means of both variables, respondents considered a one-step increase in visibility to be worth about $51. Although this provides some indication of the value of visibility, the study values discrete steps in the photographs rather than per mile changes, making it difficult to transfer. Furthermore, pollution problems in Denver are much more severe than those in the study area and are complicated by Denver's topography.

Tolley et al. (1986b) and Tolley, Frankel and Kelly (1988) conducted studies on the benefits of residential visibility in seven eastern US cities. Residents of these cities were asked their WTP for each of three changes in visibility in their cities: preventing a five-mile visibility reduction, improving visibility 10 miles and improving visibility 20 miles, each illustrated with photographs. Respondents' bids ranged from $77 per year to prevent a five-mile reduction in Cincinnati to $410 to increase visibility 20 miles in Washington, DC. This study has several methodological weaknesses, however. First, the photographs were of Chicago only and therefore were less relevant to respondents residing in the other six cities. Second, the photographs did not accurately depict the changes in visibility the respondents were asked to value. Third, because their bidding-game procedure used the same starting point, the WTP values are subject to starting-point bias (see Chapter 5). Finally, the respondents were not asked to separate other possible air-quality components, such as health and agricultural effects, from valuing the changes in visibility, which Schulze et al. (1991) showed to have an influence on estimates. These problems make this study a questionable basis for measuring the value of air quality.

Rowe, d'Arge and Brookshire (1980) estimated WTP for increased visibility in the south-western US. They showed photographs with visual ranges of 25, 50 and 75 miles to residents of Farmington, New Mexico. On average, respondents were willing to pay $97 annually to prevent a visibility reduction from 50 to 25 miles and $180 to prevent a reduction from 75 to 50 miles. On a per mile basis, these bids are low compared to other recent visibility studies. The context of these studies is much different from the case-study policy contex, however, with background visibility ranges of 25 to 75 miles being significantly greater than the visibility in Minnesota, which is typically about 15 miles.

Rae (1984) studied WTP for residential visibility in Cincinnati, using a contingent-ranking method. The midpoint estimates of Rae's contingent-ranking survey range from a WTP of $160 for an increase in visibility from 10.9 to 11.8 miles ($178 per mile) to $640 for an increase from 11.6 to 16.4 miles ($133 per mile) per year. The study also found a WTP of $357 for an increase from 10.9 to 14.4 miles ($102 per mile). These estimates of WTP suggest a U-shaped marginal WTP curve that is inconsistent with other studies' predictions of lesser WTP per mile for greater changes in visibility.

Furthermore, these high values make the study an outlier compared to other studies.

Schulze et al. (1991) conducted a CV study to measure the WTP for increased visibility in Atlanta and Chicago. They asked respondents to value a 2.4-mile increase in average visual range. Atlanta respondents valued an increase from 15.2 to 17.6 miles, whereas those from Chicago valued an increase from 20 to 22.4 miles. These distances are within the range of visibility levels in the case-study area of analysis. Photographs, which were relevant to the area the respondents lived in and were consistent as to the scene depicted, were shown to respondents so they could see baseline visibility and an actual 2.4-mile increase in visual range. Two of the four survey versions also showed the visibility change in a suburban area, where sight lines are limited. To reduce the problem of embedding, Schulze et al. asked respondents to apportion their overall WTP to each benefit of increased air quality, including better health, increased visibility and decreased materials damage. They found that an average household would be willing to pay $39 per year for a 2.4-mile increase in visibility alone ($16 per mile). Schulze et al. used a technique based on stated attitudes and demographic attributes to adjust for protest bids; with this process they concluded that a more accurate WTP figure for the 2.4-mile increase is $18 annually ($8 per mile).

None of these CV studies is ideal, with each of them having methodological problems or significant contextual differences from the case-study policy site. Although the Schulze et al. (1991) study might be the strongest candidate for choosing a single study, Smith and Osborne (1993) have performed a meta-analysis of three other urban visibility CV studies: Brookshire et al. (1979), Loehman and Boldt (1981) and Mitchell, Carson and Ruud (1989). This study has the advantage of incorporating information from each of these three studies.

The functional form of their analysis is as follows:

$$\text{Ln(monthly WTP)} = \beta \cdot \frac{\Delta V}{V} \qquad (6.9)$$

where β is the regression coefficient to be estimated, ΔV is the valued change in visibility and V is the baseline visibility, both measured in miles. They estimate β to be 0.064.

Relative to studies of the south-western US, the visibility ranges valued in each of the studies in Smith and Osborne's meta-analysis are similar to those in the policy area. And as a summary of several studies, it is preferable to any single study. Using their results to estimate WTP in the NSP service area for a one-mile increase in visibility, substitute ΔV

equal to 1 and V equal to 15, approximately the ambient visibility in Minnesota (US EPA 1979). The resulting monthly household WTP is $1.00, or about $12 annually.

NOTES

1. See Adams and Crocker (1991) for an introduction and discussion of the agricultural (and materials) aspects of the benefits of environmental quality.
2. In 1996, The United States Congress passed and the President of the United States signed the Freedom to Farm Bill, which has changed the role of some of these programmes.
3. Much of the material that follows is derived from Cochrane and Runge (1992). The reader is referred to that source for additional detail.
4. Much of this section is taken from Westhoff et al. (1990).
5. Notice that there is some tension between this view and our choice to limit other externality costs to the NSP service territory.
6. Thus, as with the health conceptual model, costs of averting behaviour or mitigating behaviour will be a lower bound on total materials damages.
7. Salmon calculates changes in cleaning frequency by employing measured relationships between cleaning frequency and pollution concentrations.
8. This averaging time was used because it was consistent with the secondary air-quality standards, the policy context for the benefits estimates.
9. We take inventories of aluminium, cement, copper, stone, carbon steel and zinc from the *Mineral Commodity Summaries* (US DOI 1993), which are based on 1992 consumption estimates. Estimates of brick inventories come from the *1987 Census of Manufactures* (US Department of Commerce 1988). The only inventory measure of paint is the value of shipments, as reported in the *Current Industrial Reports* (US Department of Commerce 1993). We shall assume that this measure is a reasonable proxy for annual consumption. In all cases, we then multiply the ratio of each receptor's population over the national population by national consumption. The product is the receptor's consumption level (1993 dollars).
10. Indeed, from one perspective visibility is as much a measure of air quality as a service of air quality. Certainly it plays an important part in people's perceptions of air quality and, as noted in Section 4.2, some objective measures of particulates observe opacity levels.

7. Results of the case study

Completing the chain of linkages among policies, environmental quality, effects on services and people's values, this chapter presents the culmination of the transfer methodology and the object of the case study: the dollar measure of potential externality costs resulting from the electricity-generating scenarios. These estimates can inform such policy decisions as where to site new power plants and which technologies to use. After the presentation of results and discussion in Section 7.1, Section 7.2 evaluates the sensitivity of these results to various judgements, comparing them to alternative estimates under different assumptions.

7.1 PRESENTATION OF RESULTS AND DISCUSSION

The case study estimates potential health, materials, visibility and agricultural externality costs for three hypothetical planning scenarios. These scenarios are mixes of existing and new power plants that could meet future demand for electricity. The technologies of the plants involved and their locations influence how much people and various natural resources are exposed, and consequently, the environmental costs of each scenario. Recall that the three scenarios are:

1. *Rural scenario*: in which a pulverized coal plant and four combined cycle plants are located in the western, rural part of Minnesota.
2. *Metropolitan fringe scenario*: in which the same plants are located just west of Minneapolis/St Paul.
3. *Urban scenario*: in which the emissions of two urban coal plants are assumed to increase.

The scenarios are described in more detail in Chapter 3. They are designed to bracket the range of likely externalities and to be generalizable to the entire study area of Minnesota, western Wisconsin and south-eastern South Dakota. Our expectation was that, relative to the other scenarios, the rural scenario would be associated with smaller potential health damages, because fewer people would be exposed to the emissions, but larger agricultural damages. By the same token we expected the urban scenario and, to a lesser extent, the metropolitan fringe scenario to be associated with relatively large health damages but smaller agricultural damages.

Recall that the first linkage in the disaggregate transfer methodology involves simulating pollution exposures throughout the study area for each scenario under 1991 weather conditions. The second linkage estimates the health, materials, visibility and agricultural effects at each location, using response functions that quantify the relationship between concentrations and effects. Finally, these effects are multiplied by the willingness to pay to avoid them.[1] This then gives the potential externality costs of each scenario annually.

In this chapter, these externality costs are reported on a dollar-per-ton basis. Although not without its limitations, this approach has the advantage of facilitating comparisons of the potential damages from a particular pollutant in one scenario to the potential damages in another scenario with different emission levels. Table 7.1 shows the most likely value of potential per ton externality costs across scenarios for PM, nitrogen oxides (NO_x), NO_x with ozone, sulphur dioxide (SO_2), carbon monoxide (CO) and lead. Because ozone is not emitted directly, it does not have its own per ton damages. However, because the atmospheric model attributes ozone formation solely to NO_x, per ton NO_x damages include the ozone damages.

Table 7.1   Externality costs per ton of pollutant emitted (1993 $)

Pollutant	Rural scenario	Metropolitan fringe scenario	Urban scenario
PM	668	2295	5128
NO_x	15	54	130
NO_x with ozone	29	84	404
SO_2	21	54	126
CO	0.29	0.99	1.57
Lead	401	1719	3302

These most likely values are the median externality costs from a distribution of possible costs estimated using a Monte Carlo simulation. With per ton values ranging from $633 to $4798, PM clearly has the largest values. Potential lead externality costs are the next highest on a per ton basis, at between $401 and $3302 per ton. Although lead externality costs are quite high on a per ton basis, lead is emitted in only very small quantities. Potential per ton NO_x, NO_x with ozone (includes both pollutants), SO_2 and CO externality costs are all much smaller than PM or lead. Comparing across scenarios, Table 7.1 indicates that the urban scenario is associated with the highest per ton externality costs, the metropolitan fringe scenario with the second highest and the rural scenario with the lowest. This is consistent with the importance of health damages in the study and the fact that the urban scenario would expose larger numbers of people to emissions.

Most likely estimates such as these can be useful in a regulatory context, where a single estimate is often used. However, it is important to stress that the externality costs listed in Table 7.1 have not all been estimated with equal certainty and some are statistically indistinguishable from zero. Thus, the most likely estimate by itself is not as informative as the 90 per cent confidence interval. Table 7.2 presents the confidence intervals

Table 7.2   Ninety per cent confidence interval for per ton damages (1993 $)

Pollutant	Rural scenario	Metropolitan fringe scenario	Urban scenario
PM			
Health	$510–$756	$1793–$2517	$4020–$5576
Soiling	$3–$30	$13–$121	$30–$285
Visibility	$17–$20	$67–$82	$156–$193
Total	$530–$806	$1873–$2720	$4206–$6054
NO_x			
Health	$7–$24	$32–$76	$83–$177
NO_x with ozone			
Health	$6–$24	$32–$85	$83–$210
Agriculture	(−$11)–$33	$21–$32	$44–$308
Total	(−$6)–$56	$53–$118	$127–$518
SO_2			
Health	$2–$4	$11–$24	$21–$40
Materials	$7–$9	$29–$37	$79–$102
Agriculture	$0–$12	$0–$46	$0–$42
Total	$9–$24	$43–$104	$106–$178
CO			
Health	$0.20–$0.39	$0.72–$1.26	$1.00–$2.14
Lead			
Health	$379–$422	$1557–$1881	$2951–$3653

for these externality costs, further analysing them by the type of effect (health, agriculture, materials or visibility).[2] The table shows that NO_x with ozone damages are statistically insignificant in the rural scenario and that SO_2 agricultural damages also are statistically insignificant in all scenarios. Nevertheless, Table 7.2 generally supports the trends indicated in Table 7.1.

These results follow several logical patterns. The most apparent pattern is a geographical one across scenarios. The tables indicate that the urban scenario has the highest per ton health and materials damages, the metropolitan fringe scenario the second highest and the rural scenario the lowest. This finding is consistent with the fact that a ton of pollution emitted over an urban area is likely to affect the most people, causing more health effects to occur and injuring more materials, resulting in higher damages. Note also that the differences can be quite significant, indicating that the location of the power plants plays an important role in the resulting damage estimates.

To further explore this geographic and demographic dimension, Figures 7.1 through 7.3 show the 30 counties with the highest health damages. The figures show that the metropolitan areas around Minneapolis/St Paul, St Cloud, Rochester, Duluth and other cities experience some of the highest health damages regardless of the placement of the emission sources. This result reflects the population distribution in the study area. Because these cities have a much higher population density than other areas, they are particularly sensitive to changes in pollution concentrations.

However, the fact that these urban areas have some of the highest externality costs, regardless of the placement of the plants, does not mean that such placement is irrelevant. To the contrary, because urban areas are particularly sensitive to changes in concentrations, siting plants in an urban area would lead to greater health damages. As shown in Table 7.2, per ton damages are highest in the urban scenario and lowest in the rural scenario for the health effects of every pollutant. Moreover, although some areas such as Minneapolis/St Paul are among the top counties in health damages in all three scenarios, some differences between the scenarios can still be seen. In the rural scenario (Figure 7.1) for example, some of the western counties experience the highest level of damages. In the urban scenario (Figure 7.3), however, the higher damages shift to the east. This follows from the location of the plants that distinguish each of these scenarios, with a new coal plant being placed in the western, rural part of Minnesota in the rural scenario and the emissions of two coal plants in Minneapolis/St Paul increasing in the urban scenario.

The importance of plant location can be seen even more clearly when

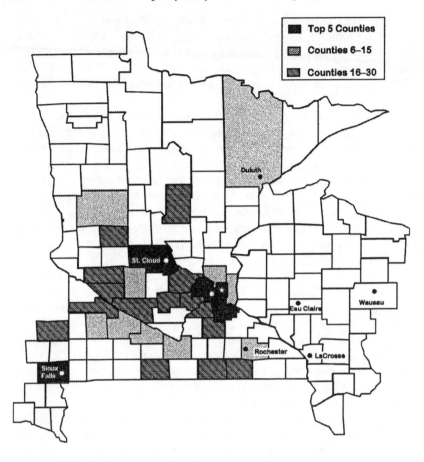

Figure 7.1   Top 30 counties: health damages, rural scenario

population differences are considered. Figures 7.4 through 7.6 show
county-level damages per capita to control for population differences.
These figures illustrate which regions would experience the largest change
in pollution concentrations under the scenarios. The rural scenario
primarily affects the south-western portion of the study area and the
urban scenario the eastern portion, as would be expected from the
locations of the relevant emission sources. The metropolitan fringe
scenario involves new plants to the west of Minneapolis/St Paul, and
Figure 7.5 shows that per capita damages are highest at points around
them. It is initially surprising that this scenario also results in predicted

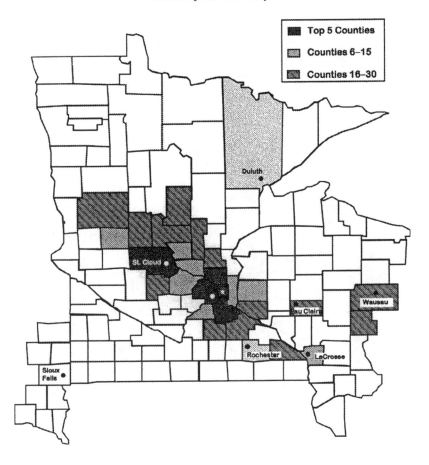

Figure 7.2   Top 30 counties: health damages, metropolitan fringe scenario

damages that extend so far to the north-west, but the meteorological data indicate that winds frequently blow in this direction. Thus the location of a plant is important not only with respect to its distance from affected resources, but also with respect to its direction from those resources.

Agricultural externalities also follow geographic patterns, although they do not necessarily follow expectations. As Table 7.2 shows, contrary to expectations agricultural externality costs are no higher in the rural scenario than in the other scenarios. In fact, ozone agricultural damages are statistically indistinguishable from zero in this scenario. This is a consequence of the atmospheric model, which predicts that NO_x emissions

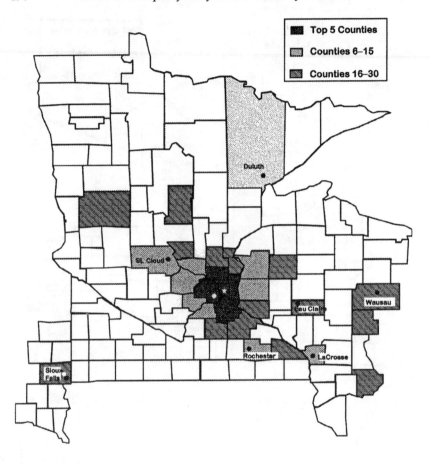

Figure 7.3   Top 30 counties: health damages, urban scenario

in the rural scenario would scavenge existing ozone in many counties so that they actually have lower predicted ozone concentrations. The model predicts that only the counties nearest the hypothetical plant would experience increases in ozone concentrations.

The geographic pattern of agricultural damages depends closely on the proximity of farmland to emission sources. Figures 7.7 through 7.9 show the top 30 counties in agricultural damages for each scenario. (Figure 7.7, for the rural scenario, shows the top 15 counties with positive damages and the top 15 counties with negative damages.) Figure 7.7 shows that the rural scenario causes the highest predicted agricultural damages in

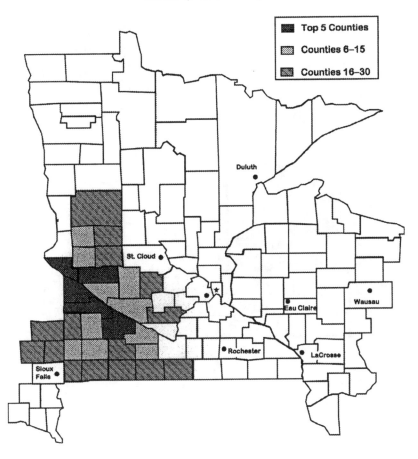

Figure 7.4   Top 30 counties: per capita health damages, rural scenario

counties close to the added power plants, which lead Minnesota in cash
farming receipts. More strikingly, despite the fact that the other two
scenarios concentrate exposure around the Minneapolis/St Paul area, they
also cause the greatest predicted agricultural damages in the important
western counties. Even Polk County in north-western Minnesota, which
has the state's second highest level of farm receipts, is among the top
counties in agricultural damages for these scenarios. This result is similar
to the persistent importance of health damages in Minneapolis/St Paul
across all scenarios.

In addition to these geographic patterns, a second type of pattern in the

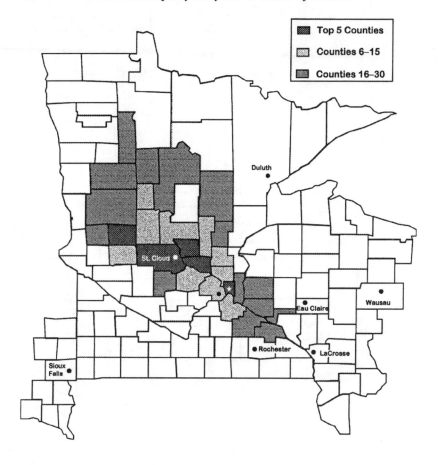

Figure 7.5   Top 30 counties: per capita health damages, metropolitan fringe scenario

results is the simple principle that more severe effects will translate into greater costs. For example, PM and lead are associated with the greatest number and most severe health effects, and accordingly have the highest predicted per ton damages. In contrast CO is associated only with head-ache, and it has the smallest predicted per ton damages. Table 7.3 further breaks the health damages into the 16 health effects transferred, along with the percentage of total health damages contributed by each effect. The table confirms that the most severe health effects from PM are responsible for the greatest share of health damages, namely mortality

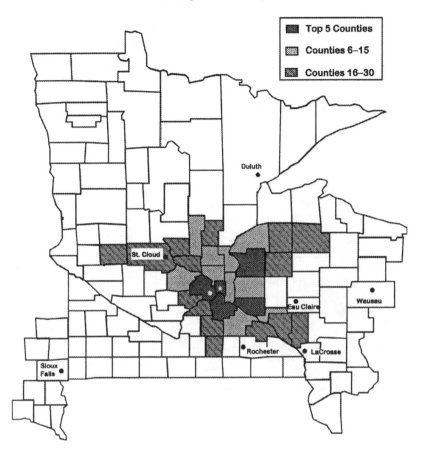

Figure 7.6   Top 30 counties: per capita health damages, urban scenario

risks (37 to 42 per cent) and an aggregate of emphysema, chronic bronchitis and asthma (15 to 18 per cent).

Table 7.4 similarly shows the percentage share of agricultural damages from each crop–pollutant combination. In the metropolitan fringe and urban scenarios, ozone soybean and corn damages make up the largest share of predicted agricultural damages, with the other crops being well behind. This result is a consequence of the relative importance of these crops in the study area and the concentration-response functions. Corn is the number one crop as measured by cash receipts for all three states in the study area. Soybeans are second in Minnesota, which makes up the

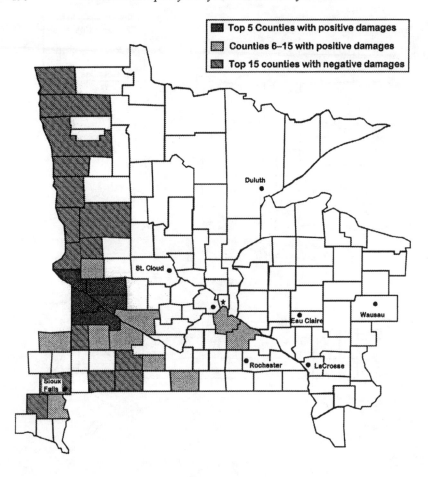

*Figure 7.7   Top 15 counties (positive and negative): agricultural damages,
rural scenario*

largest part of the study area, and third in Wisconsin and South Dakota.
As noted in Chapter 6, however, soybeans are the most sensitive of these
crops to ozone, making soybean damages larger than the predicted
damages for any other crop. Similarly, all the crops are more sensitive
to ozone than to SO_2, so ozone damages are much higher. In fact, SO_2
agricultural damages are statistically insignificant in all three scenarios.
Thus the model cannot rule out the possibility that SO_2 agricultural

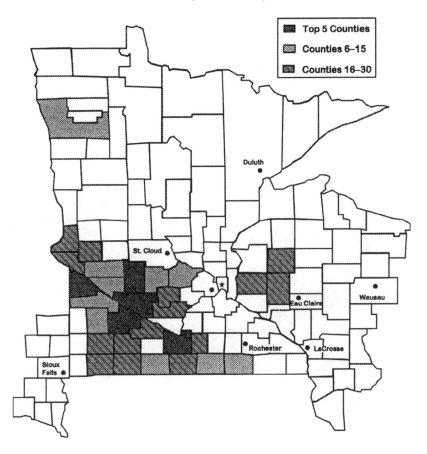

Figure 7.8 Top 30 counties: agricultural damages, metropolitan fringe scenario

externality costs could be zero or even negative. To be conservative, we censor the reported damages in Table 7.2 at zero.

These patterns are not as easy to see in the rural scenario, again because of the surprising predictions about ozone formation. Some of the ozone effects on crops are positive and some negative in this scenario, reflecting two features of the predicted changes in ozone concentrations. First, estimated ozone concentrations increase in some parts of the study area and decrease in others, affecting crops differently depending on where they are grown. Similarly, estimated ozone concentrations change by different

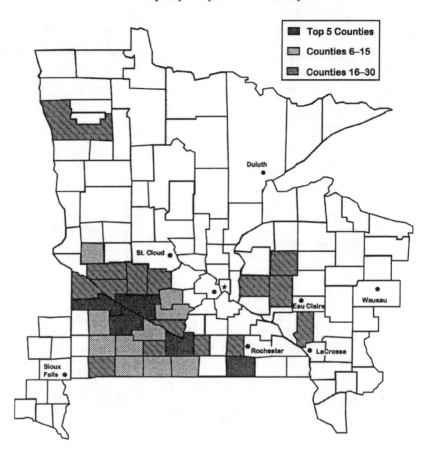

Figure 7.9   Top 30 counties: agricultural damages, urban scenario

amounts for the different relevant averaging times, which are the growing season for each crop.

A third type of pattern in the results is that greater emissions of a particular pollutant or in a particular scenario lead to greater externality costs. Although simple, this pattern can be missed when focusing on per ton damages, as do Tables 7.1 and 7.2; this is one shortcoming of reporting damages on a per ton basis. The high per ton lead damages, for example, seem to imply that lead should be a focus of electricity planning. This is a false impression. In fact, as shown in Table 7.3, lead accounts for almost none of the total health damages from the scenarios.

Table 7.3   Health damages by effect (per cent)

Health effect	Rural scenario	Metropolitan fringe scenario	Urban scenario
SO$_2$			
Chest discomfort	0.9	1.4	5.0
PM			
Mortality	41.6	37.0	38.4
Bronchitis	0.2	0.2	0.2
Chronic cough	5.4	5.8	6.4
Croup	0.0	0.0	0.0
Emphysema, chronic bronchitis and chronic asthma	15.1	16.5	18.4
Upper respiratory effects	0.0	0.0	0.0
Cough days	0.6	0.6	0.7
NO$_2$			
Eye irritation	37.0	36.4	28.9
Ozone			
Lower respiratory effects	−0.5	1.7	1.7
Upper respiratory effects	−0.1	0.2	0.2
Chronic asthma	−0.3	0.0	0.1
CO			
Headache	0.0	0.0	0.0
Lead			
IQ decrements	0.0	0.0	0.0
Hypertension	0.0	0.0	0.0
Pre-term deliveries	0.0	0.0	0.0
Total	100.0	100.0	100.0

The discrepancy arises because while lead may cause severe effects on a per ton basis, very little lead is emitted in the scenarios.

To illustrate which pollutants account for the largest share of predicted damages, Figures 7.10 through 7.12 show the percentage of total dollar damages contributed from each pollutant by scenario. From these figures, PM clearly accounts for the highest percentage of damages in all three scenarios, ranging from approximately one-third in the urban scenario to one-half in the metropolitan fringe scenario. Again, this is consistent with

Table 7.4   Agricultural damages by crop and pollutant (per cent)

Pollutant and crop	Rural scenario	Metropolitan fringe scenario	Urban scenario
SO₂			
Corn	0.2	0.6	0.3
Corn silage	0.0	0.1	0.0
Soybeans	3.9	0.1	0.4
Wheat	0.0	0.0	0.0
Ozone			
Corn	17.6	20.7	24.0
Corn silage	−4.2	1.9	3.3
Soybeans	107.5	60.6	65.3
Hay	−8.1	5.6	6.6
Wheat	−16.9	9.8	0.0
Potatoes	−0.1	0.6	0.0

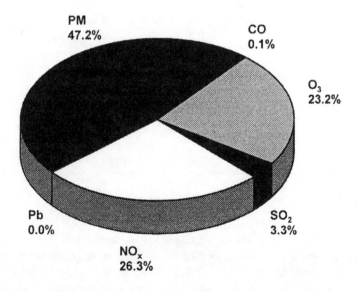

Figure 7.10   Damages by pollutant, rural scenario

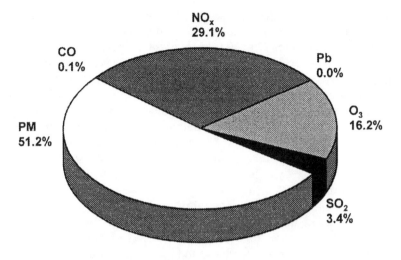

Figure 7.11 Damages by pollutant, metropolitan fringe scenario

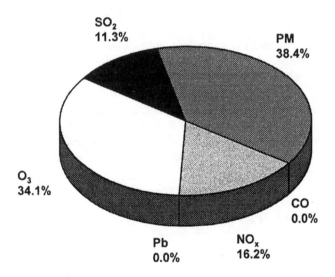

Figure 7.12 Damages by pollutant, urban scenario

the fact that PM has the most severe and greatest number of effects. But severity of effects cannot explain why NO_x, associated only with eye irritation, accounts for 17 to 30 per cent of total predicted health damages. As with the small emissions for lead, here the reason is that predicted NO_x emissions increase by 10 to 20 per cent in the hypothetical scenarios, a much larger increase compared to other pollutants such as PM or SO_2. Emission levels can help explain some of the other results of Figures 7.10 through 7.12 as well. Potential SO_2 damages, for example, are only about 3 per cent of total damages in the rural and metropolitan fringe scenarios, but about 12 per cent in the urban scenario. This is because predicted SO_2 emissions increase by only 1 per cent in the former scenarios, but by 16 percent in the latter.

In summary, the predicted externality-cost estimates follow a number of logical patterns. Furthermore, these patterns relate to the various linkages that form the structure of the transfer process. The first pattern is that the location of the power plants relative to people and resources is important. For example, the urban scenario – and to a lesser extent the metropolitan fringe scenario – results in higher health damages because of the proximity to population centres. Second, the quantity of a pollutant emitted affects the magnitude of total predicted damages. Both of these patterns relate to the initial formulation of the policies and to the linkage between the policies and environmental quality. Note too the importance of a study design that can account for different levels of environmental quality in rural and urban areas. A third pattern is that the types of effects associated with a given pollutant are important. A pollutant such as PM, which can result in severe health effects that people are willing to pay to avoid, other things being equal, is associated with higher damages than a pollutant such as CO, which is associated only with headache in our study. This pattern relates to both the linkage between environmental quality and effects and between effects and WTP. By allowing analysts to break final results down into component parts in this way, the transfer process has the advantage of being able to help identify priorities for policy making or for further research.

7.2 SENSITIVITY OF RESULTS

The estimates of the externality costs associated with a given scenario are only as good as the inputs into our model and are sensitive to our judgements about how best to transfer each input. Such sensitivity to estimation strategies is of course inherent in any kind of economic research and is not limited to transfer studies. Results can be sensitive to survey techniques, assumptions about the technical linkages and the roles of various institutions and modelling specifications for demand equations. But while all research results are sensitive to these kinds of judgements, the transfer methodology is perhaps particularly so. Not only does the methodology transfer the judgements of the original researchers, but it also adds an extra layer of uncertainty in the judgements made by the transfer analysts. These additional judgements include, among others, such overall study-design considerations as the geographic extent of the market, transfer considerations such as the appropriate studies to transfer and how to make any adjustments and, in the case of the disaggregate transfers, the matter of which effects categories to quantify. In a comparison of two separate transfer studies assessing the benefits of limiting effluent discharges into the Hudson River (Desvousges, Naughton and Parsons 1992 and Luken, Johnson and Kibler 1992), Smith (1992) identifies a number of such areas where the approaches and judgements differ and concludes that these different assumptions lead to significantly different outcomes. Smith suggests that part of the problem lies 'in the absence of a systematic protocol for benefit transfer analysis' (p. 691). While there certainly is a need for greater consensus on appropriate transfer procedures, it will always be necessary to make judgements about the quality of available information and which of several alternatives is the best way to transfer it.

These judgements add to the uncertainty of the final estimates, but in a way that is not quantified by the 90 per cent confidence intervals that the Monte Carlo simulations generate. While they reflect the (quantified) uncertainty of the estimates transferred, the confidence intervals do not reflect larger uncertainties about the appropriateness of the chosen estimates themselves. This includes uncertainty about the choice of the estimate, but also uncertainty about whether an effect should be estimated at all. Such modelling uncertainty, described in Chapter 2, really is external to the entire estimation process. Thus the entire process, including both the best estimates and the confidence intervals, is conditional on certain sets of judgements. However, analysts may assess the sensitivity of the results to these judgements by performing sensitivity analysis; that is, by comparing results to those obtained under alternative sets of assumptions. Table 7.5 reports results of some sensitivity analyses for several aspects of the transfer methodology.

Consider first three aspects of the study design: the geographic extent of the market, the geographic resolution of the analysis and the temporal resolution of the analysis. For the case study, the geographic extent of the market is largely determined by the policy context. As mentioned in Chapter 3, the goal of the study is to estimate welfare losses within

Table 7.5   Sensitivity of results to several key assumptions

Assumption	Likely impact on results
Study design issues	
Extent of the market	Geographic extent of the market is a definitional rather than judgemental issue. Estimate of market size within geographic area is based on census data and presumed accurate.
Geographic resolution	Some sensitivity to choice of Zip codes as geographic unit compared to alternative choice of counties. Difference is as much as 10 per cent.
Temperal resolution	For the range of data involved in the case study, sensitivity is very small.
Physical linkages between scenarios and air quality	
Secondary formation of PM	NO_x damages would be 1.5 to 3.1 times higher if secondary formation had been included.
Effects categories and concentration-response functions	
NO_x upper respiratory symptoms	Damages are relatively small for this effect. Including it would not noticeably alter the results.
Ozone mortality	Damages are significant for this effect. Including it would have increased estimated per ton NO_x damages as much as 8 times in one scenario, but reduced them by about 12 per cent in another.
PM mortality	Damages are not very sensitive to the choice of transferring an age-specific function versus one not controlling for age. They are more sensitive to the choice not to control for ambient air quality, with per ton PM damages increasing as much as 70 per cent.
WTP estimates	
Functional form of QWB function	Some damages are moderately sensitive to the choice of functional form.
Timing of chronic effects	Chronic effects would be 25 to 60 per cent lower if effects were spread over 10- to 20-year period.

Northern States Power's service territory. Accordingly, we limit our analysis to this area. A related issue is the estimate of the market size within this geographic area. For health effects, the market is the affected population. These data come directly from the US Census, making this an area where we have had to make few subjective judgements. Although some adjustments are necessary to ensure that all the people in the study area were represented by the 618 receptors used in the dispersion model, damages have proven to be insensitive to the methods used for doing so.

To evaluate the importance of assumptions about the appropriate geographic resolution – specifically, our approach of estimating exposures at the Zip code level – we estimate damages under an alternative assumption that county-wide averages are more appropriate. While generally a finer resolution is preferable, one could argue that if people move about sufficiently between work and home, a wider area would be more suitable for representing actual exposures. Using data from the urban scenario and examining health damages from particulates, damages would fall by approximately 3 per cent by averaging air-quality effects over the receptors within each county. While this difference is small, damages would fall by approximately 10 per cent by representing each county with only one receptor. The latter comparison is probably more informative, as any study design based on county-wide averages would probably use data from only one receptor per county. This comparison shows that the geographic resolution may be important. Averaging over space, as over time, can wash out the peaks in concentrations, which may be particularly important in the presence of non-linear response functions. In addition, there may be spatial correlations between pollutant concentrations and population densities.

A third important aspect of the study design is the temporal resolution. We estimated pollution concentrations on an hourly basis and aggregated up to the averaging times required by the original studies. Sensitivity analysis of results in this dimension indicates that using annual averages would have made little difference. Using annual averages simply linearizes the concentration-response functions, which would have been a reasonable approximation for the very small changes in pollution concentrations in this case study.

In addition to the study design, a second area where results may be sensitive to certain assumptions is the first linkage in the disaggregate methodology: estimating the air-quality impacts of the scenarios. One potentially important judgement is the choice of the Industrial Source Complex (ISC) model as opposed to other modelling regimes, such as the MESOPUFF model. Thayer (1995) estimates that PM concentrations in the transfer area would be 2.68 to 3.95 times higher in the urban scenario and 2.26 to 3.13 times higher in the other scenarios by including the PM formed by NO_x emissions. Desvousges (1995a) estimates that this indirect effect of NO_x emissions would make NO_x damages \$23 to \$40 per ton higher in the rural scenario, \$79 to \$133 higher in the metropolitan fringe scenario and \$223 to \$404 higher in the urban scenario. At a factor of about 1.5 to 2.7 times higher, this is a significant difference. On the other hand, allowing NO_x to form PM implies that NO_x concentrations themselves would be lower, so that the direct damages from NO_x would also be lower. Thus, these adjustment factors are almost certainly pessimistic.

The effects categories and concentration-response functions are areas where perhaps the greatest number of judgements are required. For health effects, Chapter 4 documents the decisions that we made based on the scientific evidence. Perhaps three of the most important judgements were deciding not to quantify NO_x lower respiratory effects in children, deciding not to quantify ozone mortality, and the particular choice of how to transfer PM mortality effects. In sensitivity tests, NO_x lower respiratory damages prove to be relatively minor; including them would have increased per ton NO_x damages only negligibly. Not surprisingly given the severity of the effect, the judgement about ozone mortality has a much more significant impact. Including ozone mortality damages would increase the per ton NO_x damages from \$404 to \$894 (121 per cent) in the urban scenario and from \$29 to \$204 (833 per cent) in the rural scenario, while reducing them from \$84 to \$74 (12 per cent) in the metropolitan fringe scenario.

With regard to transferring PM mortality, per ton PM damages would have been 1 to 5 per cent higher, if mortality effects had not controlled for age. They would also have been about 70 per cent higher using the regression analysis of mortality effects that controls background air quality instead of the mother distribution. As noted in Chapter 4, the regression actually predicts relatively more severe effects in areas with lower ambient pollution concentrations, perhaps because of an errors-in-variables problem; and transferring it would require extrapolating outside the available data to many rural Minnesota receptors with very low concentrations. For these reasons, the age-specific meta-analysis appears to be more appropriate for the transfer. Nevertheless, this judgement does significantly affect the final results. Thus meta-analysis, while a helpful transfer tool, does not relieve the transfer analyst of making important judgements.

Another important area that could be sensitive to certain judgements is the willingness-to-pay estimates. Willingness to pay per case or per episode is simply multiplied by the change in the number of cases of a symptom, so that doubling a willingness-to-pay estimate would double damages. Thus our damages are sensitive to the functional form used in the QWB analysis for valuing short-term morbidity, to the values used to value chronic morbidity and to the mortality valuation meta-analysis, all reported in Chapter 5. Alternative functional forms in the QWB analysis result in both smaller and larger estimates of potential short-term health damages. Some alternatives give estimates up to 70 per cent higher. For some pollutants, many of these effects are a relatively minor proportion of total damages when compared to such other effects as mortality, however, making total damages relatively insensitive to these judgements. Estimates for pollutants such as CO, whose damages are primarily made up of acute health effects, are thus more sensitive to the choice of functional form, while pollutants such as PM, whose damages are influenced more by chronic effects or even non-health effects, are less sensitive. Overall, total damages were most sensitive to functional forms that increase the WTP estimate for eye irritation, the most important of the acute health effects.

A final judgement that introduces uncertainty into the estimates is the rather arbitrary and conservative assumption that all chronic effects begin immediately after the scenario. As noted in Chapter 5, chronic effects would probably take place gradually, adjusting to new long-term pollution levels. Depending on the rate of discount and time horizon, this assumption greatly overstates damages. If chronic effects adjust over 10 years and are discounted at 3 per cent, damages would be about 25 per cent lower. If they adjust over 20 years and are discounted at 8 per cent, they would be about 60 per cent lower.

These sensitivity analyses indicate that final results in the transfer are indeed sensitive to various assumptions. Sensitivity analysis can identify areas where, in hindsight, the analyst could have made better decisions. Sensitivity in some areas simply reflects the uncertain state of science, such as whether ozone is linked to mortality effects. While analysts can assess these uncertainties, they cannot eliminate them. This is really a lesson that is embedded in the policy-making process and is not confined to the transfer methodology; policy makers must base their decisions on the available, imperfect information about the state of the world.

NOTES

1. As exceptions, materials and soiling damages involved transferring the last two steps simultaneously.
2. Because agricultural damages are estimated outside the Monte Carlo simulation, as noted in Chapter 6, we simply add the lower and upper bounds for each effects category to get the bounds on total damages by pollutant. As discussed in Chapter 2, this tends to overstate the width of the confidence intervals, because it is unlikely that all lower bounds or all upper bounds would occur simultaneously.

8. Assessing the transfer method

Transfer studies are widely used for policy analysis because they are more economical than original studies. Nevertheless, the quality of the outcome depends upon economic principles and statistics that must be as skilfully employed as in original studies. While it would be impossible to explore all the possible problems policy analysts may encounter in using limited information from original studies, the previous chapters have surveyed a wide range of available techniques. Still, as in much applied work, success lies as much in the art as in the science of the analysis. Thus we have also emphasized the importance of creativity and good judgement in implementing transfer methods.

Transfer studies play two important roles in applied cost–benefit analysis: either as a preliminary scoping effort to help develop an original study that will ultimately be used for the policy analysis, or as the final policy analysis itself. How successful the transfer method is in either of these roles will be a function of the demands of the analysis task, the quality of information available to meet that task, the level of complexity at which the information is transferred (for example, transferring a function versus transferring a scalar), and the required level of precision to support a policy recommendation. The case study in this book is relatively demanding, with many linkages. Other transfers may have fewer linkages, or only one. Simple transfers require less information and impose fewer requirements for consistency with other information sources. The case study also sets fairly high requirements for the precision of the estimate. Relating back to the continuum illustrated in Figure 1.3, the policy context required it to go beyond identifying priorities for future research and beyond just establishing whether benefits are greater than or less than costs. Instead, the study objective was to identify externality values used in resource planning. However, this objective is still consistent with levels of uncertainty that would not affect the choice among the set of competing plans for future electricity generation.

How successful can transfers be at these various levels? Our experience suggests that it can be quite successful. Despite a demanding task with many linkages, we found information available that could be successfully combined for many of the linkages. We also used successfully several advanced models such as the Industrial Source Complex (ISCST2) dispersion model and the FAPRI crops model, combined information from multiple studies in several meta-analyses, transferred entire equations, and quantified uncertainty using Monte Carlo methods. Furthermore, the final results of the case study follow patterns that match theoretical expectations.

However, an impression that one has successfully completed a research task can be misleading. To better assess the success of the transfer method, several researchers have undertaken tests of convergent validity, which can be divided into two types. The first type of convergent-validity test compares the results of a transfer study to those of an original study to see if they give similar estimates. It is tempting to think of the original study as a true value against which one compares the transfer estimate, but in fact each is an estimate of the unknown true value. The second type of convergent-validity test compares two transfer estimates. If the transfer method is robust to the choices made by the analyst, the studies should give approximately similar estimates.

Two points should be made about interpreting such convergent-validity tests. First, while perhaps providing some insights, tests of the similarity of parameters are not always sufficient if another value derived from those parameters determines the outcome of the policy analysis. For example, in one convergent-validity test, Downing and Ozuna (1996) find that different sites for saltwater fishing trips had similar demand-function coefficients but had statistically different consumer-surplus values (see also Adamowicz, Fletcher and Graham-Tomasi 1989 and Bockstael and Strand 1987). Second, finding statistically different estimates of either parameters or consumer surplus may not invalidate the transfer. If they have small standard errors, two estimates may be statistically different but still be quite close in magnitude. As a basis for policy recommendations, the small difference between the two estimates implies that they still could be good proxies for one another. Ben-Akiva (1981) and Lerman (1981) thus stress these so-called 'importance' tests over statistical tests.

Relating this back to some of the discussion in Chapter 1, the ideal test of a transfer would be whether the difference between expected welfare under a policy based on the transfer approximation and under a policy based on an original estimate is less than the savings provided by conducting a transfer instead of an original study. If so, the transfer analysts can accept the small bias. In other words, transfers are inherently empirical compromises, but tests requiring statistical equality are inconsistent with this spirit of compromise. The standard should not be whether transfer estimates will be as good as original estimates; in most cases, they will not be. The standard is whether the savings from performing a transfer study instead of an original study will exceed the expected benefits from the better information.

In an early test of convergent validity, Atherton and Ben-Akiva (1976) transfer a multinomial logit model of transportation choices based on Washington, DC data to New Bedford, Massachusetts, comparing it to an original model based on New Bedford data. They use a number of transfer methods discussed in Chapter 2, including a straight transfer of the Washington, DC model, a transfer with updated constants based on group New Bedford data, a transfer with updated constants based on individual-level New Bedford data, and a pooled Bayesian model using a small sample of New Bedford data. Atherton and Ben-Akiva find that the hypothesis of equal coefficients across models cannot be rejected. They also find that the percentage differences in predicted probabilities of each choice are very small, ranging from less than 0.1 per cent to 4 per cent depending on the models. This suggests that the transfer would be adequate for most policy purposes. Finally, they find that more complex transfers are more successful, with the Bayesian updating approach out-performing the others. Train (1979) and Koppelman and Wilmot (1986) perform somewhat similar tests with transportation-choice models, but Train compares the transferred probability shares only to actually observed shares and not to an original model, while Koppelman and Willmot provide only McFadden (1973) rho-square measures of goodness of fit.

Loomis (1992) conducts a convergent-validity test using data sets of ocean-salmon fishing trips in both Oregon and Washington states. He estimates both separate and pooled demand equations and tests the equality of the coefficients with a Chow test. He also repeats this test for freshwater steelhead fishing in Oregon and Idaho. At the 5 per cent level, Loomis rejects the hypothesis that the coefficients are equal across models for both types of fishing. Unfortunately, he does not report either statistical or 'importance' tests of the benefits estimates indicating how much difference the transfer would have made relative to an original model. However, Loomis does report such a test for a within-state transfer using the Oregon steelhead data. Specifically, he estimates the average per-trip consumer surplus for fishing at each of ten Oregon river sites with a multisite travel-cost model. He then drops one of the rivers from the analysis, re-estimates the model, and transfers the results to the excluded river, repeating this exercise over all ten rivers. Here, he finds that the transfer estimates are generally only one to nine percentage points away from the 'true benefits' estimated from the complete model, with one outlying case having a difference of 18 per cent.

Downing and Ozuna (1996) and Kirchhoff, Colby and LaFrance (1997) also perform convergent-validity tests of both coefficients and benefits estimates for outdoor recreation. Downing and Ozuna use contingent-valuation data of saltwater anglers off the Texas gulf coast from eight regions and three time periods (24 sub-groups in total). They find that while about half of the possible comparisons yield statistically similar coefficients, very few give statistically significant benefits estimates. However, they do not report importance tests. In addition, this test bases its analysis on transferring a simple demand equation that does not control for site differences.

Kirchhoff, Colby and LaFrance (1997) test convergent validity across each of two pairs of contingent-valuation estimates, one for the willingness to pay (WTP) to preserve riparian habitat along two Arizona rivers noted for birding, the other for a rafting trip in one of two stretches of the Rio Grande River in New Mexico. They reject the statistical equality of the coefficients for both pairs, as well as the statistical equality of consumer-surplus measures. However, they find more mixed results in the percentage differences between the estimated consumer-surplus measures. For the Arizona river habitat, differences were 2.3 per cent and 25.2 per cent when restricting the sample to birders, depending on which was taken to be the transfer model and which the original model. However, for the New Mexico raft trips, the differences were much larger – at 87.1 per cent and 210.4 per cent respectively. As the authors note, part of the problem may be the qualitative difference between the commodities. One stretch of river is a majestic canyon with strong rapids providing a difficult river-running experience, whereas the other stretch provides much less challenging rapids. Thus, this transfer may not have been advisable from the beginning, and might not have been made by analysts considering the similarity of contexts as one factor in choosing an original study to transfer.

In fact, all these studies have this problem, being somewhat artificial in so far as they test the impact of transferring a model without actually submitting the transfer to the judgements of a transfer analyst and to the standards of transfer protocols. In this way, they test the validity of specific transfers, but not necessarily the transfer method. They simply assume that analysts would transfer the model to the other context, but in an actual transfer analysts would examine the quality of the original study and its similarity to the transfer context. If the original study did not meet these standards, they might use another study instead, or, if possible, summarise several studies. Moreover, even if analysts were to transfer the models across the contexts assumed in the studies, they might do so with some adjustments. For example, a modest adjustment for the different rafting experiences across the Rio Grande River stretches might easily reduce the disparity between estimates found by Kirchhoff, Colby and LaFrance.

By comparing two actual transfer studies of a similar policy, Smith (1992) provides a different kind of test of convergent validity. Smith compares the results of Desvousges, Naughton and Parsons (1992) and Luken, Johnson and Kibler (1992), both of which use the transfer methodology to estimate the benefits from limiting the effluent discharges from pulp and paper mills. The two studies have one river in common (the Hudson), where their results are comparable. One of the most important differences between the two studies is that Desvousges et al. define the resources as river reaches, whereas Luken et al. define them as areas surrounding the regulated mills. Additionally, Desvousges et al. assume that the geographic market is captured by county boundaries; Luken et al. assume a fixed radius of 30 miles. Finally, Desvousges et al. assume that the geographical range of effects is identical to that from the original studies; Luken et al. assume a judgemental ratio based on miles of river in each area – neither recognizes the impact of the quality change. Note that both of these studies involve several linkages, and thus are more demanding transfers than those reviewed above. Analysing the consequences of different assumptions and judgements, Smith concludes that they led to results different enough to change the policy conclusions one would derive from the analysis.

Two final tests of convergent validity are provided by Brucato, Murdoch and Thayer (1990) and Smith and Huang (1995). Brucato, Murdoch and Taylor compare a disaggregate transfer of benefits for a 10 per cent reduction in ozone levels in San Francisco – a transfer very similar to our case study – with an estimate based on a hedonic regression of the San Francisco housing market. They find that the confidence intervals for the two approaches overlap, suggesting that the disaggregate transfer meets the validity test. Smith and Huang (1995) compare a disaggregate transfer of benefits for a reduction in concentrations of particulate matter to the prediction from a meta-analysis of 86 hedonic estimates. Unlike Brucato, Murdoch and Thayer, however, they find that the disaggregate transfer gives estimates as much as 5 to 15 times higher than the aggregate transfer from the hedonic studies.

To perform a validity test of our own case study, we transfer an aggregate per unit value of particulate matter concentrations from the Smith and Huang meta-analysis.[1] Transferring the mean value of $14.10 (1993 dollars) for a one-unit change in annual average TSP, the particulate damages would be $132 per ton in the rural scenario, $531 in the metropolitan fringe scenario, and $1248 in the urban scenario. Consistent with the findings of Smith and Huang, these values are only one-fifth to one-quarter of the disaggregate point estimates reported in Chapter 7 and one-quarter to one-third of the lower bounds. Transferring their entire meta-equation increases the estimates of the aggregate transfer over a simple transfer of the mean value, largely because real income is slightly higher and background air quality slightly better in the case study than the mean values in the regression.[2] Transferring the meta-equation leads to estimates of per ton particulate damages of $272 for the rural scenario, $984 for the metropolitan fringe scenario, and $2296 for the urban scenario. These values are a little more than half the disaggregate lower bounds reported in Chapter 7. This discrepancy may be within acceptable limits for the policy question. Generally speaking, the externalities found in the aggregate transfer are small enough to suggest that they would not play a large role in the siting of future power plants. The even smaller aggregate transfer simply confirms this finding. The differences between them may reflect conservative assumptions embedded in the disaggregate transfer, particularly the assumption that WTP per statistical life for the elderly and infirm population affected by particulate matter is equal to those in wage-risk studies and the assumption that chronic conditions such as emphysema occur immediately.

The results of this and previous convergent-validity tests illustrate several principles discussed in Chapter 2. First, transfers are more likely to be accurate if they use higher-quality original studies, as seen in the successful transfers of the transportation random-utility models. Similarly, transfers are also more accurate across similar contexts. For example, Kirchhoff, Colby and LaFrance (1997) find that the transfer across relatively similar Arizona birding sites was better than the transfer across relatively different New Mexico rafting sites. Another principle is that more complex transfers of functions are preferable to simple transfers of scalar values. Downing and Ozuna (1996), who conclude that the transfer method does not meet a test of convergent validity, transfer simple demand equations without controlling for site or population differences across contexts. In direct comparisons of different levels of transfer complexity, Loomis (1992) finds more success in transferring an entire equation than just means, as do we in our convergent-validity test of aggregate and disaggregate WTP for air quality. Similarly, Atherton and Ben-Akiva (1976) find transferring a pooled model with Bayesian updating is more successful than transferring a function without updating.

These patterns indicate that rather than being a mechanical procedure for mass-producing benefit–cost estimates, the transfer method is a creative endeavour that requires skill and judgement on the part of the analyst. This does not imply that transfers are entirely subjective and arbitrary; practical policy analysis need not imply slipshod policy analysis.

As with any research, analysts must base their judgements on the information available to them. They can also choose conservative assumptions that shield policy conclusions from doubt over the assumptions. However, the role of skill and judgement does imply that, because information will vary on a case-by-case basis, analysts must use creatively the tools at their disposal. Probably the most important example of this is using meta-analysis to summarise the results of many studies and to take advantage of inter-study variation in some variables.

In addition, analysts must make their judgements open and explicit and test their impact with sensitivity analyses. Of course, sensitivity analyses make the results reported more honest and complete. But they are also an important part of the transfer method because they are part of the learning process. They help to identify the structure of the policy context and the variables that can have the biggest impact on outcomes. For this reason sensitivity analyses are built into the transfer process, with qualitative or back-of-the-envelope calculations being used to inform judgements during the study design. In addition, sensitivity analyses performed at the end of the research can help identify priorities for future research designed to reduce the uncertainty. Greater uncertainty and sensitivity to assumptions will always be the price for practical policy analysis such as transfers. However, in our view, a carefully crafted transfer can provide sufficient information to make well-informed policy recommendations in many cases. In cases where the uncertainty is judged to be too great, it can also provide an important first cut to identify the priorities for original studies.

Probably the greatest limitation facing many transfers is the quality and sheer availability of original studies. Some possible health effects could not be valued in the case study because of a lack of original studies, and others could be valued only with less than ideal proxies. Transfer studies are only as good as the information on which they are based. Accordingly, one focus of future efforts to improve transfers should be on the original studies themselves.

In general, the prospects for successful transfers should improve as the stock of existing studies continues to build and as experience with non-market valuation grows. This process could be accelerated if applied economists continue to update existing compilations of hard-to-locate materials in the grey literature, making original studies more accessible. It could also be accelerated if there were a market for applied studies that replicate existing results. While incentives exist for such studies in the natural sciences, the valuation linkage of transfers suffers from current practices which discourage replication. Although we do not have delusions about the chances of journals changing their practices, journals could take other steps to make the articles they publish more useful for transfers. High on this list would be requiring better reporting of the assumptions underlying empirical analyses, as well as full reporting of covariances, perhaps making complete variance–covariance matrices available electronically.

The contribution to future transfer studies could also be one goal when designing original studies. A recent study of health effects, for example, uses flexible methods provided by conjoint surveys, allowing it to value many health states, and surveys two very different populations, steps taken explicitly with transfers in mind (Desvousges et al. 1996). A first step in making original studies more useful for transfers may come in the choice of method to use. In valuation studies, conjoint surveys and discrete-choice models allow values to be modelled as a function of choice attributes. This makes it possible to control for differences in commodity attributes across contexts when making a transfer. In contrast, traditional contingent-valuation surveys can only value one or a few commodities, making it difficult to control for differences in commodity attributes.

A second step toward making original studies more useful in transfers would be to use variables that are both relevant to policy makers and available in other contexts. If this is not possible, using variables that have a measured relationship to variables available elsewhere may be sufficient. This allows transferring more terms of the equation and controlling for more variables than would otherwise be possible. Even in cases where analysts desire to test more esoteric variables or specially constructed indices, they could also report additional models without these variables.

With these and other improvements in original studies and in tools used in transfers, such as meta-analysis techniques, the prospects for transfer studies should continue to improve. This does not mean that transfers will always be the best research strategy. In some cases, the available information simply may not support the requirements for a transfer. And progress in any science requires that new research be conducted. The valuable role played by transfers, however, is to inform policy making. If designed to exploit fully the existing information, transfer studies can provide a rigorous way of evaluating policy proposals in light of the current stock of knowledge.

NOTES

1. We thank Kerry Smith for providing us with these data.
2. To characterize background particulate levels, the case study uses annual average PM_{10} levels by receptor, estimated from a kriging model of air-quality receptors. However, this

measure is not consistent with the second-high 24-hour TSP level used by Smith and Huang (1995). To rescale our data, we regressed second-high PM levels on the annual average at 55 midwestern air quality monitors. The regression with the best fit is:

$$Ln(\text{second-max}) = 0.61829 + 1.0661 * Ln(\text{annual average})$$

with an R^2 of 0.64. We used this to predict second-maximum concentrations at each receptor and then converted PM_{10} to TSP by dividing by 0.55, the metric used in Chapter 4 and by Smith and Huang. To test the sensitivity of the estimates to this adjustment process, we also estimated damages by assuming that background concentrations at all receptors are equal to the average of the second-high values reported at the 55 monitors. This increased damages by another 20 to 30 per cent, making them still closer to our disaggregate estimates.

Bibliography

Abbey, D.E., F. Peterson, P.K. Mills and W.L. Beeson (1993), 'Long-term ambient concentrations of total suspended particulates, ozone, and sulfur dioxide and respiratory symptoms in a nonsmoking population', *Archives of Environmental Health*, **48** (1), 33–46.

Abdalla, C.W., B.A. Roach and D.J. Epp (1992), 'Valuing environmental quality changes using averting expenditures: An application to groundwater contamination', *Land Economics*, **68** (2), 163–9.

Acres International Limited (1991), *The Effects and Social Costs of Fossil-Fired Generating Station Emissions on Structural Materials (Update)*, Niagara Falls, Ontario, prepared for Ontario Hydro.

Adamowicz, W.L., J.J. Fletcher and T. Graham-Tomasi (1989), 'Functional form and the statistical properties of welfare measures', *American Journal of Agricultural Economics*, **70**, 414–21.

Adams, K.F., G. Koch, B. Chatterjee, G.M. Goldstein, J.J. O'Neil, P.A. Bromberg, D.S. Sheps, S. McAllister, C.J. Price and J. Bissette (1988), 'Acute elevation of blood carboxyhemoglobin to 6 percent impairs exercise performance and aggravates symptoms in patients with ischemic heart disease', *Journal of American College of Cardiology*, **12**, 900–906.

Adams, R.M. and T.D. Crocker (1991), 'Materials damages', in John B. Braden and Charles D. Kolstad (eds), *Measuring the Demand for Environmental Quality*, Amsterdam: North-Holland.

Adams, R.M., T.D. Crocker and N. Thanavibulchai (1982), 'An economic assessment of air pollution damages to selected annual crops in southern California', *Journal of Environmental Economics and Management*, **9**, 42–58.

Adams, R.M., J.D. Glyer and B.A. McCarl (1988), 'The NCLAN economic assessment: Approach, findings, and implications', in W.W. Heck, O.C. Taylor and D.T. Tingey (eds), *Assessment of Crop Loss from Air Pollutants*, London: Elsevier Applied Science Publishing.

Aigner, D.J. and E.E. Leamer (1984), 'Estimation of time-of-use response in the absence of experimental data', *Journal of Econometrics*, **26**, 205–27.

Åkerman, J., F.R. Johnson and L. Bergman (1991), 'Paying for safety: voluntary reduction of residential radon risks', *Land Economics*, **67** (4), 435–46.

Alberini, A., M.L. Cropper, T.T. Fu, A.J. Krupnick, J.T. Liu, D. Shaw and W. Harrison (1994), 'Valuing health effects of air pollution in developing countries: The case of Taiwan', Resources for the Future Discussion Paper 95-01.

Allred, E.N., E.R. Bleecker, B.R. Chaitman, T.E. Dahms, S.O. Gottlieb, J.D. Hackney, D. Hayes, M. Pagano, R.H. Selvester, S.M. Walden and J. Warren (1989a), *Acute Effects of Carbon Monoxide Exposure on Individuals With Coronary Artery Disease*, Research Report no. 25, Cambridge, MA: Health Effects Institute.

Allred, E.N., E.R. Bleecker, B.R. Chaitman, T.E. Dahms, S.O. Gottlieb, J.D. Hackney, M. Pagano, R.H. Selvester, S.M. Walden and J. Warren (1989b), 'Short-term effects of carbon monoxide exposure on the exercise performance of subjects with coronary artery disease', *The New England Journal of Medicine*, **321** (21), 1426–32.

Amemiya, T. (1985), *Advanced Econometrics*, Cambridge, MA: Harvard University Press.

Anderson, E.W., R.J. Andelman, J.M. Strauch, N.J. Fortuin and J.H. Knelson (1973), 'Effect of low-level carbon monoxide exposure on onset and duration of angina pectoris', *Annals of Internal Medicine*, **79**, 46–50.

Arnould, R. and L.M. Nichols (1983), 'Wage-risk premiums and workers' compensation: A refinement of estimates of compensating wage differentials', *Journal of Political Economy*, **91** (2), 332–40.

Aronow, W.S. and M.W. Isbell (1973), 'Carbon monoxide effect on exercise-induced angina pectoris', *Annals of Internal Medicine*, **79**, 392–5.

Aronow, W.S., C.N. Harris, M.W. Isbell, S.N. Rockaw and B. Imparato (1972), 'Effect of freeway travel on angina pectoris', *Annals of Internal Medicine*, **77**, 669–79.

Arrow, K., R. Solow, E. Leamer, P. Portney, R. Radner and H. Shuman (1993), 'Report of the NOAA Panel on contingent valuation', *Federal Register*, **58** (10).

Atherton, T.J. and M.E. Ben-Akiva (1976), 'Transferability and updating of disaggregate travel demand models', *Transportation Research Record*, **610**, 12–18.

Baker, J.B. and T.F. Bresnahan (1988), 'Estimating residual demand facing a single firm', *International Journal of Industrial Organization*, **6**, 283–300.

Bartik, T.J. (1987), 'The estimation of demand parameters in hedonic price models', *Journal of Political Economy*, **95** (1), 81–8.

Bartik, T.J. (1988a), 'Evaluating the benefits of non-marginal reductions in pollution using information on defensive expenditures', *Journal of Environmental Economics and Management*, **15** (1), 111–27.

Bartik, T.J. (1988b), 'Measuring the benefits of amenity improvements in hedonic price models', *Land Economics*, **64** (2), 172–83.

Battye, B. (1983), 'Lead Emissions Inventory (1981)', Memorandum to John Haines, 31 January. Available for inspection at US Environmental Protection Agency, Environmental Criteria and Assessment Office, Research Triangle Park, NC.

Bedi, J.F., L.J. Folinsbee and S.M. Horvath (1984), 'Pulmonary function effects of 1.0 and 2.0 ppm Sulfur Dioxide exposure in active young male nonsmokers', *Journal of the Air Pollution Control Association*, **34**, 1117–21.

Bellinger, D.C., K.M. Stiles and H.L. Needleman (1992), 'Low-level lead exposure, intelligence, and academic achievement: A long-term follow-up study', *Pediatrics*, **90** (6), 855–61.

Ben-Akiva, M.E. (1981), 'Issues in transferring and updating travel-behavior models', in P.R. Stopher, A.H. Meyburg and W. Börg (eds), *New Horizons in Travel-Behavior Research*, Lexington, MA: Lexington Books.

Ben-Akiva, M. and S.R. Lerman (1985), *Discrete Choice Analysis: Theory and Application to Travel Demand*, Cambridge, MA: MIT Press.

Berger, M.C., G.C. Blomquist, D. Kenkel and G.S. Tolley (1987), 'Valuing changes in health risks: a comparison of alternative measures', *Southern Economic Journal*, **53** (4), 967–84.

Bjornstad, D.J. and J.R. Kahn (1996), *The Contingent Valuation of Environmental Resources*, Cheltenham, UK: Edward Elgar.

Blomquist, G. (1979), 'Value of life saving: Implications of consumption activity', *Journal of Political Economy*, **96** (4), 675–700.

Bockstael, N.E. and I.E. Strand (1987), 'The effect of common sources of regression error on benefit estimates', *Land Economics*, **63**, 11-20.

Bockstael, N.E., K.A. McConnell, and I.E. Strand (1991), 'Recreation', in J.B. Braden and C.D. Kolstad (eds), *Measuring the Demand for Environmental Quality*, Amsterdam: North-Holland.

Bohm, P. (1975), 'Option demand and consumer's surplus: Comment', *American Economic Review*, **65** (4), 733–6.

Bornschein, R.L., J. Grote, T. Mitchell, P.A. Succop, K.N. Dietrich, K.M. Krafft and P.B. Hammond (1989), 'Effects of prenatal lead exposure on infant size at birth', in M.A. Smith, L.D. Grant and A.I. Sors (eds), *Lead Exposure and Child Development: An International Assessment*, Dordrecht, The Netherlands: Kluwer Academic Publishers, pp. 307–19.

Boyle, K.J. and J.C. Bergstrom (1992), 'Benefit transfer studies: Myths, pragmatism, and idealism', *Water Resources Research*, **28** (3), 657–63.

Boyle, K.J., R.C. Bishop and M.P. Welsh (1985), 'Starting point bias in contingent valuation surveys', *Land Economics*, **61**, 188–94.

Boyle, K.J., G.L. Poe and J.C. Bergstrom (1994), 'What do we know about groundwater values? Preliminary implications from a meta analysis of contingent-valuation studies', *American Journal of Agricultural Economics*, **76**, 1055–61.

Boyle, K.J., F.R. Johnson, D.W. McCollum, W.H. Desvousges, R.W. Dunford and S.P. Hudson (1996), 'Valuing public goods: Discrete versus continuous contingent-valuation responses', *Land Economics*, **72** (3), 381–96.

Braden, J.B. and C. Kolstad (eds) (1991), *Measuring the Demand for Environmental Quality*, Amsterdam and New York: Elsevier Science Publishers.

Braun-Fahrländer, C., U. Ackermann-Liebrich, J. Schwartz, H.P. Gnehm, M. Rutishauser and H.U. Wanner (1992), 'Air pollution and respiratory symptoms in preschool children', *American Review of Respiratory Disease*, **145**, 42–7.

Brewer, R.F. and R. Ashcroft (1982), *The Effects of Ozone and SO₂ on Alfalfa Yields and Hay Quality*, report prepared for the California Air Resources Board, no. A1-038-33.

Brookshire, D.S. (1992), 'Issues regarding benefits transfer', paper presented at the 1992 Association of Environmental Resource Economists Workshop, Snowbird, Utah, 3–5 June.

Brookshire, D.S. and H.R. Neill (1992), 'Benefit transfers: Conceptual and empirical issues', *Water Resources Research*, **28** (3), 651–5.

Brookshire, D.S., A. Randall and J. R. Stoll (1980), 'Valuing increments and decrements in natural resource service flows', *American Journal of Agricultural Economics*, **62**, 478–88.

Brookshire, D.S., R. d'Arge, W. Schulze and M. Thayer (1979), *Experiments in Valuing Non-Market Goods: A Case Study of Alternative Benefit Measures of Air Pollution Control in the South Coast Air Basin of Southern California, Vol. II: Methods Development for Assessing Air Pollution Control Benefits*, report prepared for the US EPA, Washington, DC.

Brown, C. (1980), 'Equalizing Differences in the Labor Market', *The Quarterly Journal of Economics*, 113–34.

Brown, C., C. Gilroy and A. Kohen (1982), 'The effect of the minimum wage law on employment and unemployment', *Journal of Economic Literature*, **20** (2), 487–528.

Brown, J.N. and H.S. Rosen (1982), 'On the estimation of structural hedonic price models', *Econometrica*, **50** (3), 764–8.

Brucato, P.F., J.C. Murdoch and M.A. Thayer (1990), 'Urban air quality improvements: A comparison of aggregate health and welfare benefits to hedonic price differentials', *Journal of Environmental Management*, **30** (3), 265–79.

Brunekreef, B. (1984), 'The relationship between air lead and blood lead in children: a critical review', *The Science of the Total Environment*, **38**, 79–123.

Burt, O. and D. Brewer (1971), 'Evaluation of net social benefits from outdoor recreation', *Econometrica*, **39** (5), 813–27.

Bush, J.W., S. Fanshel and M.M. Chen (1972), 'Analysis of a tuberculin testing program using a health status index', *Socio-Economic Planning Sciences*, **6** (1), 49–68.

Bush, J.W., M.M. Chen, D.L. Patrick and W.R. Blischke (1973), *Linear Models of Social Preferences for Constructing a Health Status Index*, report prepared for the Bureau of Health Services Research, La Jolla, CA: University of California at San Diego.

Butler, R.J. (1983), 'Wage and injury rate responses to shifting levels of workers' compensation', in John D. Worral (ed.), *Safety and the Work Force*, Ithaca, NY: Cornell University, ILR Press.

Cameron, T.A. (1992), 'Issues in benefits transfer', paper presented at the 1992 Association of Environmental Resource Economists Workshop, Snowbird, Utah, 3–5 June.

Card, D.E. and A.B. Krueger (1995), *Myth and Measurement: The New Economics of the Minimum Wage*, Princeton, NJ: Princeton University Press.

Carson, R.T., J. Wright, A. Alberini, N. Carson and N. Flores (1994a), *A Bibliography of Contingent Valuation Studies and Papers*, Natural Resource Damage Assessment, Inc., La Jolla, CA.

Carson, R.T., W.M. Hanemann, R.J. Kopp, J.A. Krosnick, R.C. Mitchell, S. Presser, P.A. Ruud and V.K. Smith (1994b), *Prospective Interim Lost Use Value Due to DDT and PCB Contamination in the Southern California Bight*, two volumes, report prepared for the National Oceanic and Atmospheric Administration, La Jolla, CA, Natural Resource Damage Assessment, Inc.

Chai, S. and R.C. Webb (1988), 'Effects of lead on vascular reactivity', in W. Victery (ed.),

'Symposium on Lead–Blood Pressure Relationships' and *Environmental Health Perspectives*, **78**, 77–83.

Chestnut, L.G. and D.M. Violette (1984), *Estimates of WTP for Changes in Morbidity: A Critique of Benefit–Cost Analysis of Pollution Regulation*, draft final report prepared for US Environmental Protection Agency.

Chestnut, L.G., S.D. Colome, L.R. Keller, W.E. Lambert, B. Ostro, R.D. Rowe and S.L. Wojciechowski (1988), *Heart Disease Patients' Averting Behavior, Costs of Illness and Willingness to Pay to Avoid Angina Episodes*, final report prepared for US Environmental Protection Agency. Document no. EPA-230-10-88-042.

Cicchetti, C.J., A.C. Fisher and V.K. Smith (1976), 'An econometric evaluation of a generalized consumer surplus measure: The Mineral King controversy', *Econometrica*, **44** (6), 1259–76.

Clarke, B.B., M.R. Henninger and E. Brennan (1983), 'An assessment of potato losses caused by oxidant air pollution in New Jersey', *Phytopathology*, **73**, 104–8.

Clawson, M. and J.L. Knetsch (1966), *Economics of Outdoor Recreation*, Baltimore, MD: Johns Hopkins University Press for Resources for the Future.

Coburn, R.F., R.E. Forster and P.B. Kane (1965), 'Considerations of the physiological variables that determine the blood carboxyhemoglobin concentration in man', *Journal of Clinical Investigation*, **44** (11), 1899–910.

Cochrane, W.W. and C.F. Runge (1992), *Reforming Farm Policy: Toward a National Agenda*, Ames, IA: Iowa State University Press.

Colombo, A. (1985), 'The underdefined nature of the blood lead–air relationship from biological and statistical grounds', *Atmospheric Environment*, **19**, 1485–93.

Consineau, J., R. Lacroix and A. Girard (1988), 'Occupational hazard and wage compensating differentials', working paper, University of Montreal.

Constantinou, E. and C. Seigneur (1991), 'Multimedia health risk assessment model', Santa Clara, CA: ENSR Consulting and Engineering.

Consumer Energy Council of America (1990), *Incorporating Environmental Externalities into Utility Planning*, draft report.

Cooper, J. and J. Loomis (1992), 'Sensitivity of willingness-to-pay estimates to bid design in dichotomous choice contingent valuation models', *Land Economics*, **68** (2), 211–24.

Courant, P.N. and R.C. Porter (1981), 'Averting expenditure and the cost of pollution', *Journal of Environmental Economics and Management*, **8** (4), 321–9.

Crocetti, A.F., P. Mushak and J. Schwartz (1990), 'Determination of numbers of lead-exposed children in areas in the U.S.: An integrated summary of a report to the U.S. Congress on childhood lead poisoning', *Environmental Health Perspectives*, **89**, 109–20.

Cropper, M.L. (1981), 'Measuring the benefits from reduced morbidity', *American Economic Review*, **71**, 235–40.

Cropper, M.L. and A.M. Freeman III (1991), 'Environmental health effects', in J.B. Braden and C.D. Kolstad (eds), *Measuring the Demand for Environmental Quality*, Amsterdam: North-Holland.

Cropper, M.L. and A.J. Krupnick (1989), 'The social costs of chronic heart and lung disease', paper presented at the 1989 AERE workshop, 'Estimating and Valuing Morbidity in a Policy Context', Research Triangle Park, NC, 8–9 June.

Cruz, M.L. (1986), 'Product and geographical market measurements in the merger of hospitals', *Dickinson Law Review*, **91**, 497–527.

Dardis, R. (1980), 'The value of life: new evidence from the marketplace', *American Economic Review*, **70** (5), 1077–82.

Dasgupta, P., A.K. Sen and S. Marglin (1972), *Guidelines for Project Evaluation*, New York: United Nations.

Deck, L.B. and L.G. Chestnut (1992), 'Benefit transfer: How good is good enough?', paper presented at the 1992 Association of Environmental Resource Economists Workshop, Snowbird, Utah, 3–5 June.

Desvousges, W.H. (1995a), 'Sur-rebuttal testimony of Dr. William H. Desvousges', submitted to the Minnesota Public Utilities Commission, in the matter of *The Investigation of the*

Minnesota Public Utilities Commission Into the Quantification of Environmental Costs, Docket no. E999/CI-93-583.

Desvousges, W.H. (1995b), 'Volume V: Report on economic losses associated with groundwater', Expert report of Dr William H. Desvousges in the matter of *State of Montana v. Atlantic Richfield Company*, US District Court, District of Montana, Helena Division, no. CV-83-317-HLN-PGH.

Desvousges, W.H., M.C. Naughton and G.R. Parsons (1992), 'Benefit transfers: Conceptual and empirical issues', *Water Resources Research*, **28** (3), 675–83.

Desvousges, W.H., V.K. Smith and M.P. McGivney (1983), *A Comparison of Alternative Approaches for Estimation of Recreation and Related Benefits of Water Quality Improvements*, US EPA Report no. EPA-230-05-83-0001, Washington, DC: US EPA.

Desvousges, W.H., F.R. Johnson, H.S. Banzhaf, R.R. Russell, E.E. Fries, K.J. Dietz, S.C. Helms, D. Keen, J. Snyder, H. Balentine, V. Sadeghi and S.A. Martin (1995a), *Assessing Environmental Externality Costs for Electricity Generation*, seven-volume final report prepared for Northern States Power Company, Durham, NC: Triangle Economic Research.

Desvousges, W.H., F.R. Johnson, H.S. Banzhaf, R.R. Russell, E.E. Fries, K.J. Dietz, S.C. Helms, D. Keen, J. Snyder, H. Balentine, V. Sadeghi and S.A. Martin (1995b), *Assessing Environmental Externality Costs for Electricity Generation in Wisconsin*, seven-volume final report prepared for the Task Force on Externality Costing, Durham, NC: Triangle Economic Research.

Desvousges, W.H., F.R. Johnson, S.P. Hudson, A.R. Gable and M.C. Ruby (1996), *Using Conjoint Analysis and Health-State Classifications to Estimate the Value of Health Effects of Air Pollution: Pilot Test Results and Implications*, final report prepared for Environment Canada, Health Canada, Ontario Hydro, Ontario Ministry of Environment and Energy, and Quebec Ministry of Environment, Durham, NC: Triangle Economic Research.

Diamond, P.A. and J.A. Hausman (1994), 'Contingent valuation: is some number better than no number?', *Journal of Economic Perspectives*, **8** (4), 45–64.

Dickie, M., S. Gerking, W. Schulze, A. Coulson and D. Tashkin (1986), 'Value of symptoms of ozone exposure: An application of the averting behaviour method', in *Improving Accuracy and Reducing Cost of Environmental Benefit Assessments*, US Environmental Protection Agency.

Dickie, M., S. Gerking, D. Brookshire, D. Coursey, W. Schulze, A. Coulson and D. Tashkin (1987), 'Reconciling averting behaviour and contingent valuation benefit estimates of reducing symptoms of ozone exposure', in *Improving Accuracy and Reducing Costs of Environmental Benefit Assessment*, Washington, DC: US Environmental Protection Agency.

Dickie, M., S. Gerking, G. McClelland and W. Schulze (1988), 'Contingent valuation: The value formation process', unpublished manuscript, University of Wisconsin, Department of Economics.

Dillingham, A.E. (1979), 'The injury risk structure of occupations and wages', unpublished Ph.D. dissertation, Cornell University, Ithaca, New York.

Dillingham, A.E. (1985), 'The influence of risk variable definition on value of life estimates', *Economic Inquiry*, **24**, 277–94.

Dockery, D.W., J. Schwartz and J.D. Spengler (1992), 'Air pollution and daily mortality: Associations with particulates and acid aerosols', *Environmental Research*, **59**, 362–73.

Dockery, D.W., F.E. Speizer, D.O. Stram, J.H. Ware, J.D. Spengler and B.G. Ferris (1989), 'Effects of inhalable particles on respiratory health of children', *American Review of Respiratory Disease*, **139**, 587–94.

Downing, M. and T. Ozuna Jr (1996), 'Testing the reliability of the benefit function transfer approach', *Journal of Environmental Economics and Management*, **30** (3), 316–22.

Dunford, R.W., K.E. Mathews and H.S. Banzhaf (1995), 'A co-operative approach for measuring direct-use damages: The 1992 Avila Beach (CA) oil spill', paper presented at the 1995 International Oil Spill Conference, Long Beach, CA, 27 February–2 March.

Eckstein, O. (1958), *Water-Resource Development: The Economics of Project Evaluation*, Cambridge, MA: Harvard University Press.

Eddy, D.M., V. Hasselblad and R. Shachter (1992), *Meta-Analysis by the Confidence Profile Method*, Boston: Academic Press.

Efron, B. and R.J. Tibshirani (1993), *An Introduction to the Bootstrap*, Chapman and Hall: New York.

Elkiey, T., D.P. Ormrod and B.A. Marie (1988), 'Growth responses of crop plants in the vegetation stage to sulphur dioxide and nitrogen dioxide', *Gartenbauwissenschaft*, **53**, 61–4.

Elzinga, K.G. and T.F. Hogarty (1973), 'The problem of geographic market delineation in antimerger suits', *Antitrust Bulletin*, **18** (1), 45–81.

Epple, D. (1987), 'Hedonic prices and implicit markets: estimating demand and supply functions for differentiated products', *Journal of Political Economy*, **87** (1), 59–80.

European Commission (1995), *Externalities of Energy: ExternE Project*, report for the Directorate General XII, prepared by Metroeconomica, CEPN, IER, Eyre Energy-Environment, ETSU, and the Ecole des Mines.

Fairley, D. (1990), 'The relationship of daily mortality to suspended particulates in Santa Clara County, 1980–1986', *Environmental Health Perspectives*, **89**, 159–68.

Fanshel, S. and J.W. Bush (1970), 'A health-status index and its application to health-services outcomes', *Operations Research*, **18** (6), 1021–966.

Farrell, B.P., H.D. Kerr, T.J. Kulle, L.R. Sauder and J.L. Young (1979), 'Adaptation in human subjects to the effects of inhaled ozone after repeated exposure', *American Review of Respiratory Disease*, **119**, 725–30.

Finkel, A.M. (1990), 'A simple formula for calculating the "mass density" of a log normally distributed characteristic', *Risk Analysis*, **10** (2), 291–301.

Fischhoff, B. (1991), 'Value elicitation: is there anything in there?', *American Psychologist*, **46**, 835–47.

Fisher, A., L.G. Chestnut and D.M. Violette (1989), 'The value of reducing risks of death: A note on new evidence', *Journal of Policy Analysis and Management*, **8** (1), 88–100.

Fishman, G.S. (1996), *Monte Carlo: Concepts, Algorithms, and Applications*, New York: Springer-Verlag.

Folinsbee, L.J. and S.M. Horvath (1986), 'Persistence of the acute effects of ozone exposure', *Aviation, Space, and Environmental Medicine*, **57** (12), 1136–43.

Folinsbee, L., J.F. Bedi and S. Horvath (1985), 'Pulmonary response to threshold levels of sulfur dioxide (1.0 ppm) and ozone (0.3 ppm)', *Journal of Applied Physiology*, **58**, 1783–7.

Foster, K.W., H. Timm, D.K. Labanauskas and R.J. Oshima (1983), 'Effects of ozone and sulphur dioxide on tuber yield and quality of potatoes', *Journal of Environmental Quality*, **12** (1), 75–80.

Freeman, A.M. III (1984), 'On the tactics of benefit estimation under executive order 12291', in V.K. Smith (ed.), *Environmental Policy Under Reagan's Executive Order: The Role of Benefit–Cost Analysis*, Chapel Hill, NC: University of North Carolina Press.

Freeman, A.M. III (1989), '*Ex ante* and *ex post* values for small changes in risks', *Risk Analysis*, **9** (3), 309–17.

Freeman, A.M. III (1993), *The Measurement of Environmental and Resource Values: Theory and Methods*, Washington, DC: Resources for the Future.

Froberg, D.G. and R.L. Kane (1989), 'Methodology for measuring health-state preferences-II: Scaling methods', *Journal of Clinical Epidemiology*, **42** (5), 459–71.

Gaver, D.P., D. Draper, P.K. Goel, J.B. Greenhouse, L.V. Hedges, C.N. Morris and C. Watemaux (1992), *Combining Information: Statistical Issues and Opportunities for Research*, Washington, DC: National Research Council.

Gegax, D., S. Gerking and W. Schulze (1985), 'Perceived risk and the marginal value of safety', working paper prepared for the US Environmental Protection Agency, August.

Gerking, S. and L.R. Stanley (1986), 'An economic analysis of air pollution and health: The case of St. Louis', *The Review of Economics and Statistics*, **68** (1), 115–21.

Gerking, S., M. de Haan and W. Schulze (1988), 'The marginal value of job safety: A contingent valuation study', *Journal of Risk and Uncertainty*, **1** (2), 185–200.

Glass, G.V. (1976), 'Primary, secondary, and meta-analysis of research', *Educational Researcher*, **5**, 3–8.

Gold, D.R., A. Rotnitzky, A.I. Damokosh, J.H. Ware, F.E. Speizer, B.G. Ferris Jr and D.W. Dockery (1993), 'Race and gender differences in respiratory illness prevalence and their relationship to environmental exposures in children 7 to 14 years of age', *American Review of Respiratory Disease*, **148**, 10–18.

Graham, D.A. (1981), 'Cost–benefit analysis under uncertainty', *American Economic Review*, **71** (4), 715–25.

Graziano, J., D. Popovac, M.J. Murphy, A. Mehmeti, J. Kline, G. Ahmedi, P. Shrout, Z. Zvicer, G. Wasserman, E. Gashi, Z. Stein, B. Rajovic, L. Belmont, B. Colakovic, R. Bozovic, R. Haxhiu, L. Radovic, R. Vlaskovic, D.U. Nenezic and N.J. Loiacono (1989), 'Environmental lead, reproduction, and infant development', in M.A. Smith, L.D. Grant and A.I. Sors (eds), *Lead Exposure and Child Development: An International Assessment*, Dordrecht, The Netherlands: Kluwer Academic Publishers, pp. 379–86.

Greene, W.H. (1993), *Econometric Analysis*, Englewood Cliffs, NJ: Prentice Hall.

Greenley, D.A., R.G. Walsh and R.A. Young (1981), 'Option value: Empirical evidence from a case study of recreation and water quality', *Quarterly Journal of Economics*, **96**, 657–74.

Grossman, M. (1972), 'On the concept of health capital and the demand for health', *Journal of Political Economy*, **80**, 223–55.

Grubb, W.N., D. Whittington and M. Humphries (1984), 'The ambiguities of benefit–cost analysis: An evaluation of regulatory impact analyses under Executive Order 12291', in V.K. Smith (ed.), *Environmental Policy Under Reagan's Executive Order: The Role of Benefit–Cost Analysis*, Chapel Hill, NC: University of North Carolina Press.

'Guidelines as to what constitutes an adverse respiratory health effect with special reference to epidemiologic studies of air pollution' (1985), *American Review of Respiratory Disease*, **131**, 666.

Gupta, G. and S. Sabaratnam (1988), 'Reduction in soya-bean yield after a brief exposure to nitrogen dioxide', *Journal of Agricultural Science*, **110**, 399–400.

Halton, J. (1970), 'A retrospective and prospective survey of the Monte Carlo method', *SIAM Review*, **12**, 1–63.

Hanemann, W.M. (1991), 'Willingness to pay and willingness to accept: How much can they differ?,' *American Economic Review*, **81** (3), 635–47.

Hanemann, W.M. (1994), 'Valuing the environment through contingent valuation', *Journal of Economic Perspectives*, **8** (4), 19–43.

Harford, J.D. (1984), 'Averting behavior and the benefits of reduced soiling', *Journal of Environmental Economics and Management*, **11**, 296–302.

Harrington, W. and P. Portney (1987), 'Valuing the benefits of health and safety regulation', *Journal of Urban Economics*, **22**, 101–12.

Harrington, W., A.J. Krupnick and W.O. Spofford (1989), 'The economic losses of a waterborne disease outbreak', *Journal of Urban Economics*, **25**, 116–37.

Harrison, D., A.L. Nichols, S.L. Bittenbender and M.L. Berkman (1993), 'External costs of electric utility resource selection in Nevada', report to Nevada Power Company, March, Cambridge, MA: National Economic Research Associates.

Harrod, R.F. (1938), 'Scope and method in economics', *The Economic Journal*, **48**, 383–412.

Hasselblad, V., D.M. Eddy and D.J. Kotchmar (1992), 'Synthesis of environmental evidence: Nitrogen dioxide epidemiology studies', *Journal of the Air and Waste Management Association*, **42** (5), 662–71.

Hausman, J. (1978), 'Specification tests in econometrics', *Econometrica*, **46**, 1251–71.

Haveman. R. (1965), *Water Resource Investment and the Public Interest*, Nashville, TN: Vanderbilt University Press.

Hazucha, M.J. (1987), 'Relationship between ozone exposure and pulmonary function changes', *Journal of Applied Physiology*, **62** (4), 1671–80.

Heck, W.W. and D.T. Tingey (1979), *Nitrogen Dioxide: Time-Concentration Model to Predict Acute Foliar Injury*, report no. EPA-600/3-79-057, Corvallis, OR: US Environmental Protection Agency, Corvallis Environmental Research Laboratory.

Heck, W.W., O.C. Taylor, R. Adams, G. Bingham, J. Miller, E. Preston and L. Weinstein (1982), 'Assessment of crop loss from ozone', *Journal of the Air Pollution Control Association*, **32** (4), 353–61.

Heck, W.W., W.W. Cure, J.O. Rawlings, L.J. Zaragoza, A.S. Heagle, H.E. Heggestad, R.J. Kohut, L.W. Kress and P.J. Temple (1984), 'Assessing impacts of ozone on agricultural crops: Crop yield functions and alternative exposure statistics', *Journal of the Air Pollution Control Association*, **34** (8), 810–17.

Hicks, J.R. (1939), 'Foundations of welfare economics', *The Economic Journal*, **49**, 696–712.

Hirshliefer, J. and J.G. Riley (1992), *The Analytics of Uncertainty and Information*, Cambridge: Cambridge University Press.

Hixson, J. (1993), Environmental Toxicologist for Radian Corporation, personal communication on 17 January 1993, with the authors at Research Triangle Institute, Research Triangle Park, NC.

Hoehn, J.P. and A. Randall (1989), 'Too many proposals pass the benefit cost test', *American Economic Review*, **79** (3), 544–51.

Horst, R.L. (1995), Personal correspondence with H.S. Banzhaf, 25 April 1995.

Horvath, S.M., J.A. Gliner and L.J. Folinsbee (1981), 'Adaptation to ozone: duration of effect', *American Review of Respiratory Disease*, **123**, 496–9.

Huang, K.S. (1985), *US Demands for Food: A complete System of Price and Income Effects*, US Department of Agriculture, Economic Research Service, Technical Bulletin no. 1714.

Irving, P.M., J.E. Miller and P.B. Xerikos (1982), 'The effect of NO_2 and SO_2 alone and in combination on the productivity of field-grown soybeans', in T. Schneider and L. Grant (eds), *Air Pollution by Nitrogen Oxides*, Amsterdam, The Netherlands: Elsevier Scientific Publishing, pp. 521–31.

Irwin, J., D. Schenk, G.H. McClelland, W.D. Schulze, T. Stewart and M. Thayer (1989), 'Urban visibility: Some experiments on the contingent valuation method', in C.V. Mathai (ed.), *Visibility and Fine Particles: Transactions*, Pittsburgh, PA: Air and Waste Management Association, pp. 647–58.

Johannesson, M. (1992), 'Economic evaluation of hypertensive treatment', *International Journal of Technology Assessment in Health Care*, **8** (3), 506–23.

Johannesson, M. (1996), *Theory and Methods of Economic Evaluation of Health Care*, Dordrecht, The Netherlands: Kluwer Academic Publishers.

Johannesson, M., B. Jönsson and L. Borgquist (1991), 'Willingness to pay for antihypertensive therapy: results of a Swedish pilot study', *Journal of Health Economics*, **10**, 461–73.

Johannesson, M., P. Jöhansson, B. Kriström and U. Gerdtham (1993), 'Willingness to pay for antihypertensive therapy: Further results', *Journal of Health Economics*, **12**, 95–108.

Johnson, F.R., E.E. Fries and H.S. Banzhaf (1997), 'Valuing morbidity: An integration of the willingness-to-pay and health status index literatures', *Journal of Health Economics*, **16**, 641–65.

Johnson, F.R., M.C. Ruby, W.H. Desvousges and A.R. Gable (1996), 'Using stated preferences and health-state classifications to value the health benefits of air quality programs', paper presented at the 1997 annual meeting of the American Agricultural Economics Association, Toronto, July.

Johnson, F.R., W.H. Desvousges, M.C. Ruby, D. Stieb and P. De Civita (1998), 'Eliciting stated health preferences: an application to willingness to pay for longevity', *Medical Decision Making*, forthcoming.

Jones-Lee, M.W., M. Hammerton and P.R. Philips (1985), 'The value of safety: Results of a national sample survey', *Economic Journal*, **95**, 49–72.

Judge, G.G., R.C. Hill, W.E. Griffiths, H. Lutkepohl and T.C. Lee (1988), *Introduction to the Theory and Practice of Econometrics*, New York: John Wiley & Sons.

Kahneman, D. and A. Tversky (1979), 'Prospect theory: An analysis of decisions under risk', *Econometrica*, **47**, 263-91.

Kaldor, N. (1939), 'Welfare propositions of economics and inter-personal comparisons of utility', *The Economic Journal*, **49**, 549–53.

Kalkstein, L.S. (1991), 'A new approach to evaluate the impact of climate on human mortality', *Environmental Health Perspectives*, **96**, 145–50.

Kalvins, A. (1985), *Effects and Social Costs of Fossil–Fired Emissions Due to Electrical Exports on Structural Materials*, Ontario Hydro Research Division, Report No. 84–210-k.

Kanemoto, Y. (1988), 'Hedonic prices and the benefits of public projects', *Econometrica*, **56** (4), 981–9.

Kanninen, B.J. (1995), 'Bias in discrete response contingent valuation', *Journal of Environmental Economics and Management*, **28** (1), 114–25.

Kaplan, R.M. and J.P. Anderson (1988), 'A general health policy model, update and applications', *Health Services Research*, **23** (2), 203–35.

Kaplan, R.M. and J.P. Anderson (1990), 'The general health policy model, an integrated approach', in B Spilker (ed.), *Quality of Life Assessments in Clinical Trials*, New York: Raven Press, pp. 131–49.

Kaplan, R.M. and J.W. Bush (1982), 'Health-related quality of life measurement for evaluation research and policy analysis', *Health Psychology*, **1** (1), 61–80.

Kaplan, R.M. and J.A. Ernst (1983), 'Do category rating scales produce biased preferences weights for a health index?', *Medical Care*, **21** (2), 193–207.

Kaplan, R.M., J.P. Anderson and T.G. Ganiats (1993), 'The Quality of Well-Being Scale: Rationale for a single quality of life index', in S.R. Walker and R.M. Rosser (eds), *Quality of Life Assessment: Key Issues in the 1990s*, Boston: Kluwer Academic.

Kaplan, R.M., J.W. Bush and C.C. Berry (1976), 'Health status: Types of validity and the index of well-being', *Health Services Research*, **11** (4), 478–507.

Kaplan, R.M., J.W. Bush and C.C. Berry (1978), 'The reliability, stability, and generalizability of health status index', paper presented at the annual meeting of the American Statistical Association, Social Statistics Section.

Kaplan, R.M., J.P. Anderson, T.L. Patterson, J.A. McCutchan, J.D. Weinrich, R.K. Heaton, J.H. Atkinson, L. Thal, J. Chandler, I. Grant and HNRC Group (1995), 'Validity of the quality of well-being scale for persons with human immunodeficiency virus infection', *Psychosomatic Medicine*, **57**, 138–47.

Kask, S.B. (1992), 'Long-term health risks valuation: Pigeon River, North Carolina', paper presented at the 1992 Association of Environmental Resource Economists Workshop, Snowbird, Utah 3–5 June.

Katsouyanni, K., A. Pantazopoulou, G. Touloumi, I. Tselepidaki, K. Moustris, D. Asimakopoulos, G. Poulopoulou and D. Trichopoulos (1993), 'Evidence for interaction between air pollution and high temperature in the causation of excess mortality', *Archives of Environmental Health*, **48** (4), 235–42.

Keller, L.R. and R. Staelin (1987), 'Effects of quality and quantity of information on decision effectiveness, *Journal of Consumer Research*, **114**, 200–213.

Kendall, M. and A. Stuart (1963), *The Advanced Theory of Statistics*, New York: Hafner Publishing.

Kinney, P.L. and H.K. Özkaynak (1991), 'Associations of daily mortality and air pollution in Los Angeles County', *Environmental Research*, **54**, 99–120.

Kinney, P.L., J.H. Ware and J.D. Spengler (1988), 'A critical evaluation of acute ozone epidemiology results', *Archives of Environmental Health*, **43** (2), 168–73.

Kirchhoff, S., B.G. Colby and J.T. LaFrance (1997), 'Evaluating the performance of benefit transfer: An empirical inquiry', *Journal of Environmental Economics and Management*, **33** (1), 75–93.

Klein, H., H.-J. Jäger, W. Domes and C.H. Wong (1978), 'Mechanisms contributing to differential sensitivities of plants to SO_2', *Oecologia* (Berlin), **33**, 203–8.

Kleinman, M. and J. Whittenberger (1985), *Effects of Short-Term Exposure to Carbon Monoxide in Subjects With Coronary Artery Disease*, Report no. ARB-R-86/176, Sacramento, CA: California State Air Resources Board.

Kneese, A.V. (1964), *The Economics of Regional Water Quality Management*, Baltimore, MD: The Johns Hopkins University Press for Resources for the Future.

Kniesner, T.J. and J.D. Leeth (1991), 'Compensating wage differentials for fatal injury risk in Australia, Japan, and the United States', *Journal of Risk and Uncertainty*, **4** (1), 75–90.

Kopp, R.J. and A.J. Krupnick (1987), 'Agricultural policy and the benefits of ozone control', *American Journal of Agricultural Economics*, **69** (5), 956–62.

Kopp, R.J., J.T. Barron and J.P. Tow (1988), 'Cardiovascular actions of lead and relationship to hypertension: a review', in W. Victery (ed.), 'Symposium on Lead–Blood Pressure Relationships' and *Environmental Health Perspectives*, **78**, 77–83.

Kopp, R.J., W.J. Vaughan and M. Hazilla (1984), *Agricultural Sector Benefits Analysis for Ozone: Methods Evaluation and Demonstration*, final report submitted to the Office of Air Quality Planning and Standards, US Environmental Protection Agency, Research Triangle Park, NC.

Koppelman, F.S. and C.G. Wilmot (1986), 'The effect of omission of variables on choice model transferability', *Transportation Research B*, **20B** (3), 205–13.

Krupa, S.V. (1987), *Responses of Alfalfa to Sulphur Dioxide Exposures from the Emissions of the NSP-SHERCO Coal-Fired Power Plant Units 1 and 2*, report to Northern States Power Company.

Krupa, S.V. and M. Nosal (1989), 'A multivariate, time series model to relate alfalfa responses to chronic, ambient sulphur dioxide exposures', *Environmental Pollution*, **61**, 3–10.

Krupnick, A.J. (1986), *Benefit Estimation and Environmental Policy: Setting the NAAQS for Photochemical Oxidants*, Resources for the Future, Quality of the Environment Division, Washington, DC.

Krupnick, A.J. (1992), 'Benefit transfer and social costing', paper presented at the 1992 Association of Environmental Resource Economists Workshop, Snowbird, Utah, 3–5 June.

Krupnick, A.J. and M.L. Cropper (1992), 'The effect of information on health risk valuations', *Journal of Risk and Uncertainty*, **5** (1), 29–48.

Krupnick, A.J. and R.J. Kopp (1988), *The Health and Agricultural Benefits of Reductions in Ambient Ozone in the United States*, discussion paper QE88-10, Washington, DC: Resources for the Future.

Krupnick, A.J., W. Harrington and B. Ostro (1990), 'Ambient ozone and acute health effects: Evidence from daily data', *Journal of Environmental Economics and Management*, **18** (1), 1–18.

Krupnick, A.J., M.L. Cropper, M. Hagan, M. Eiswerth, J. Kurl, S. Radin and C. Harnett (1989), *Valuing Chronic Morbidit Damages: Medical Costs, Labor Market Effects, and Individual Valuations*, interim report for the US Environmental Protection Agency.

Krutilla, J.V. (1972), *Natural Environments: Studies in Theoretical and Applied Analysis*, Baltimore, MD: The Johns Hopkins University Press for Resources for the Future.

Krutilla, J.V. (1981), 'Reflections of an applied welfare economist', presidential address from the annual meeting of the Association of Environmental and Resource Economists, 6 September 1980, Denver, Colorado, reprinted in *Journal of Environmental Economics and Management*, **8**, 1–10.

Krutilla, J.V., and A.C. Fisher (1975), *The Economics of Natural Environments*, Baltimore, MD: Johns Hopkins University Press.

Leamer, E.E. (1995), 'Pooling Noisy Data Sets', in T. Url and A. Wörgötter (eds), *Econometrics of Short and Unreliable Time Series*, Heidelberg: Physica-Verlag.

Lee, R., A.J. Krupnick and D. Burtraw (1995), 'Estimating externalities of electric fuel cycles: Analytical methods and issues', Washington, DC: McGraw-Hill/Utility Data Institute.

Leigh, J.P. and R.N. Folsom (1984), 'Estimates of the value of accident avoidance at the job depend on concavity of the equalising differences curve', *The Quarterly Review of Economics and Business*, **24** (1), 56–66.

Lerman, S.R. (1981), 'A comment on interspatial, intraspatial, and temporal transferability', in P.R. Stopher, A.H. Meyburg and W. Börg (eds), *New Horizons in Travel-Behaviour Research*, Lexington, MA: Lexington Books.

Leung, S.K., W. Reed and S. Geng (1982), 'Estimations of ozone damage to selected crops grown in southern California', *Journal of the Air Pollution Control Association*, **32** (2), 160–64.

Levin, R. (1987), *Reducing Lead in Drinking Water, A Benefits Analysis*, revised final report, EPA Document no. EPA/230/09-86-019.

Li, Y., T.E. Powers and H.D. Roth (1994), 'Random-effects linear regression meta-analysis models with application to the nitrogen dioxide health effects studies', *Journal of Air & Waste Management Association*, **44** (March), 261–70.

Lindquist, O., R.E. Manglo, L.E. Olsson and J. Rosvall (1988), 'Case study on the deterioration of stone: The Cathedral Well (Domkyrkobrunnen) in Goteborg', *Durability of Building Materials*, **5**, 581–611.

Lipfert, F.W., R.G. Malone, M.L. Daum, N.R. Mendell and C.C. Yang (1988), *A Statistical Study of the Macroepidemiology of Air Pollution and Total Mortality*, Report prepared for the US Department of Energy, Office of Environmental Analysis, Washington, DC, under Contract no. DE-ACO2-76CH00016, Upton, Long Island, NY: Brookhaven National Laboratory.

Little, I.M.D. and J.A. Mirlees (1969), *Manual of Industrial Project Analysis in Developing Countries*, Paris: Organization for Economic Cooperation and Development.

Loehman, E.T. and D. Boldt (1981), 'Willingness to pay for gain and losses in visibility and health', unpublished paper, Purdue University and West Georgia College.

Loehman, E.T., D. Boldt and K. Chaikin (1984), *Measuring the Benefits of Air Quality Changes in the San Francisco Bay Area*, US EPA project no. EPA-230/07-83-009, Washington, DC: US EPA Office of Policy Analysis.

Loehman, E.T., S.V. Berg, A.A. Arroyo, R.A. Hedinger, J.M. Schwartz, M.E. Shaw, R.W. Fahien, V.H. De, R.P. Fishe, D.E. Rio, W.F. Rossley and A.E.S. Green (1979), 'Distributional analysis of regional benefits and cost of air quality control', *Journal of Environmental Economics and Management*, **6**, 222–43.

Loomis, J.B. (1992), 'The evolution of a more rigorous approach to benefit transfer: Benefit function transfer', *Water Resources Research*, **28** (3), 701–5.

Loomis, J.B. and D.S. White (1996), 'Economic benefits of rare and endangered species: summary and meta-analysis', *Ecological Economics*, **18**, 197–206.

Low, S.A. and L.R. McPheters (1983), 'Wage differentials and risk of death: an empirical analysis', *Economic Inquiry*, **21**, 271–80.

Luken, R.A., F.R. Johnson and V. Kibler (1992), 'Benefits and costs of pulp and paper effluent controls under the clean water act', *Water Resources Research*, **28** (3), 665–74.

Machina, M.A. (1983), 'Generalized expected utility analysis and the nature of observed violations of the independent axiom', in B.P. Stigum and F. Wenstop (eds), *Foundations of Utility and Risk Theory with Applications*, Dordrecht, The Netherlands: D. Reidel.

Machina, M.A. (1984), 'Temporal risk and the nature of induced preferences', *Journal of Economic Theory*, **33**, 199–231.

MacNair, D. (1993), 'RPA recreation values database', mimeo.

Magat, W.A., W.K. Viscusi and J. Huber (1988), 'Paired comparison and contingent valuation approaches to morbidity risk valuation', *Journal of Environmental Economics and Management*, **15** (4), 395–411.

Manski, C. and S. Lerman (1977), 'The estimation of choice probabilities from choice-based samples', *Econometrica*, **45**, 1977–88.

Manuel, E.H., R.L. Horst, K.M. Brennan, W.N. Lanen, M.C. Duff and J.K. Tapiero (1982), *Benefits Analysis of Alternative Secondary National Ambient Air Quality Standards for Sulphur Dioxide and Total Suspended Particulates*, report prepared for the US Environmental Protection Agency, Princeton, NJ: Mathtech, Inc.

Marin, A. and G. Psacharopoulos (1982), 'The reward for risk in the labour market: Evidence from the United Kingdom and a reconciliation with other studies', *Journal of Political Economy*, **90** (4), 827–53.

McConnell, K.E. (1992), 'Model building and judgment: Implications for benefit transfers with travel cost models', *Water Resources Research*, **28** (3), 695–700.

McConnell, K.E. and T.T. Phipps (1987), 'Identification of preference parameters in hedonic models: Consumer demands with nonlinear budgets', *Journal of Urban Economics*, **22** (1) 35–52.

McFadden, D. (1973), 'Conditional logit analysis of qualitative choice behaviour', in P. Zarembka (ed.), *Frontiers in Econometrics*, New York: Academic Press.

McFadden, D. and G.K. Leonard (1993), 'Issues in the contingent valuation of environmental goods: Methodologies for data collection and analysis', in J.A. Hausman (ed.), *Contingent Valuation, A Critical Assessment*, Amsterdam: North-Holland.

McMichael, A.J., G.V. Vimpani, E.F. Robertson, P.A. Baghurst and P.D. Clark (1986), 'The Port Pirie cohort study: Maternal blood lead and pregnancy outcome', *Journal of Epidemiology and Community Health*, **40**, 18–25.

Mehrez, A. and A. Gafni (1989), 'Quality-adjusted life years, utility theory, and healthy-years equivalents', *Medical Decision Making*, **9** (2), 142–9.

Miller, T. (1990), 'The plausible range for the value of life: Red herrings among the mackerel', *Journal of Forensic Economics*, **3** (3), 17–39.

Milon, J.W. (1989), 'Contingent valuation experiments for strategic behaviour', *Journal of Environmental Economics and Management*, **17**, 293–308.

Mishan, E.J. (1971), 'Evaluation of life and limb: A theoretical approach', *Journal of Political Economy*, **79**, 687–705.

Mitchell, R.C. and R.T. Carson (1989), *Using Surveys to Value Public Goods: The Contingent Valuation Methods*, Washington, DC: Resources for the Future.

Mitchell, R., R. Carson and P. Ruud (1989), 'Cincinnati visibility valuation study: Pilot study findings', unpublished draft, Clark University, University of California–San Diego, and University of California–Berkeley.

Moore, M.J. and W.K. Viscusi (1988a), 'Doubling the estimated value of life: Results using new occupational fatality data', *Journal of Policy Analysis and Management*, **7** (3), 476–90.

Moore, M.J. and W.K. Viscusi (1988b), 'The quantity-adjusted value of life', *Economic Inquiry*, **26** (3), 369–88.

Moore, M.J. and W.K. Viscusi (1990), *Compensating Mechanisms for Job Risks: Wages, Workers' Compensation, and Product Liability*, Princeton, NJ: Princeton University Press.

Morgan, M.G. and M. Henrion (1990), *Uncertainty: A Guide to Dealing with Uncertainty in Quantitative Risk and Policy Analysis*, Cambridge: Cambridge University Press.

Morgenstern, R.D. (1997), *Economic Analysis at EPA: Assessing Regulatory Impact*, Washington, DC: Resources for the Future.

Morris, R., T.C. Myers, E.L. Carr, M.C. Causley, S.G. Douglas and R.D. Scheffe (1990), *User's Guide for the Urban Airshed Model*, Vol. 1–5, EPA-450/4-90-007, Research Triangle Park, NC: US Environmental Protection Agency.

Morton, B.J. and A.J. Krupnick (1987), *Estimation of Concentration-Response Functions for Respiratory Symptoms Using Data From Four Controlled Human Exposure Studies of Acute Responses to Ozone*, Research Triangle Park, NC: US Environmental Protection Agency.

Morton, B.J. and A.J. Krupnick (1988), 'Ozone acute health dose-response functions: Combined results from four clinical studies', mimeo.

National Research Council (1993), *Protecting Visibility in National Parks and Wilderness Areas*, Washington, DC: National Academy Press.

Needleman, H.L. and C.A. Gatsonis (1990), 'Low-level lead exposure and the IQ of children', *Journal of the American Medical Association*, **263**, 673–8.

Needleman, H.L., A. Schell, D. Bellinger, A. Leviton and E.N. Allred (1990), 'The long-term effects of exposure to low doses of lead in childhood', *New England Journal of Medicine*, **322**, 83–8.

Olson, C.A. (1981), 'An analysis of wage differentials received by workers on dangerous jobs', *Journal of Human Resources*, **16**, 167–85.

Ontario Hydro (1990), *Social Cost Studies*, six vols, Toronto.

Oregon Health Services Commission (1991), *Prioritization of Health Services: A Report to the Governor and Legislature*, Portland, Oregon.

Oshima, R.J., M.P. Poe, P.K. Braegelmann, D.W. Baldwin and V. Van Way (1976), 'Ozone dosage-crop loss function for alfalfa: A standardized method for assessing crop losses from air pollutants', *Journal of the Air Pollution Control Association*, **26** (9), 861–5.

Ostro, B.D., California Environmental Protection Agency, 9 December 1993, personal communication with H.S. Banzhaf, Research Triangle Institute, Research Triangle Park, NC.

Ostro, B.D. and S. Rothschild (1989), 'Air pollution and acute respiratory morbidity: An observational study of multiple pollutants', *Environmental Research*, **50**, 238–47.

Ostro, B.D., M.J. Lipsett and N.P. Jewell (1989), 'Predicting respiratory morbidity from pulmonary function tests: A reanalysis of ozone chamber studies', *Journal of the Air Pollution Control Association*, 39 (10), 1313–18.

Ostro, B.D., M.J. Lipsett, J.K. Mann, A. Krupnick and W. Harrington (1993), 'Air pollution and respiratory morbidity among adults in southern California', *American Journal of Epidemiology*, 137 (7), 691–700.

Özkaynak, H. and G.D. Thurston (1987), 'Associations between 1980 U.S. mortality rates and alternative measures of airborne particle concentration', *Risk Analysis*, 7 (4), 449–61.

Palmquist, R.B. (1991), 'Hedonic methods', in J.B. Braden and C.D. Kolstad (eds), *Measuring Demand for Environmental Improvement*, Amsterdam: North-Holland.

Parkinson, D.K., M.J. Hodgson, E.J. Bromet, M.A. Dew and M.M. Connell (1987), 'Occupational lead exposure and blood pressure', *British Journal of Industrial Medicine*, 44, 744–8.

Patrick, D.L., J.W. Bush and M.M. Chen (1973), 'Methods for measuring levels of well-being for a health status index', *Health Services Research*, 8 (2), 228–45.

Peterson, J.E. and R.D. Stewart (1970), 'Absorption and elimination of carbon monoxide by inactive young men', *Archives of Environmental Health*, 21, 165–71.

Pocock, S.J., A.G. Shaper, D. Ashby and T. Delves (1985), 'Blood lead and blood pressure in middle-aged men', in T.D. Lekkas (ed.), *International Conference: Heavy Metals in the Environment*, Edinburgh: CEP Consultants, Ltd, pp. 303–5.

Pocock, S.J., A.G. Shaper, D. Ashby, T. Delves and T.P. Whitehead (1984), 'Blood lead concentrations, blood pressure, and renal function', *British Medical Journal*, 289, 872-4.

Pope, C.A., J. Schwartz and M.R. Ransom (1992), 'Daily mortality and PM_{10} pollution in Utah Valley', *Archives of Environmental Health*, 47 (3), 211–17.

Porter, T. (1995), *Trust in Numbers: The Pursuit of Objectivity in Science and Public Life*, Princeton, NJ: Princeton University Press.

Portney, P.R. and J. Mullahy (1986), 'Urban air quality and acute respiratory illness', *Journal of Urban Economics*, 20, 21–38.

Portney, P.R. and J. Mullahy (1990), 'Urban air quality and chronic respiratory disease', *Regional Science and Urban Economics*, 20, 407–18.

Pratt, G.C. (1982), 'Effects of ozone and sulphur dioxide on soybeans', Ph.D. thesis, University of Minnesota.

Quackenboss, J.J., J.D. Spengler, M.S. Kanarek, R. Letz and C.P. Duffy (1986), 'Personal exposure to nitrogen dioxide: Relationship to indoor/outdoor air quality and activity patterns', *Environmental Science and Technology*, 20 (8), 775–83.

Rae, D.A. (1984), *Benefits of Visual Air Quality in Cincinnati: Results of a Contingent Ranking Survey*, report prepared for Electric Power Research Institute, Boston, MA: Charles River Associates.

Ramberg, J.S., E.J. Dudewicz, P.R. Tadikamalla and E.F. Mykytka (1979), 'A probability distribution and its uses in fitting data', *Technometrics*, 21 (2), 201–14.

Randall, A. (1991), 'Total and nonuse values', in J.B. Braden and C.D. Kolstad (eds), *Measuring the Demand for Environmental Quality*, Amsterdam: North-Holland, pp. 303–21.

Reardon, Gregory and D.S. Pathak (1989), 'Contingent valuation of pharmaceuticals and pharmacy services – methodological considerations', *Journal of Social and Administrative Pharmacy*, 6 (2), 83–91.

Robbins, L. (1938), 'Interpersonal comparisons of utility: Comment', *The Economic Journal*, 48, 635–41.

Rosen, S. (1974), 'Hedonic prices and implicit markets: Product differentiation in price competition', *Journal of Political Economy*, 82 (1), 34–55.

Rosenthal, R. (1991), *Meta-Analytic Procedures for Social Research*, London: Sage Publications.

Rosenthal, R. and D.B. Rubin (1988), 'Comment: Assumptions and procedures in the file drawer problem', *Statistical Science*, 3, 120–25.

Rousseeuw, P.J. and A.M. Leroy (1987), *Robust Regression and Outlier Detection*, New York: John Wiley and Sons.

Rowe, R.D. and L.G. Chestnut (1985a), *Oxidants and Asthmatics in Los Angeles: A Benefits Analysis*, final report prepared for US EPA, Document no. EPA/230/7-85/010.

Rowe, R.D. and L.G. Chestnut (1985b), 'Economic assessment of the effects of air pollution on agricultural crops in the San Joaquin Valley', *Journal of the Air Pollution Control Association*, **35**, 728–34.

Rowe, R.D., R.C. d'Arge and D.S. Brookshire (1980), 'An experiment on the economic value of visibility', *Journal of Environmental Economics and Management*, **7**, 1–19.

Rowe, R.D., S. S. Benow, L.A. Bird, J.M. Callaway, L.G. Chestnut, M.M. Eldridge, C.M. Lang, D.A. Latimer, J.C. Murdock, B.D. Ostro, A.K. Patterson, D.A. Rae and D.E. White (1994), *New York State Environmental Externalities Cost Study*, report prepared for Empire State Electric Energy Research Corporation and New York State Energy Research and Development Authority, Boulder, CO: RCG/Hagler, Bailey, Inc.

Salmon, R.L. (1970), *Systems Analysis of the Effects of Air Pollution on Materials*, final report prepared for Economic Effects Research Division, National Air Pollution Control Administration, Raleigh, NC, Kansas City, MO: Midwest Research Institute.

Schkade, D.A. and J.W. Payne (1994), 'Where do the numbers come from? How people respond to contingent valuation questions', in J. Hausman (ed.), *Contingent Valuation: A Critical Assessment*, Amsterdam: North-Holland.

Schmalensee, R. (1972), 'Option demand and consumer's surplus: Valuing price changes under uncertainty', *American Economic Review*, **62** (5), 813–24.

Schulze, W.D., G. McClelland, D. Waldman, J. Irwin, D. Schenk, T. Stewart, L. Deck and M. Thayer (1991), *Valuing Eastern Visibility: A Field Test of the Contingent Valuation Method*, report prepared for the US Environmental Protection Agency.

Schwartz, J. (1991a), 'Particulate air pollution and daily mortality in Detroit', *Environmental Research*, **56**, 204–13.

Schwartz, J. (1991b), 'Particulate air pollution and daily mortality: a synthesis', *Public Health Reviews*, **28**, 39–60.

Schwartz, J. (1991c), 'Lead, blood pressure, and cardiovascular disease in men and women', *Environmental Health Perspectives*, **91**, 71–5.

Schwartz, J. (1993a), 'Air pollution and daily mortality in Birmingham, Alabama', *American Journal of Epidemiology*, **137** (10), 1136–47.

Schwartz, J. (1993b), 'Particulate air pollution and chronic respiratory disease', *Environmental Research*, **62**, 7–13.

Schwartz, J. and D.W. Dockery (1992a), 'Increased mortality in Philadelphia associated with daily air pollution concentrations', *American Review of Respiratory Disease*, **145**, 600–604.

Schwartz, J. and D.W. Dockery (1992b), 'Particulate air pollution and daily mortality in Steubenville, Ohio,' *American Journal of Epidemiology*, **135** (1), 12–19.

Schwartz, J. and A. Marcus (1990), 'Mortality and air pollution in London: A time series analysis', *American Journal of Epidemiology*, **31** (1),185–94.

Schwartz, J. and S. Zeger (1990), 'Passive smoking, air pollution, and acute respiratory symptoms in a diary study of student nurses', *American Journal of Respiratory Disease*, **141** (1), 62–7.

Schwartz, J., V. Hasselblad and H. Pitcher (1988), 'Air pollution and morbidity: A further analysis of the Los Angeles student nurses data', *Journal of the Air Pollution Control Association*, **38**, 158–62.

Schwarz, N., H. Hippler, B. Deutsch and F. Strack (1985), 'Response scales: Effects of category range on reported behavior and comparative judgments', *Public Opinion Quarterly*, **49** (3), 388–95.

Schwartz, J., C. Spix, H.E. Wichmann and E. Malin (1991), 'Air pollution and acute respiratory illness in five German communities', *Environmental Research*, **56**, 1–14.

Shachter, E.N., T.J. Witek, G.J. Beck, H.R. Hosein, G. Colice, B.P. Leaderer and W. Cain (1984), 'Airway effects of low concentrations of sulfur dioxide: Dose-response characteristics', *Archives of Environmental Health*, **39** (1), 34–42.

Shepard, R.N. (1964), 'On subjectively optimum selections among multiattribute alternatives', in M.W. Shelby and G.L. Bryan (eds), *Human Judgments and Optimality*, New York: Wiley.

Sheps, D.S., K.F. Adams, P.A. Bromberg, G.M. Goldstein, J.J. O'Neil, D. Horstman and G. Koch (1987), 'Lack of effect of low levels of carboxyhemoglobin on cardiovascular function in patients with ischemic heart disease', *Archives of Environmental Health*, **42** (2), 108–16.

Shields, M.D. (1983), 'Effects of information supply and demand on judgment accuracy: evidence from corporate managers', *Accounting Review*, **58**, 284–303.

Shumway, R.H., A.S. Azari and Y. Pawitan (1988), 'Modeling mortality fluctuations in Los Angeles as functions of pollution and weather effects', *Environmental Research*, **45**, 224–41.

Sillman, S., J.A. Logan and S.C. Wofsy (1990), 'The sensitivity of ozone to nitrogen oxides and hydrocarbons in regional ozone episodes', *Journal of Geophysical Research*, **95**, 1837–51.

Sinn, J.P. and E.J. Pell (1984), 'Impact of repeated nitrogen dioxide exposures on composition and yield of potato foliage and tubers', *Journal of American Horticultural Science*, **109**, 481–4.

Slovic, P., D. Griffin and A. Tversky (1990), 'Compatibility effects in judgment and choice', in Robin Hogarth (ed.), *Insights in Decision Making*, Chicago: University of Chicago Press.

Slovic, P., B. Fischhoff and S. Lichtenstein (1979), 'Rating the risks', *Environment*, **21** (3), 14–20, 36–39.

Smith, R.S. (1974), 'The feasibility of an "injury tax" approach to occupational safety', *Law and Contemporary Problems*, **38** (4), 730–44.

Smith, R.S. (1976), *The Occupational Safety and Health Act: Its Goals and Achievements*, Washington: American Enterprise Institute.

Smith, V.K. (1983), 'The role of site and job characteristics in hedonic wage models', *Journal of Urban Economics*, **13**, 296–321.

Smith, V.K. (1991), 'Household production functions', in J.B. Braden and C.D. Kolstad (eds), *Measuring the Demand for Environmental Quality*, Amsterdam: North-Holland.

Smith, V.K. (1992), 'On separating defensible benefit transfers from smoke and mirrors', *Water Resources Research*, **28** (3), 685–94.

Smith, V.K. (1996), 'Environmental costing: Experience and prospects', *Resource and Energy Economics*, **18**.

Smith, V.K. and W.H. Desvousges (1986), *Measuring Water Quality Benefits*, Boston: Kluwer–Nijhoff Publishing.

Smith, V.K. and W.H. Desvousges (1987), 'An empirical analysis of the economic value of risk changes', *Journal of Political Economy*, **95** (1), 89–114.

Smith, V.K. and J. Huang (1983), *Can Markets Value Air Quality? A Meta-Analysis of Hedonic Property Value Models*, Discussion Paper QE93-17, Washington, DC: Resources for the Future, Inc.

Smith, V.K. and J. Huang (1995), 'Can markets value air quality? A meta-analysis of hedonic property value models', *Journal of Political Economy*, **103** (1), 209–27.

Smith, V.K. and Y. Kaoru (1990), 'Signals or noise? Explaining the variation in recreation benefit estimates', *American Journal of Agricultural Economics* (May), 419–33.

Smith, V.K. and L. Osborne (1993), *Do Contingent Valuation Estimates Pass a 'Scope' Test? A Preliminary Meta-Analysis*, working paper, Raleigh, NC: North Carolina State University, Department of Economics.

Smith, V.K. and L. Osborne (1996), 'Do contingent valuation estimates pass a "scope" test? A meta-analysis', *Journal of Environmental Economics and Management*, **31**, 287–301.

Smith, V.K., W.H. Desvousges and A. Fisher (1986), 'A comparison of direct and indirect methods for estimating environmental benefits', *American Journal of Agricultural Economics*, **68** (2), 280–90.

Sommerville, M.C., S.E. Spruill, J.O. Rawlings and V.M. Lesser (1989), *Impact of Ozone and Sulphur Dioxide on the Yield of Agricultural Crops*, North Carolina Agricultural Research Service Technical Bulletin 292.

Sundstrom, G.A. (1987), 'Information search and decision making: the effects of information displays', *Acta Psychologica*, **65**, 165–79.

Sussman, F.G. (1984), 'A note on the willingness to pay approach to the valuation of longevity', *Journal of Environmental Economics and Management*, **11**, 84–9.

Thacker, S.B. (1988), 'Meta-analysis: A quantitative approach to research integration', *Journal of the American Medical Association*, **259** (11), 1685–9.

Thaler, R. and S. Rosen (1976), 'The value of saving a life: Evidence from the labor market', in N. Terleckyz (ed.), *Household Production and Consumption*, New York: Columbia University Press.

Thayer, M. (1995), 'Rebuttal exhibit of Dr. Mark Thayer', submitted to the Minnesota Public Utilities Commission, in the matter of *The Investigation of the Minnesota Public Utilities Commission Into the Quantification of Environmental Costs*, Docket no. E999/CI-93-583.

Thayer, M.A., F.D. Sebold, J.C. Murdock, T.A. Mayer, D.R. Murray, S.R. Tracy and J. Zapert (1994), *The Air Quality Valuation Model*, report prepared for California Energy Commission, San Diego, CA: Regional Economic Research.

Thompson, M.S. (1986), 'Willingness to pay and accept risks to cure chronic disease', *American Journal of Public Health*, **76** (4), 392–6.

Thompson, M.S., J.L. Read and M. Liang (1984), 'Feasibility of willingness to pay measurement in chronic arthritis', *Medical Decision Making*, **4**, 195–215.

Tolley, G., A. Frankel and A. Kelly (1988), 'Estimation of the basic visibility value function', in George Tolley and Robert Fabien (eds), *The Economic Value of Visibility*, Mount Pleasant, MI: Blackstone Company.

Tolley, G., D. Kenkel and R. Fabian (eds) (1994), *Valuing Health for Policy An Economic Approach*, Chicago: The University of Chicago Press.

Tolley, G., L. Babcock, M. Berger, A. Bilotti, G. Blomquist, M. Brien, R. Fabian, G. Fishelson, C. Kahn, A. Kelly, D. Kenkel, R. Krumm, T. Miller, R. Ohsfeldt, S. Rosen, W. Webb, W. Wilson and M. Zelder (1986a), 'Valuation of reductions in human health symptoms and risk', in *Vol. 1: Contingent Valuation Study of Light Symptoms and Angina*, final report prepared for US Environmental Protection Agency.

Tolley, G.A., A. Randall, G. Blomquist, R. Fadian, G. Fishelson, A. Frankel, J. Hoehn, R. Krumm, E. Mensah and T. Smith (1986b), *Establishing and Valuing the Effects of Improved Visibility in Eastern United States*, report prepared for the US Environmental Protection Agency.

Torrance, G.W. (1986), 'Measurement of health state utilities for economic appraisal', *Journal of Health Economics*, **5**, 1–30.

Train, K.E. (1979), 'A comparison of the predictive ability of mode choice models with various levels of complexity', *Transportation Research A*, **13A**, 11–16.

Trainer, M., M.P. Buhr, C.M. Curran, F.C. Fehsenfeld, E.Y. Hsie, S.C. Liu, R.B. Norton, D.D. Parrish, E.J. Williams, B.W. Gandrud, B.A. Ridley, J.D. Shelte, E.J. Allwine and H.H. Westberg (1991), 'Observations and modeling of the reactive nitrogen photochemistry at a rural site', *Journal of Geophysical Research*, **96**, 3045–63.

Trainer, M., D.D. Parrish, M.P. Buhr, R.B. Norton, F.C. Fehsenfeld, K.G. Anlauf, J.W. Bottenheim, Y.Z. Tang, H.A. Wiebe, K.J. Olszyna, M.O. Rodgers, T. Wang, H. Barreshe, K.L. Demerjian and U.K. Roychowdhury (1993), 'Correlation of ozone with NO_y in photochemically aged air', *Journal of Geophysical Research*, **96**, 3045–63.

TRC Environmental Consultants, Inc. (1984), *Damage Cost Models for Pollution Effects on Materials*, report prepared for Environmental Sciences Research Lab, East Hartford, CT: TRC Environmental Consultants, Inc.

Trijonis, J. and K. Yuan (1978), *Visibility in the Northeast: Long-Term Visibility Trends and Visibility/Pollutant Relationships*, report prepared for Environmental Sciences Research Lab, Santa Monica, CA: Technology Service Corporation.

Trumbull, W.N (1990), 'Who has standing in cost–benefit analysis?', *Journal of Policy Analysis and Management*, **9** (2), 201–18.

Tversky, A., S. Sattah and P. Slovic (1988), 'Contingent weighting in judgment and choice', *Psychological Review*, **95** (3), 371–84.

US Council on Environmental Quality (1991), *National Acid Precipitation Assessment Program*.

US Department of Commerce, Bureau of the Census (1988), *1987 Census of Manufacturers*, Washington, DC: Government Printing Office.

US Department of Commerce (1993), *Current Industrial Reports*, Washington, DC: Bureau of the Census, Economics and Statistics Administration.

US Department of Health and Human Services (1988), *The Nature and Extent of Lead Poisoning in Children in the United States: A Report To Congress*.

US Department of the Interior (1993), *Mineral Commodity Summaries 1993*, Washington, DC: Government Printing Office.

US Department of Labor (1993), *Consumer Expenditure Survey, 1990–91*, Bulletin 2425, Washington, DC: Bureau of Labor Statistics.

US Environmental Protection Agency (1977), 'User's manual for single-source (CRSTER) model', EPA-450/2-77-013.

US Environmental Protection Agency (1979), *Protecting Visibility: An EPA Report to Congress*, EPA-450/5-79-008, Research Triangle Park, NC: Office of Air Quality Planning and Standards.

US Environmental Protection Agency (1982), *Air Quality Criteria for Particulate Matter and Sulfur Oxides*, vols 1–3, Research Triangle Park, NC: US EPA.

US Environmental Protection Agency (1984), 'User's guide to the MESOPUFFII model and related processor programs', EPA-600/8-84-013, Research Triangle Park, NC: Office of Research and Development.

US Environmental Protection Agency (1986a), *Air Quality Criteria for Ozone and Other Photochemical Oxidants*, 5 vols, Document no. EPA/600/8-84/020, Research Triangle Park, NC: US EPA.

US Environmental Protection Agency (1986b), *Air Quality Criteria for Lead*, 4 vols, Document no. EPA/600/8-89/049.

US Environmental Protection Agency (1990), *Air Quality Criteria for Lead: Supplement to the 1986 Addendum*, Document no. EPA/600/8-89/049.

US Environmental Protection Agency (1992a), 'User's guide for the industrial source complex (1SC2) dispersion models', EPA-450/4-92-008, Research Triangle Park, NC: Office of Air Quality Planning and Standards.

US Environmental Protection Agency (1992b), 'SCREEN2 model user's guide', EPA-450/4-92-06, September, Research Triangle Park, NC: Office of Air Quality Planning and Standards.

US Environmental Protection Agency (1995), *National Air Quality and Emission Trend Report, 1995*, Research Triangle Park, NC: Office of Air Quality Planning and Standards.

Vander, A.J. (1988), 'Chronic effects of lead on the renin–angiotension system', in W. Victery (ed.), 'Symposium on Lead–Blood Pressure Relationships', and Environmental Health Perspectives, **78**, 77–83.

Viscusi, W.K. (1978), 'Labor market valuations of life and limb: Empirical estimates and policy implications', *Public Policy*, **26** (3), 359–86.

Viscusi, W.K. (1981), 'Occupational safety and health regulation: Its impact and policy alternatives', in J. Crecine (ed.), *Research in Public Policy Analysis and Management, Vol. 2*, Greenwich, CT: JAI Press.

Viscusi, W.K. (1992), *Fatal Tradeoffs: Public and Private Responsibilities for Risk*, New York: Oxford University Press.

Viscusi, W.K. (1993), 'The value of risks to life and health', *Journal of Economic Literature*, **31**, 1912–46.

Viscusi, W.K. and W.N. Evans (1990), 'Utility functions that depend on health status: Estimates and economic implications', *American Economic Review*, **80** (3), 353–74.

Viscusi, W.K. and M. Moore (1989), 'Rates of time preference and valuations of the duration of life', *Journal of Public Economics*, **38**, 297–317.

Viscusi, W.K., W.A. Magat and J. Huber (1991), 'Pricing environmental health risks: Survey assessments of risk–risk and risk–dollar trade-offs for chronic bronchitis', *Journal of Environmental Economics and Management*, **21**, 32–51.

Wachter, K.W. (1988), 'Disturbed by meta-analysis?', *Perspective*, **16**, 1407–8.

Walsh, R.G., D.M. Johnson and J.R. McKean (1992), 'Benefit transfer of outdoor recreation demand studies, 1968–1988', *Water Resources Research*, **28** (3), 707–13.

Watson, W.D. and J.A. Jaksch (1982), 'Air pollution: Household soiling and consumer welfare losses', *Journal of Environmental Economics and Management*, **9**, 248–62.

Westhoff, P., R. Baur, D.L. Stephens and W.H. Meyers (1990), *FAPRI U.S. Crops Model Documentation*, Technical Report 90-TR 17, Center for Agricultural and Rural Development, Ames, Iowa.

Whitfield, R.G. and T.S. Wallsten (1988), 'A risk assessment for selected lead-induced health effects: an example of a general methodology', *Risk Analysis*, **9** (2), 197–207.

Whitten, G.Z. and H. Hogo (1978), 'User's manual for kinetics model and ozone isopleth plotting package', EPA-600/8-78-014a, Research Triangle Park, NC: US Environmental Protection Agency.

Whittington, D. and D. MacRae, Jr (1986), 'The issue of standing in benefit–cost analysis', *Journal of Policy Analysis and Management*, **5** (4), 665–82.

Whittington, D. and D. MacRae, Jr (1990), 'Comment: Judgments about who has standing in benefit–cost analysis', *Journal of Policy Analysis and Management*, **9** (4), 536–47.

Williams, R.L., R.K. Creasy, G.C. Cunningham, W.E. Hawes, F.D. Norris and M. Tashiro (1982), 'Fetal growth and perinatal viability in California', *Obstetrics and Gynecology*, **59** (5), 624–32.

Willig, R.D. (1976), 'Consumers' surplus without apology', *American Economic Review* **66** (4), 589–97.

Zellner, A. (1971), *Introduction to Bayesian Inference in Econometrics*, New York: Wiley.

Index